Emergent Quilombos

Joe R. and Teresa Lozano Long Series
in Latin American and Latino Art and Culture

Emergent Quilombos

BLACK LIFE AND HIP-HOP IN BRAZIL

Bryce Henson

University of Texas Press
Austin

Copyright © 2023 by the University of Texas Press
All rights reserved
Printed in the United States of America
First edition, 2023

Requests for permission to reproduce material from this work should be
　　sent to:
　　Permissions
　　University of Texas Press
　　P.O. Box 7819
　　Austin, TX 78713-7819
　　utpress.utexas.edu

♾ The paper used in this book meets the minimum requirements of ANSI/
NISO Z39.48-1992 (R1997) (Permanence of Paper).

Library of Congress Cataloging-in-Publication Data

Names: Henson, Bryce, author.
Title: Emergent quilombos : Black life and hip-hop in Brazil / Bryce Henson.
Description: First edition. | Austin : University of Texas Press, 2023. |
　　Includes bibliographical references and index.
Identifiers: LCCN 2023013421 | ISBN 978-1-4773-2809-5 (cloth) |
　　ISBN 978-1-4773-2810-1 (paperback) | ISBN 978-1-4773-2811-8 (PDF)
　　| ISBN 978-1-4773-2812-5 (ePub)
Subjects: LCSH: Hip-hop—Social aspects—Brazil. | Hip-hop—Political
　　aspects—Brazil. | Black people—Brazil—Ethnic identity. | Black people—
　　Race identity—Brazil. | Black people—Brazil—Social conditions. |
　　Working class—Brazil—Social conditions. | Quilombos.
Classification: LCC F2510 .H46 2023 | DDC 305.896/081—
　　dc23/eng/20230419
LC record available at https://lccn.loc.gov/2023013421

doi:10.7560/328095

Para todos os quilombolas do passado, do presente e do futuro.

Contents

Acknowledgments   ix

Introduction   1

Chapter 1.   Racial Conditions   27

Chapter 2.   Hip-Hop *Aquilombamento*   53

Chapter 3.   Black Spaces of Culture   77

Chapter 4.   Intimacy   107

Chapter 5.   Artifice   131

Chapter 6.   Mediating *Quilombo* Politics   157

Chapter 7.   Real Women   189

Coda: A Diasporic Love Letter   219

Notes   225 | *Reference List*   235 | *Index*   255

Acknowledgments

At so many stages, I have marveled at my embarrassment of riches while writing this book. This has not been an easy and straightforward process. Still, I am beyond thankful for the love, encouragement, and nourishment that so many friends, family, and community members have graciously given me. Honestly, the word "acknowledgment" does not seem sufficient for what the people below have done for me.

First, I must express my deepest gratitude to the members of the Bahian hip-hop movement. I am constantly amazed at their kindness—how they have opened up their lives, street philosophies, and worlds to me. Sometimes I came recommended by someone they knew. Often I just reached out into nowhere on social media because I had heard of them. Regardless, they welcomed me, a stranger, with open arms, showing me their homes, their communities, their archives, and their stories. More importantly, they shared with me a different way to move in this world: privileging the collective, embracing the ancestral and the diasporic, and acting on a desire to transform reality. I still cannot believe it sometimes, but I have never taken their generosity for granted. I hope this book does justice to what they have taught me and done for me. *Axé*.

In Salvador, my Bahian people are irreplaceable. I must start with Belinha Reis, César Costa Ramos, and Jizelli Brito Sampaio. I met these three during a study abroad program as an undergraduate. Over the past fifteen years, they bestowed on me their friendship, guidance, shelter, food, and community. Even when my Portuguese was rough in the early stages, they were patient and kind. Belinha Reis graciously welcomed me into her home in 2013 during my preliminary research and introduced me to my first research participants. Similarly, César

Costa Ramos has been a friend and brother, making sure I do not spend holidays in Brazil alone. Both Belinha and César have been the greatest teachers of Bahian culture and society: Belinha teaching me about graffiti and visual cultures, and César about music. I mustn't forget about Jamille Santana as well. Sedrick Miles, Luciana Brito, and Lonan Miles-Brito always provide excellent companionship over pizza, football games, and a few cold beers. Finally, thank you to Walter Paim, his Soweto School, and his students for welcoming me into their classrooms and coming virtually to so many of my talks.

My Seattle community means the world to me. Thank you Chris Dunford, Zorn Taylor, Jamil Suleman, Aaron Jacob, Camille Trummer, Daniel Trummer, Valentina Alvarez, Jennifer Moore, Yumi Sullivan, Serg Khandzhayan, Pary Khandzhayan, Will Chu, Katie Rocha, Marco Martinez, Adrien Montalvo, Omitosin King, Damon Bomar, Kristi Brown, Vanessa Wilkin, Toby Crittenden, Sam Terry, Jonathan Cunningham, Sarah Feldman, Andre Jackson, Chris Shaw, Alberto Mejia, the Nishimotos, Alaya Carr, Tarik Abdullah, Sean Thayer, Brianna Vazquez, Jaylon Nazario, and Ben Yisrael. Big shoutout to Luis Rodriguez and Leona Moore-Rodriguez, who have become family. Their care and support have been nothing short of a lifeline.

I cannot imagine a better place to do my PhD than at the Institute of Communications Research at the University of Illinois, Urbana-Champaign. To this very day, I am still reaping the benefits from a world-class doctoral committee: Cameron McCarthy, Junaid Rana, Isabel Molina-Guzmán, and Norman Denzin. Cameron has exceeded his charge as an adviser and continues to be an inspiring teacher, mentor, thinker, interlocutor, and friend. Angharad Valdivia, my unofficial fifth committee member, has supported and championed my work with vigor and enthusiasm for well over a decade. I'd also like to acknowledge my outstanding colleagues and friends from Illinois: John Nerone, Shantel Martinez, Myra Washington, Carolyn Randolph, Diana Leon-Boys, Ergin Bulut, Karla Palma, Darren Stevenson, Veronica Mendes, and Christine Peralta. While in the Chambana, I established many friends in Chicago, especially Mike Staudenmaier, Anne Carlson, and their awesome kids Sofia, Niko, and Malcolm. There is no way I would have survived the cornfields without my brothers, Kyle Mays, Eduardo Coronel, and Kevin Whalen. We made ample time at Murphy's to support one another over Irish nachos (with no swine), chicken wings, Midwest beers, and some Catholic whiskey.

I was fortunate to spend an extra year in Urbana-Champaign as a postdoctoral research associate in the Department of African American

Studies. Erik McDuffie, Faye Harrison, Desiree McMillion, Merle Bowen, Ron Bailey, and Robin Jarrett welcomed me into their intellectually vibrant community. In particular, Erik has strongly supported me in numerous ways, from the final stages of my dissertation to my work as a junior professor. I extend my gratitude to the fellow members of that postdoc community: José de la Garza Valenzuela, Balbir Singh, Chris Eng, and Charisse Burden-Stelly.

The University of Texas Press team has been nothing less than superb. During the 2018 American Studies Association conference, Kerry Webb approached me, wanting to know more about my work. She immediately understood the book project and its significance. Along the way, she has kindly answered every question I had, demystifying the book publishing process and guiding me through it. In addition, Dawn Durante, Christina Vargas, and Andrew Hnatow have provided enthusiastic support for this book. I would like to thank the two reviewers who offered valuable and generous feedback. This book would not be possible without the services of the mighty Laura Helper, who helped me ensure that it pays proper respects to those who are in it. I would also like to acknowledge the Melbern G. Glasscock Center for Humanities Research at Texas A&M University for a publication support grant.

Outside of Illinois, I am grateful for an academic community across the country that I get to learn with and from all the time. First off... Jenn M. Jackson is a national treasure, and I'm lucky to be their friend. I am also indebted to Ralina Joseph, Manoucheka Celeste, Jonathan Warren, Omaris Zamora, Geneva Smitherman, Angela Hudson, Ivan Chaar-Lopez, Francheska Roja Alers, Douglas Ishii, Antonio La Pastina, Darrel Wanzer-Serrano, Asha Winfield, Christen Smith, Nicole Ramsey, Emilce Santana, Portia Owusu, Jenn McClearan, and Rachel Afi Quinn. The Association for the Study of the Worldwide African Diaspora (ASWAD) has been a nurturing intellectual space in which to broaden and sharpen my thinking. Many thanks to Robert Trent Vinson, Erik McDuffie, Kim D. Butler, Leslie Alexander, Minkah Makalani, Sonya Maria Johnson, Reighan Gillam, Herman Bennett, and Ben Talton for their camaraderie, friendship, and support.

Finally, I'd like to thank my family for their support. While my mother has not always understood what I have done or what I do, she has always supported my pursuit of knowledge, first as a young child and today as an adult.

Emergent Quilombos

Introduction

July 25, 2014: Thousands of Black youths descend on Salvador da Bahia's historic center, Pelourinho, for a special night. As part of the Panorama Percussivo Mundial (Global Percussion Panorama, or Perc-Pan), Racionais MC's lead rapper, Mano Brown, is performing, for free no less, at the Praça de Cruz Caída (Fallen Cross Plaza). Even though Brown's mother is from Bahia, opportunities to see Brazil's most well-known MC are a special occasion in this Brazilian city nestled in the Northeast region. This is a chance to see a living legend, a Black man whose voice has conjured and amplified the struggles, experiences, hopes, and dreams of millions of Black youths in Brazil's peripheral communities. Brazilians do not show up early for anything! But tonight, they do. No one wants to miss even a second of Brown performing. Everyone comes correct. All the youths dress up for the occasion, pulling out their best hip-hop gear to wear on the deck that overlooks *cidade baixa* (the lower city). In the sea of Black bodies of various brown hues, women wear short shorts, denim skirts, tights, tank tops that show off their midriffs, and high-top shoes or Chuck Taylors. They came to impress. Men are wearing NBA jerseys that droop to the mid-thigh, baggy T-shirts, and denim shorts. They know they look fly. The range of Black hairstyles is wide and beautiful: fades, dreadlocks, Afros, cornrows, twists, and curls. And let's not forget the New Era baseball hats worn by women and men alike: New York Yankees, New York Knicks, Brooklyn Nets, Los Angeles Lakers, Atlanta Hawks, Orlando Magic, and Miami Heat. The people look good.

The air is a mix of sweet and savory. Cologne and perfume circulate within the convivial crowd. Gotta smell good. Whiffs of lager beer, *cravinho*, and Coca-Cola emanate from small plastic cups. Gotta feel good. Salt from bodily sweat and the seawater underneath the deck meld together. The sound of excitement is in heavy rotation. A chorus of *periferia* slang rings loud and poetic. Waves of Black youths are still arriving on buses from the Comércio or Praça da Sé stations nearby. They casually talk with their friends, acquaintances, coworkers, lovers, and romantic interests. Youths trade their best freestyle rhymes with their coperformers on the streets. There's a special energy in the air. Everyone can feel it.

On the large stage, the lights go off, silence hits, and the DJ initiates the transition to the show. The music blares. The bass booms. Everyone knows what time it is. Brown is about to emerge on stage and finally perform. Collectively, eyes get bigger; anticipation rises; stomachs get tighter. Brown walks out wearing sunglasses, denim jeans, a gray blazer, a gray shirt, and a gray tie. He is clearly in charge of this operation. The excitement explodes. Like a sacred chant, thousands of people say "poooooooooorra" (holy shit!). Yells, chants, and screams raise the decibel meter higher and higher. All eyes are fixed on the stage. Everyone rushes over, getting close to the beloved MC who, for decades, has rapped about racial, social, and spatial exclusion—which is also the vantage point of his audience. Brown performs mostly his solo music on his not-yet-released album *Boogie Naipe*, a tribute to the *bailes black* (Black parties) of the 1970s and 1980s that combine soul, disco, and boogie. Anyone who goes to a concert also wants to hear an artist or group play their classic cuts. Brown knows this, rapping through his discography from Racionais MC's 1997 album *Sobrevivendo no Inferno* (Surviving in hell) to the present. Nothing—and I mean nothing—is more deafening than when he performs "Negro Drama" (Black drama) from Racionais MC's 2001 album *Nada como um dias após o outro dia* volumes 1 and 2 (Nothing like a day after the other day). You would think this is the Black Brazilian national anthem. And you know what? It just might be. Brown raps about life as a Black man in São Paulo's periphery that includes crime, football, music, single Black mothers with their "vagabond" children, Tupac Shakur influences, the stench, the unfair life chances given to poor and working-class Black people, and racist institutions like schooling. He rhymes about the allure of whiskey and Red Bull drinks, Nike shoes, guns, and fancy cars in the all-too-familiar concrete jungle. At the end, Brown asserts his humanity as a Black man from the *gueto* (ghetto). Everyone in the crowd is rapping along, verse for verse, word for word, beat for beat. There's no delay. No forgetting. No trying to remember. They know it by heart. They feel it in their soul. The song rests in their bellies. The lyrics flow effortlessly from their gut to their lips. He is them. And they are him. Black drama is a collective experience.

This scene highlights the importance of hip-hop in Salvador da Bahia, frequently referred to as Brazil's most African city. Hip-hop cultures like rap music are vessels that amplify Black Bahians' communal practices and resistance to their racialized oppression. For these Black youths, African-derived cultures are political, providing Black people with an ideological weapon of social critique, a basis for alternative systems, and a model of belonging that is both diasporic and antithetical to the nation-state's normative regimes. Hip-hop challenges the Brazilian mythology that a mythical and timeless African past feeds seamlessly into a racially harmonious and mixed-race Brazilian present. Hip-hop in Bahia also opposes the idea that Salvador is a harbor of pure Africanisms and a racial paradise where Black people embrace their ethnic background without prejudice. Instead, marginalized Black urban youths breathe new life into African-derived cultures through modern forms, like hip-hop, to connect them to other Black populations in the African Diaspora that are similarly socially and politically disenfranchised in their respective national locations. They portray Salvador specifically and Brazil more generally as anything but a Black utopia. And these youths use hip-hop to construct Black life as a radical ensemble of alternative lifeways and political possibilities in the midst of deeply entrenched national structures of anti-Black racism, sexism, and class exploitation.

In this book I argue for a simple yet critical claim: the Bahian hip-hop movement nourishes, maintains, and retools the *quilombo* (maroon community) blueprint to assert Black life and diasporic cultures in and against contemporary Brazil. Just as enslaved people formed historical *quilombos* under enslavement, Bahian hip-hop creates Black political and cultural spaces of refuge and communal creation to develop and protect the collective. In these radical practices of possibility, Black people have been able to cultivate Black life in the midst of political death (Moten, 2018; Weheliye, 2014). Throughout Brazilian history, Black people have re-created the *quilombo* model, occupying different spaces, configurations, names, and cultures. The *quilombo* baton has circulated through Candomblé territories, Black parties, samba schools, periphery communities of mostly poor and working-class Black people, and urban cultural centers. Today, Bahian hip-hop carries that baton.

Emergent *Quilombos*

Without a doubt, *quilombos* are a part of the Black radical tradition, places where Black people have sought liberation on their own terms (Robinson, 2021). The Black radical tradition does not seek to eradicate racism through inclusion into the very apparatus that oppresses them: the modern world, the nation-state, and a Eurocentric consciousness. Instead, it pursues alternatives. As the conceptual engine that drives this book, *quilombos* are local, living, emergent, and creative processes and practices (B. Nascimento, 2018f). By emergent, I mean that people wrest new meanings, values, practices, ideologies, positions, geographies, politics, aesthetics, and relationships from past experiences, aspirations, human configurations, achievements, societies, cosmologies, rituals, and expressions that the dominant sociocultural group neglects, stigmatizes, represses, or simply cannot fathom (R. Williams, 1978). Whether in 1605 or 2023, Black people create *quilombos*, manifesting spaces of rest, refuge, creation, and communion through a culture of reimagination, reinvention, and reconnection. *Quilombos* are neither simply a relic of the past nor a scholarly term of inquiry. They are always active practices, constructed from historical elements and retooled to intervene and disrupt a given conjuncture, whether that is against the anti-Black colony or now the anti-Black nation.

Black people have continued to dig into the crates of the past and pull out necessary and relevant social, cultural, and political elements to construct *quilombos* as radical Black spaces and systems. *Quilombos* are never static. They are malleable, fluid, and disruptive, building off the past, intervening in the present, and setting forth alternative directions for a liberatory future. In emergent *quilombos*, Black people continue to develop alternative social, cultural, and political systems that center their humanity, communities, and spaces. In Salvador, many of them are doing it with hip-hop, combining its four elements—rapping, DJing, breakdancing, and graffiti murals—with social justice, forming what they conceive of as the Bahian hip-hop movement. The Bahian hip-hop movement is an emergent *quilombo* that puts into praxis a choreography of ideologies, cultural politics, and social practices that organizes the Black masses into a different set of relationships to themselves, to each other, to space, to aesthetics, to Black people around the globe, to politics, and even to the very idea of the human. Most importantly, the Bahian hip-hop movement produces an alternative Blackness that rests neither on resistance to anti-Black violence solely nor on nationally acceptable forms of Blackness that do not disturb the racialized and gendered human hierarchy.

The Bahian hip-hop movement produces this emerging *quilombo* through media and popular culture—that dirty and vulgar terrain of the common folk, the lower classes, the mass-produced, and the widely liked (Storey, 2015). Artists like the rap group Quilombo Vivo explicitly identify the Bahian hip-hop movement as a *quilombo* in the contemporary era. It shows that the Black radical tradition is not distant and elusive but rather near, present, and accessible, ready to be mobilized at a moment's notice. For Black people around the diaspora, media and popular culture can be and often are intense sites of political mobilization, thought, and action (Iton, 2008). Black media and popular culture, hip-hop included, are no less innovative, political, and important than other Black cultural expressive forms that Black people around the diaspora have elevated to high culture.

Understanding the Bahian hip-hop movement as an emergent *quilombo* requires some brief historical context. First, there was the Imbangala group (also known as Jagas) in Angola and their institution called the *kilombo*, which literally translates to "war encampment" (B. Nascimento, 2021). As the first enslaved Africans arrived in Brazil in the first half of the sixteenth century (E. Carneiro, 1980), the *kilombo* almost instantaneously reemerged and transformed against Brazilian colonialism. Black people refused slavery as a social condition and a way of life (Moura, 1981), escaping the plantation and fleeing for the hillsides to secure their freedom and construct their own societies. In hard-to-reach places, Black people created *quilombos*, based on the *kilombo* model (B. Nascimento, 2021). They sought to strongly and boldly claim their emancipation, and with it their dignity (Mintz and Price, 1992). These fugitives mobilized the cosmological elements they brought with them from Africa, using them to construct a different social world and alternative systems outside of Brazilian colonialism and plantocratic society. Black people blended practices from various African national origins to rupture the very foundations of colonialism and its power structures of white supremacy, anti-Blackness, capitalistic exploitation, and heteropatriarchy. In *quilombos*, Black people politically emerged as a unified African people, rather than people from disparate nations, in their fight for freedom from enslavement (Robinson, 2021, p. 169). Transforming within and transformed by the social conditions of Brazilian colonialism and plantocratic society, the *quilombo* blossomed into a social, cultural, and political system that provided rest and a coordinated effort to undermine coloniality (Gomes and Reis, 2016). Certainly, *quilombos* were historically important social spaces and cultural creations. They were also extremely political. For example, *quilombos* like Palmares operated as a state, exercising political sovereignty and negotiating with Brazilian colonial administrations.

Over time, the *quilombo* became an ideal, a practice, and a system by which Black people re-created a sense of African community, belonging, and culture (J. J. Reis and Gomes, 2016). These restorations are never exact duplicates of the original (Mintz and Price, 1992), nor are they based just on heritage. They are built on the African-based symbolic, cosmological, psychic, ideological, and material pieces Black people have had at their disposal. Black people modified *quilombos* over time, often through contact with Africans from other nations or Indigenous groups, and in response to the social conditions constructed by colonialism and slavery in the Brazilian environment.

The transformation of the *kilombo* in Africa into the *quilombo* in Brazil exemplifies maroon malleability. Over time, Black people continue to modify the *quilombo*; different times, environments, and needs engender novel configurations that tend to their social, cultural, and political exigencies. No one has theorized more beautifully and poetically about *quilombo* liquidity than Black Brazilian feminist Beatriz Nascimento. Regardless of era, for her, *quilombos* are assemblies of Black people who are not accepted by society, whose Black cultures are stigmatized, and who are under attack by white society and its military forces (B. Nascimento, 2018b). Then and now, a *quilombola* (maroon inhabitant) is one who chooses liberation on their terms, yet is shunned, repressed, stigmatized, and even criminalized by those in the Brazilian community, Black and non-Black people alike. *Quilombos* are a practice of encampment and resistance against racialized poverty, the derision of Black aesthetics, urban segregation, and the erasure of Black history (C. Smith, 2016c). *Quilombos* are necessary because they are "alternative social systems organized by Black people—from the *quilombos* or the favelas" (B. Nascimento, 2005, p. 109). And every *quilombo* is a "transmigration, escape, and refuge" (C. Smith, 2016c, p. 81) from the suffocating weight of anti-Black racism, sexism, and class exploitation, whether caused by the unbearable conditions of slavery or ongoing state-sanctioned and socially enacted anti-Black violence. *Quilombos* are Black assemblies, cultural geographies, and political actions that emerge when Black people refuse the racialized exclusions of Brazil, fleeing to spaces where they can freely congregate, produce communal safe havens, and love and embrace a Blackness that Brazil can never and will never embrace.

Emerging *quilombos* like the Bahian hip-hop movement trace the political possibilities of Black social life and diasporic cultural formation after fugitivity. *Quilombos* are composed of fugitives fleeing slavery as a condition and a way of life. In Black studies, fugitivity is an important conceptual tool and mode of praxis to describe Black life amid political death (Gumbs, 2016b; Harney and Moten, 2013; Sojoyner, 2017). By fugitivity, I mean a set of unruly Black people's criminalized politics and practices that refuse captivity, escape from spaces of confinement, and flee into the unknown abyss. For good reason, Fred Moten refers to fugitivity as "stolen life" (2018) because Black people have had to steal back their bodies to secure their liberation. *Quilombos* illustrate what occurs after refusal, escape, and flight. They give us the blueprint, literally a whole history, of how we create new worlds from the past for the present and the future.

A *quilombo* contains its own epistemologies, a belief system, or what some theorists call *quilombismo*, a source of energy articulated through dynamic collectivization and expressed through ways of life, cultural expression, and political thought (A. Nascimento, 1980). It is also a verb, *aquilombar-se*, an action that creates autonomous gatherings through Black customs and cultures that struggle against the multilayered and interlocking forces of violent Black subjugation (B. O. Souza, 2008). *Quilombos* are not just an ideology and a verb; they are also a state, a condition, and a practice: *aquilombamento*. As Joselicio Junior (2019) writes, "the *aquilombamento* was a concrete experience that demonstrated, in practice, that it was possible to construct another more humane, more just, and more environmentally viable society." *Quilombos* are "anti-colonial" organizations that disrupt the hegemony of coloniality, enslavement, and the modern world (Silva de Oliveria et al., 2021; Bispo dos Santos, 2015, 2020). The *quilombo* is not just a historical fact; it is an ongoing march toward more capacious conceptions of humanity, freedom, and a just world.

As an emergent *quilombo*, the Bahian hip-hop movement continues to build on this legacy of Black political and cultural resistance. Black hip-hop artists, activists, and intellectuals now create their own *quilombo* in the Bahian hip-hop movement, building new institutions, cultures, geographies, and social relations based on carefully curated

African origins and diasporic connections. *Quilombos* are mechanisms of reorganization assembled through social unity and egalitarianism that stand in opposition to the dominant racial order that has written out Black people's role in pursuing freedom on their own terms and beyond simple abolition (B. Nascimento, 2018g, 2018b). The *quilombo*, then, is a political action of assembly, even if ephemeral: a collective created by Black people where they can take refuge, reunite, recharge, and relate in ways that are unfathomable in Brazil.

The Terrain of Blackness(es)

Besides *quilombo*, two other important terms appear throughout this book: Blackness and diaspora. To discuss Blackness, we must start with race. Race is a slippery term that is too often subsumed under other terms like culture, nation, class, biology, genetics, ethnicity, and other social categories of classification and ordering. Race is not an ethnic or biological category; it is a political category disguised as a biological category that is instrumental to creating human hierarchies (Roberts, 2012). Politically, race informs and shapes who is human, almost human, and nonhuman/subhuman (Weheliye, 2014). Race is central to human hierarchies that privilege whiteness and degrade Blackness (as well as Indigeneity). At the same time, race is never a given and static category. It is a social construction filled with specific and even contradictory meanings across a variety of representations and everyday scenarios. Even though it is socially constructed, race is material; it is a formation that sits between social structure and cultural representation (Omi and Winant, 2014). And race changes—both in meaning and as a political category—because it must adapt to different "racial projects" (Omi and Winant, 2014) that distribute social, economic, and political resources to various groups at different times and in varying spaces.

When people talk about race, they often mean Black people and Blackness. Yet they frequently convey it in uncertain terms. Blackness is polysemic: people assign it multiple and contradictory meanings. In Brazil, as elsewhere around the globe, Blackness is plural, fissuring those who belong and those who do not. Regardless of location, people contest what Blackness means, where it stands, and to whom it belongs. Instead of one Blackness, there are multiple Blacknesses that symbolize, represent, and are enacted differently according to context and people. Among Black people, Blackness has its own "non-synchrony" (McCarthy, 1998); Black racial difference carries varying meanings that groups wield to express divergent and competing interests, needs, and desires, cutting across class, gender, sexuality, and geography.

As an emergent *quilombo*, the Bahian hip-hop movement exposes the multiple Blacknesses in Brazil. It is an alternative to the prevailing three types of Blackness that occupy the Brazilian imaginary: abject Blackness, folkloric Blackness, and mixed Blackness. These Blacknesses are in some ways unique to Brazil; they are also quite like Blackness(es) around the diaspora and on the continent. Abject Blackness is social death, derision, repression, incommunicability, accumulation, and fungibility (O. Patterson, 1982; Wilderson, 2003, 2010).[1] It dates back to the earliest days of enslavement, justifying the commodification and dehumanization of Black people as chattel property. This abject Blackness continues today through "anti-Black solidarity" between whites, non-Black people of color, and even some Black people (Sexton, 2008, 2010; Wilderson, 2010). Anti-Black solidarity is also gendered, displacing Black people from hegemonic constructions of "masculine" and "feminine," whether on the plantation (Burdick, 1998; Davis, 1998; O. Pinho, 2008) or in modern society (Bailey, 2021; Bey, 2019; Gonzalez, 2021; Spillers, 1987). While no doubt atrocious in its production and consequences, abject Blackness is useful for understanding how a Eurocentric white conceptual map negates Blackness over and over again, while overrepresenting Western, white, propertied "Man" as the human (Weheliye, 2014; Wynter, 2003), as if no other possibilities already exist. Abject Blackness establishes the boundaries of modern belonging at the same time it is constantly constructing who is nonhuman. Often, but not always, some Black people have sought to escape the social stigma under the sign of abject Blackness, fleeing toward colonial/modern ideologies, consciousness, and structures, seeking to be seen as individually exceptional, an exception to the rule of abject Blackness. Yet we do not want to reduce Blackness simply to the abject, a condition of despair, misery, poverty, stigma, and injury, or what Fanon calls the "veritable hell" in the "zone of non-being" (2008, p. xii).

For well over a century, numerous nations in the Americas with atrocious histories of slavery have sought to portray themselves as multicultural communities that are now tolerant and inclusive. They wish to demonstrate that they have moved on from their production and maintenance of abject Blackness and its manifestations through racial prejudice, violence, and exploitation.[2] This began with various treaties to end the transatlantic slave trade and moved to abolition and later to celebrating multicultural inclusion. Nations have tried to show this progress by including some ethnic difference that diverges from the dominant group(s). However, the acceptance of ethnic difference is permissible only if it promotes acculturation to a Eurocentric consciousness. Accepting ethnic difference is not the same as accepting racial difference.[3] In Brazil, a national narrative, known as the racial democracy mythology, includes Black ethnic symbols and romanticizes colonial-modern *mestiçagem*, or racial mixing.[4] It contends that everyone in Brazil is racially mixed, is somewhat ethnically African, and holds no cultural prejudice; thus there is no racism in Brazil. This mythology privileges what I refer to as mixed Blackness throughout the book. Mixed Blackness is the ideology that Blackness can be included in the Brazilian nation so long as it is biologically diluted and culturally hybrid. However, Blackness, especially a social and political Blackness, cannot be its own entity and exist within the nation, as that would suggest there is a racialized experience and reality outside of the Brazilian consciousness.

Biologically, mixed Blackness centers on the *mulata*, the interracial product of the white slave owner and the nonconsenting enslaved African woman. Hegemonic groups, institutions, and public discourse offer her up as proof of Brazil as a racial democracy. The *mulata* is praised for combining the desirable attributes of African women (hypersexuality, voluptuous bodies, and passionate nature) with features such as curly hair, lighter skin tone, slimmer waists, narrow noses, and smaller lips that position her closer to white womanhood and away from the supposed ugliness of abject Blackness. Today, she is packaged as a national product, ready to be culturally and sexually consumed by Brazilians and those abroad. Culturally, mixed Blackness elevates certain Afro-Brazilian cultures to national symbols available for the use, production, and consumption of all Brazilians, most notably samba, capoeira, and feijoada. Yet mixed Blackness reduces Black cultural contributions to Brazilian civilization to folkloric elements and cultural expressions. These contributions are valuable only because the white *senhor*, whether he be the Portuguese colonizer or the Brazilian creole, selected and modified them to be part of the national fabric.

In Brazil, Black people fought to signify Blackness as something other than abject while refusing the notion that Blackness is valuable only when it is hybridized. This was especially true in 1970s Brazil, notably in Salvador da Bahia and the surrounding Reconcâvo region, resulting in what I deem a folkloric Blackness, or a Blackness associated with an African cultural purity that is timeless and homogenous. For centuries, the state heavily repressed, outlawed, and even violently policed African cultural practices like Candomblé (an Afro-Brazilian religion). People, places, and things associated with Africa were officially and generally viewed as ugly, inferior, and morally depraved. In the 1970s, during the "reafricanization" (Paschel, 2009; O. Pinho, 2005), Black Brazilians touted African styles, aesthetics, cultures, and belief systems as beautiful and positive. Black people created Afroblocs (Black organizations and cultural spaces that uplift the Black community) like Ilê Aiyê and Olodum. These were critical and valuable forms of resistance that upended how Blackness was understood, enacted, and positioned in Brazil. However, forms of resistance are susceptible to incorporation (Hall, 1981). Since the 1970s, the state, nonprofit organizations, the tourism industry, and cultural agencies have neutralized reafricanization cultures, hollowing out their political impetus and emphasis on systemic racism. The cultures remain, but the political exigency behind them—exerting pressure on the nation-state for its gendered anti-Blackness—has diminished. Today, this African cultural purity easily slips into ideas of Blackness as a set of essences, tendencies, and appearances (P. Pinho, 2010). Folkloric Blackness homogenizes Black people as Africans with a timeless and static culture, with a presocial identity and culture. Black people must return to their roots and recuperate their lost selves. It is as if Africa, with all fifty-four of its nation-states, has stood still in the winds of time for the last five hundred years.

The mixed Blackness camp and the folkloric Blackness camp have come to an agreement of sorts: folkloric Blackness can be included as *ethnically* different from Brazilian identity and culture as long as the elements of its African culture, ancestry, and heritage funnel into mixed Blackness. Abject Blackness remains tethered to the popular cultures and social practices of the Black masses that deviate from both mixed and folkloric Blackness. This also reifies Brazil as a great racial democracy, a mixed-race nation without racism that now also includes ethnically differentiated peoples. Bahia is notorious for celebrating, even though it is contradictory, African cultural purity, interracial mixture, and intercultural syncretism (Paschel, 2009). It serves as a model of harmonious race relations that supplies Brazil with an ideological cover against accusations of racism. Moreover, people, agencies, and institutions use folkloric and mixed Blackness to hide ethnic and class conflicts (Armstrong, 2001). For them, racism is a matter of individual prejudice rather than a structural vulnerability that produces the premature death of differentiated peoples without political uproar (Ferreira da Silva, 2001; Gilmore, 2007).

Emergent *quilombos* like the Bahian hip-hop movement generate another option beyond abject Blackness, mixed Blackness, and folkloric Blackness: a diasporic Blackness that establishes a Black refuge and opposes the nation as an "imagined community" (Anderson, 2006) as well as anti-Black racism, sexism, and class exploitation. The Bahian hip-hop movement is diasporic in that it weaves together US Black popular culture, African ancestrality, *négritude*, and other Black forms of cultural and political resistance from around the globe. A diasporic Blackness challenges the limited forms of Blackness, in this case folkloric and mixed Blacknesses, that the nation will permit only because they fortify romantic national narratives and do not upset Black people's structural positions across various economies. A diasporic Blackness is not just a condition grounded in racial and gender hierarchies but also a set of processes within a matrix of movement, migration, political struggle, cultural production, and intellectual thought (T. R. Patterson and Kelley, 2000, p. 20). It is in movement, always in flight, and always reconfiguring. In diasporas, scattered people forge relations with the homeland, the hostland, and other diasporic groups that are built upon memories of exile and longing for (re)connection (K. Butler, 2001).

The Bahian hip-hop movement, as an emergent *quilombo*, uses the diaspora to queer the nation's bourgeois logics of gender and sexuality that produce the family as the atomized unit of the nation-state (Gopinath, 2005). My use of queer does not mean simply a set of sexual identifications, desires, and practices, but rather a praxis that upends specific structures of heteronormativity that are tied to racialized morality (Ferguson, 2014; Somerville, 2014). Queer actions do not have to be undertaken by nonheterosexual people; heterosexual people can also queer regimes of normativity (Cohen, 1997). Emergent *quilombos* bring forth a queer diasporic Blackness that disrupts the machinations of violence within the normative order; they afford Black people connections, spaces, and refuge to love one another in ways that were supposed to have been eradicated and resist coloniality's insatiable thirst for Black social death (Tinsley, 2008).

Diasporic Blackness pursues three objectives that interrupt the Brazilian terrain of Blackness. First, diasporic Blackness challenges the nation as the primary site of identity, subjectivity, and belonging. The nation is an "imagined community" (B. Anderson, 2006) that ideologically and culturally unites disparate people into a political bloc as citizens with particular rights and values as humans. Yet citizenship is granted for locally somatic white men who establish and maintain the social contract of society and government (Mills, 1997). Those who are able to socially, culturally, and politically belong to the nation, claiming full citizenship, do so by demonstrating their supposed racial and cultural superiority over abject Blackness. Diasporic Blackness points to other imagined communities beyond the nation and white citizenship. Second, it refuses mixed and folkloric Blacknesses because each furnishes ideological covers for the Brazilian nation-state's anti-Black ideologies, representations, and systems that structurally push Black people to the figurative and literal margins of society. Mixed and folkloric Blacknesses reduce race to culture, heritage, and biology, negating it as a political category and perceiving racism as a matter of individual prejudice rather than a structure of suffering. Finally, diasporic Blackness chooses, embraces, and loves the excluded forms of Blackness that are reduced to an abject zone. It does not reify abject Blackness. Instead, diasporic Blackness sees abject Blackness as a radical site of possibility and transformation by attempting to claim other meanings for those marked as nonnormative, noncitizen, and nonhuman without redeeming them through the nation. Within emerging *quilombos*, a diasporic Blackness forges solidarity with other Black populations who are similarly marginalized and looking for other ways of being and belonging that do not rely upon the anti-Black nation-state and the limited scripts of Blackness it will permit.

Bahian Hip-Hop: Diasporic Media and Popular Culture

I offer here the first book-length study of the Bahian hip-hop movement in English. Unfortunately, many people are unaware of Bahian hip-hop's very existence. Bahia and hip-hop may even seem counterintuitive: the former linked to an African past, and the latter associated with a Black cultural modernity. Like historical *quilombos*, the Bahian hip-hop movement is outside the purview of most, hard to find because its people usually occupy Black communities in peripheries away from tourist zones and white middle-class areas. In Salvador, people, agencies, tourists, and institutions are heavily invested in the city's reputation as a locale of premodern African culturalisms. There is seemingly no room for modern Black cultures such as hip-hop. Scholarly works mirror this: they often focus Candomblé, samba schools, Afro-blocs, and capoeira and tie these cultural expressions and Black Bahians to a folkloric Blackness. Both cultural and scholarly attention focuses heavily on Black Bahians' cultural expression that relies on the body as the only medium of representation. As a result, Black Bahians are assumed to be cut off from modern media and popular culture, such as hip-hop, not to mention shielded from structural racism and other such modern problems.

Conversely, Brazilian media and popular culture represent the country's South as the Brazilian hip-hop center, as if nothing else matters. The South is where modern Blackness is to be found, and the Northeast is where one locates a folkloric Blackness. Indisputably, São Paulo and Rio de Janeiro hip-hop are important to Brazil's hip-hop history, but there is more to Brazilian hip-hop. Most Brazilian hip-hop scholars also focus on the South, analyzing hip-hop communities among urban Black communities that confront racial exclusion, social stigma, and urban segregation. Brazilian hip-hop fans and scholars usually find Bahia in hip-hop only when Southern artists sample traditional Afro-Bahian music, reference Bahia in lyrics or graffiti, or use Afro-Bahian iconography. My work shows Bahian hip-hop disrupts both the conflation of Bahia with a romantic African past and harmonious race relations and the South as the only site of Black modernity.

Hip-hop is one way we can understand how Black people culturally and politically confront oppression while also fostering other possibilities. In Brazil, "hip-hop . . . emerges as a movement of young victims of urban racial and class violence [and] serves as an instrument of social transformation through its alternate expressions of aesthetics, culture, and social protest" (J. L. Santos, 2016, p. 164). The racial conditions that afflict Rio de Janeiro and São Paulo hip-hop artists and communities also afflict Bahian hip-hop artists and communities. Even in Bahia, the state and elites view hip-hop as the culture of criminality, violence, drug use, the periphery and marginals—all threats to Brazilian civilization (J. C. Gomes da Silva, 2015; Herschmann, 2005; Messias, 2015; Pardue, 2008; Sobral Freire, 2018). They perceive hip-hop artists, intellectuals, and fans alike as agents of abject Blackness, dangerous simply because they are poor, Black, and from the periphery.

These racial conditions and hip-hop cultures are not unique to Brazil. Hip-hop itself bloomed out of diasporic connections and structural anti-Black racism. On August 11, 1973, Black diasporic youths in the (Boogiedown) Bronx gave birth to hip-hop with a "back to school jam" hosted by DJ Kool Herc. Black youths from the United States, the English Caribbean, and the Spanish Caribbean electronically blended their various African-derived cultures together to articulate their everyday experiences, material conditions, hopes, dreams, and visions for a better world than the one they were born in. This all happened in the context of deindustrialization, the fall of the social welfare system, advances in global telecommunications, and the intensification of state surveillance and policing of Black urban communities (Chang, 2005; Neal, 2001). Marginalized urban Black youth developed hip-hop as a symbolic and ideological weapon to combat the multifaceted war being waged on the Black underclass in urban cities (T. Rose, 1994). Since that fateful August day in 1973, hip-hop transformed US popular culture and the cultural industry. It also exploded across the globe (Alim, Ibrahim, and Pennycook, 2009). Jeff Chang (2007) makes it plain: "It's a hip-hop world." Hip-hop has become a connective force that binds the African Diaspora through culture, politics, and identification by those who are racialized as Black and pushed to the margins of their respective societies (M. Perry, 2008).

As a Black diasporic cultural conduit, hip-hop's political currency derives from its ability to powerfully and with magnificent nuance renarrate the experiences of the Black masses, who are socially stigmatized and politically criminalized; brilliantly deliver cultural critiques of society and the state; and offer utopic visions of a better world. Hip-hop's power unfolds precisely because it emerges from the margins, with an ability to speak back from the periphery and contest binary oppositions such as white/Black, masculine/feminine, high class/low class, etc. that organize human life and structure economies according to ideas of superiority and inferiority (Hall, 1992). Hip-hop's ideological assault is parallel to that of historical *quilombos*: they interrupt human hierarchies and Western societies while also crafting alternative systems for excluded Black people. These similarities are why we can view the Bahian hip-hop movement as an emergent *quilombo* in the contemporary conjuncture.

As a *quilombo*, Bahian hip-hop creates alternative social, cultural, and political systems that function as a sanctuary from the cascading forces of gendered anti-Blackness in Brazilian society. In Bahia, hip-hop is a street culture based on urban Black experience, negritude, and African ancestrality that welcomes, educates, and mobilizes the Black masses around social in/justices. Social injustices include themes like structural racism, violence, segregation, and their systemic effects on society and individuals (Teperman, 2015). Bahian hip-hop artists portray Black people's everyday experiences from their vantage point rather than that of the state, the elite, or more privileged Black social segments. Telling their stories rather than having their stories told for them, these artists reveal the societal burden of their Blackness in the most quotidian tasks, like taking the bus, grocery shopping, walking down the street, going to work, hanging with the homies, or going out to party. They also use their Blackness to create different kinds of community spaces and social relationships.

The Bahian hip-hop movement brings a novel element into our idea of *quilombos*: the importance of media and popular culture as pedagogical tools. Black people are using various technological apparatuses and digital platforms to produce *quilombismo* and *aquilombamento* (G. S. L. Santana and Sobrinho, 2020). Black people find value in Bahian hip-hop because it speaks to and listens from the cultural forms that are important, accessible, and meaningful to a Black underclass that heavily engages with technology, media, and popular culture. The Bahian hip-hop movement has music, online videos, social media, style, the body, visual arts, and everyday cultural performances in its repertoire. Bahian hip-hop artists use media to create diasporic identities, cultural meanings, and social communities that oppose the nation and acceptable forms of Blackness.

The Bahian hip-hop movement also demonstrates the political stakes and tensions between high cultures and popular cultures in Brazil and around the African Diaspora. High culture is often assumed to be the forms, texts, and expressions that are individually created, difficult to achieve, rare to experience, and thus superior to popular culture, which is deemed low-brow or inferior (Storey, 2015). In this case, emergent *quilombos*, like the Bahian hip-hop movement, disrupt how many powerful actors, agencies, and state institutions elevate premodern Africanisms to high culture in contrast to the mass-produced, mediated, and ordinary popular cultures of the Black masses that Brazilian society deems inferior and abject. The Brazilian nation-state and its permissible Black segments represent these African culturalisms as rare and elusive, and unique to Salvador and only a few other places in the Western Hemisphere. Black Bahian hip-hop artists do not reject the symbols, narratives, and practices of their African heritage. They are just more interested in harnessing the spirit of this heritage in their own political identifications, cultural practices, and social behaviors. They reject how African culturalisms have become viewed as high culture, available for a respectable Black social segment and wielded against the Black underclass, who are perceived as lost without their African heritage. In that regard, they are also refusing the permissible forms of Blackness that Brazil accepts and values.

Black Diasporic Feminist Orientations

My own approach to understanding emergent *quilombos* such as the Bahian hip-hop movement is guided by a Black diasporic feminist approach. If *quilombos* are formed to produce new possibilities of becoming, ideologies, territoriality, and relation-making, we must unravel not only the colonial logics that subjugate Blackness but also how Blackness is intertwined with gender, sexuality, class, and middle-class morality (Ferguson, 2014). When we *aquilombar-se*, the dilemma becomes what forms of colonial human hierarchies we bring with us, unknowingly incorporating into our assemblies of supposed radical spaces, movements, and cultures. Too often, we elevate certain Black people above others because they have more money or nicer things, perform gender and sexuality respectfully, travel across borders, or obtain social or cultural capital. Put differently, we must learn to love one another not for how well we fit into bourgeois logics of respectability, modesty, and heteronormativity, plugging colonial relationalities back into Black communal creation. We must rethink the very logics of relation-making so that *aquilombamento* does not end up reproducing the coloniality of class, gender, and sexuality in Black communities.

The Bahian hip-hop movement is an exemplar of this necessity. Repeatedly, we have witnessed Black radical organizations, movements, and practices being hindered by their blind spots when it comes to gender, sexuality, and even class. There must be emergent modes of Black social life and cultural formation that rethink gender, sexuality, and class outside of Western modalities. We cannot simply be ethnically and racially Black while adopting Eurocentric standards of gender, sexuality, and class. In my almost decade-long research on the movement, I have learned from brilliant Black hip-hop artists, intellectuals, and activists that there is zero, and I mean zero, reason to create emergent *quilombos* if we are to continue colonial logics that reproduce human hierarchies around gender and sexuality and ultimately reproduce the structures, conditions, and ways of life we are attempting to get away from.

Many emergent *quilombo* spaces have struggled with sexism, homophobia, and transphobia. This includes the Black Movement (Hanchard, 1994; Pacheco, 2013); African-based religious communities, like Candomblé (K. dos R. A. Soares and Ferreira, 2021); and Afro-blocs like Ilê Aiyê (P. Pinho, 2010). We can more fully comprehend and create emergent *quilombos* such as the Bahian hip-hop movement only by drawing on Black feminist theory that tackles interlocking systems of oppression. In *quilombos*, Black women like Dandara and Tereza de Benguela are important historical figures in the fight against Brazilian colonialism and slavery (Leite, 2020). Dandara was a fearless warrior and agricultural leader in Palmares (Henrique, 2011). She was also the wife of Zumbí, Palmares's leader. Benguela commanded the Quariterê *quilombo*, which consisted of Black fugitives and local Indigenous people along the Guaporé River in the state of Mato Grosso. There, Benguela developed a cultivation system and commerce system to feed and nourish the *quilombolas* (Lacerda, 2019). Today, Black women are leaders in remnant *quilombos* (S. da Silva, 2019), the communities that continue to exist on the lands of historical *quilombos* dating back hundreds of years (e.g., Bowen, 2021). Black women are also leaders in contemporary social movements, like those that center on land justice (K.-K. Perry, 2013) and "urban *quilombos*" (Pereira, 2015) such as Aparelha Luzia, a Black cultural center in São Paulo created by Erica Malunguinho, the first Black trans person elected to a Brazilian state legislature (Nito and Scifoni, 2018; Seigel, 2020). Black women are leading the way in the fight for interlocking forms of justice and liberation that cut across a variety of social categorizations (Barreto, 2005; Caldwell, 2006, 2017; Gonzalez, 1988b; E. Williams, 2013).

In conversation with other Black feminists around the diaspora, Black Brazilian feminists have developed their own intellectual ideas and political theories that intervene in local conditions and broader global forces. They find the pulse of interlocking systems of oppression: in Brazil, Black women experience both racism and sexism (Gonzalez, 2021). This is ingrained in Brazil's national culture. Black women are often reduced to hypersexual *mulatas*, domestic workers, mammies, bad mothers, or Mama Africa (S. Carneiro, 2019b; Gonzalez, 1984; P. Pinho, 2010; Preta-rara, 2019). Structural oppression goes beyond just cultures of racism and sexism to afflict Black women. Capitalism, class exploitation, and socioeconomic marginalization work by and through racism and sexism as well. Many Black women are shunned in the workforce, pushed to do menial jobs (S. Carneiro, 1995, 2011; Gonzalez, 2018b; B. Nascimento, 2018a). The history of Black women as domestic workers is an inherited legacy and condition from slavery (B. Nascimento, 2018a; Preta-rara, 2019). This all pushes Black women to the lower rungs of income earners, and a cocktail of classism, sexism, and racism makes them less desirable to potential romantic partners (S. Carneiro, 2019c). These combined forces of racism, sexism, and class exploitation amount to "super-exploitation" (Jones, 2009).

Beyond challenging interlocking systems of oppression, Black feminists also produce ideas and practices of alternative social connection, political identification, and cultural activity. These are for everyone, not just Black women. They are especially for Black men who are caught between anti-Black racism, white supremacy, and heteropatriarchal power. And these insights call out the racist construction of gender—of masculinity—that affects Black men. In relation to white men, Black men are often violently relegated to a subordinate, emasculated, and feminized position (O. Pinho, 2008). Black men also confront "controlling images" (P. Collins, 2000); media, the state, and society represent them as being childlike (J. J. Carvalho, 1996), hypersexual brutes (J. J. Carvalho, 1996), criminals or traffickers (Messias, 2015), noble warriors (Hanchard, 2008), or cultural entertainers (Lima, 2001). At the same time, and in response, Black men desire to occupy an elevated social class position above Black women. Even though Black men, like Black women, confront an abject Blackness that is inherently gendered (which is not to say they experience sexism), they also desire the position of white men and subsequently dominant relations with white women, Black women, and other Black men. Imitating white manhood, Black men pursue white women, who are seen as virtuous, pure, and pious, as possessions that symbolize their heteropatriarchal power (S. Carneiro, 2019c). This excludes Black women as romantic partners (Pacheco, 2013). Interlocking forces of oppression are not constructed based on an additive model (McCarthy, 1998). Black people can mobilize these systems to turn them against more marginalized Black people.

In the Middle Passage, Black people were "ungendered," a process that ensured they would not adhere to hegemonic ideals and embodiments of masculinity and femininity (Spillers, 1987). No matter how hard we try, Black men do not conform to hegemonic constructions of masculinity and Black women do not conform to hegemonic constructions of femininity. Throughout the Americas, Black people have struggled against the ways we have been displaced from normative ideations of masculinity and femininity. It is not masculinity and femininity that are the problem per se, but rather the hegemonic constructions that ensure white people are the template for those social categorizations. This is part of a broader coloniality of the human, where "Man," that is, a Western, white, masculine, bourgeois male subject, is overrepresented as the human, as if that were the only possible model we could have and thus should aspire to (Wynter, 2003). Many attempt to compensate for racial and ethnic deviations from Man by adhering strongly to his gendered, classed, sexual, and moral configurations. Yet this racial calculus of the human is not a formula to be balanced on a scale. Whiteness constructs the sheer force of Blackness as not only a racial and ethnic deviation from Man but also a gendered, sexual, class, and moral deviation.

I make this point to also think of this ungendering as a point of *aquilombamento* rather than stigma and derision. Black people's ungendering opens other possibilities of masculinity and femininity and thus relationships and communal creation that do not rest upon Western colonial logics. It veers toward a queer diaspora that opposes the nation-state and its colonial logics of human subjectivity. Emergent *quilombos* confront, refuse, and escape from Western logics of gender that are instrumental in creating abject Blackness and denying Black people full human status. In this book, I highlight the ways that Black Bahian hip-hop artists are creating emergent genres of the human that rethink both race and gender. How are Black Bahian hip-hop artists trying to rethink, re-narrate, rewrite, re-perform, and represent Blackness in ways that more fully foster a wide range of human possibilities which would benefit us all? This means refusing both the "coloniality of gender" (Oyěwùmí, 1997) and "plantation patriarchy" (hooks, 2003). Marquis Bey (2019) calls for a "fugitive un/gendering [that] attempts to vitiate the regime of gender by way of an unyielding, radically opening ungendering" (p. 56). My point here is we must go beyond refusal, escape, and flight as fugitives: we must consider *how* we create emergent *quilombos* based on alternative social, cultural, and political systems that cut across race, gender, sexuality, and class. We cannot always be in flight. We must also stop, rest, nourish, love, and care for ourselves and one another. Thus, I want to think of a radically opening ungendering as instrumental to *aquilombamento*, key to the way it bestows upon Black people other modes of collectivizing, assembling, and forging communal spaces that protect and shield Black people.

A Note on Method

In the pages to follow, I offer a critical ethnographic study of the Bahian hip-hop movement as it constructs an emergent *quilombo* through Black hip-hop members' material conditions, lived experiences, everyday ideologies, social relations, aesthetics, media representations, and visual arts. By critical ethnography, I mean that I address injustices, oppression, and unfairness, analyzing the political stakes of cultural practices and social behaviors at the lived level (Conquergood, 2013; Madison, 2005). My own approach engages anthropology traditions grounded in decolonization, activism, and social justice (Berry et al., 2017; Hale, 2008; Harrison, 1997, 2008; K.-K. Perry, 2012; Rana, 2020; Sojoyner, 2017). I also draw on communication and media studies approaches to ethnography that analyze the mediated circulation of cultural meanings in visual symbols, lyrical soundscapes, and televisual representations (Báez, 2018; Bobo, 1998; Dimitriadis, 1996; Durham, 2014; Gibson, 2000; Jackson, 2008). No ethnographic account can be accurate or fully representative. Rather, this book is a reflection and mediation based on my own interactions, performances, subjectivity, political orientations, metaphysical beliefs, and interpretations based on extended fieldwork.

In the ensuing chapters, I detail the lives, communities, spaces, practices, and cultural texts of Black female, male, and nonbinary hip-hop artists, intellectuals, and activists in Salvador da Bahia. I draw on nineteen months of ethnographic research with Black Bahian hip-hop artists as well as textual analyses of their rap songs, music videos, and graffiti murals. My research began in summer 2012 and has continued annually, with research trips of between one and three months. My research coperformers are Black MCs, graffiti artists, and DJs who are from or have been living in Salvador for extensive periods of time (at least ten years, but often much more). Their ages range from eighteen to the mid-forties. Some of them have completed high school. Many have bachelor's degrees. Some even have or are doing master's and doctoral degrees. Regardless of education, many still live in peripheries or working-class neighborhoods, often for economic, social, or political reasons.

My ethnographic methods include participant observation, semi-structured interviews, and cultural document collection (CDs, graffiti mural pictures, advertisements, clothing, and hip-hop art). Over this time, I conducted twenty-nine interviews with Black hip-hop artists (women, men, and nonbinary people) and spent countless hours in participant observation. The semi-structured interviews focused on members' own personal histories; the Bahian hip-hop movement; issues of race and racism, class and urban segregation, and misogyny and sexism; Afro-Bahian culture; and Brazilian hip-hop. As a participant-observer, I accompanied my coperformers to their homes; getting ice cream or coffee; sharing meals; riding raggedy city buses; grabbing a cold beer at a local bar; going to festivals, concerts, shows, and events; kickin' it at their jobs; to studio recordings; and as an observer (and participant) in graffiti mural paintings. I also made use of informal conversations in person and digitally to stay informed of ongoing events in the Bahian hip-hop community.

It is still important to critically reflect on one's own positionality and its implications for performing research.[5] As a light-skinned multiracial Black man from the United States, my racialization in Brazil fluctuates according to various social contexts. Usually I am hailed colorwise as *pardo*, a "brown" or "mixed" intermediate color-coded category between *preto* (black/dark in skin tone) and *branco* (white). Many times I am hailed as *nego* or *negão*, an informal way of saying "Black man." Due to various middle-class markers like education, income, and my passport, some wish to make me an honorary "white" in Brazil, a supposed compliment meant to convey that I am not like most Black people because Black is a bad thing or because I do not suffer the same conditions and prejudices as poor and working-class Black Brazilians. This is what many mean when they say that "money whitens." In the eyes of the state and civil society, however, I am still a Black man. On a recent trip, I rented a room from a friend in a building in a middle-class neighborhood. White neighbors in the building expressed their concern to my roommate about the big suspicious man with a beard and tattoos whom they did not know who had a key to the apartment complex. Still, this does not compare to the everyday realities of many Black Brazilians, especially darker folks.

With Bahian hip-hop artists, I negotiated my positionality in multiple ways. I drew on my personal history with hip-hop culture, talking about using rap music to understand my own Blackness. I explained how hip-hop taught me to push back against the racist attitudes of white family and community members. I also drew on my experiences of the stigma of growing up Black and part of the working class. All this resonated with many Bahian hip-hop artists who experience anti-Blackness from their own families, white or not, and society at large. I conveyed how hip-hop culture helped me develop my own Black identity as well as critique the systemic and structural racism in the United States. Often, I cited as counterparts MC Marechal and Mano Brown, two lighter Black male MCs who are regularly perceived to be "brown" in skin tone but "Black" in political identity. These strategies do not mean negotiating my positionality as a Black man is always smooth. Some saw me as Black in Brazil. Some saw me as *pardo* or even white because I am not dark (*preto*). Some later came to see me as Black. One's own Blackness does not always travel neatly across borders and into different contexts. As many of us know, this stuff is messy and complicated.

Key Terms

Translating concepts from one context and language into another is difficult. I wish to define some key terms so that they are understood within their Brazilian contexts. Throughout the book, I capitalize "Black," which I translate from *negrx/a/o*. In Brazil, it is common in both activist circles and social science research to use *negrx/a/o* to encompass both darker Brazilians (*pretx/a/o*) and lighter African-descended Brazilians (*pardx/a/o*). I use Black because lighter and darker African-descended Brazilians occupy similar socioeconomic and political positions in Brazil, especially in contrast to white Brazilians (e.g., Telles, 2004). I also use Black to disrupt Brazilian colorism that favors *pardx/a/os* and denies them their Blackness.

Residents use several terms to describe poor and working-class Black communities that are in hard-to-reach hillside neighborhoods, with mostly self-constructed homes. There is *bairro* (district), community, *gueto* (ghetto), *subúrbio* (suburb), and favela. A *gueto* is the Brazilianization of the US term "ghetto." A *subúrbio* sits on the outskirts of the city. A favela sits inside the city. In these areas, many of the residents do not have land rights and are overpoliced. For the sake of simplicity, I use periphery, or *periferia*, to encompass all these spaces. The periphery is both a symbolic and spatial marginalization; it refers to communities pushed to the outskirts of society.

Last, here is some much-needed context on what "Bahia" represents. In general, Bahia refers to the Brazilian state in the Northeast. Bahian, or *baiana/o* in Portuguese, is used to refer to people, places, and things from or in the state of Bahia. Salvador is the capital city of Bahia (and was the first capital city of Brazil). Often, Salvador becomes conflated with Bahia, with people saying they are going to Bahia when they mean Salvador. When most people think of Bahia, they think of Salvador da Bahia and the Reconcâvo region that surrounds the Bay of All Saints. Technically, someone from Salvador is a Soterpolitan, or *soteropolitanx/a/o*. However, I follow local conventions that just refer to people, things, and places in Salvador as Bahian.

Chapter Overview

The following chapters cover how Black Bahian hip-hop artists, intellectuals, and activists adopt, retool, and expand the *quilombo* model as they construct alternative social, cultural, and political systems for marginalized Black people. In chapter 1, I draw on fieldwork and interviews to illustrate how Black Bahian hip-hop artists understand their racial conditions. I trace how the *quilombo* is first and foremost a condition structured by Brazilian coloniality, whether produced in the colony or the contemporary moment. This chapter illustrates how race is not a matter of prejudice or cultural inclusion but rather an organizing principle in what Stuart Hall calls "societies structured in dominance" (1980b). I pay close attention to where Black Bahians live, their positions in the economy and workforce, and their experiences with state violence. This chapter depicts Brazil from the vantage point of socially excluded Black people rather than those who are accepted owing to folkloric or mixed Blackness.

Black people's socioeconomic positions and material conditions do not define them. Chapter 2 explores how Black Bahian hip-hop artists imagine themselves and their communities as more than just marginalized people who are lost in misery, poverty, and criminality. Hip-hop artists extend *quilombo* ideologies to raise a Black *conscientização* (critical consciousness) among the Black underclass. They utilize a diasporic political and cultural matrix that weaves together *ancestralidade* (ancestrality), negritude, and US Black popular culture to foment racial pride, cultural heritage, and alternative social, cultural, and political systems among themselves and their communities. Just as *quilombos* historically provided Black people with an alternative to enslavement, the hip-hop movement is providing them with an alternative to abject Blackness and permitted forms of Blackness on a national scale.

An *emergent quilombo* exceeds Black people's conditions, their racial consciousness, and their political ideologies, additionally providing a Black sociality of alternative modes for relating to one another. Chapters 3 and 4 turn to emergent *quilombos* as central to Black social life. In chapter 3, I explore how Black Bahian hip-hop artists reterritorialize the *quilombo* onto their own spaces, where Black people can find refuge, rest, cultural creativity, and communion in contrast to violent Brazilian spaces that construct white civil society. I illustrate how Black space is mobile and even ephemeral in cultivating the needs of Black sociality. Black people may be in flight, but when they converge and commune with one another, they are creating a *quilombo*. It is important to understand the alternative socialities in these *quilombo* spaces. In chapter 4, I reveal how Black men are refusing Western heteropatriarchy and instead loving and protecting one another. Afro-Brazilian cosmologies of age and seniority lay out a matrix that Black men are using to rearrange Black masculine social life to permit intimacy rather than hostility toward one another. I name this as queer to explain how Black men form unconventional social bonds that are antithetical to the racial moral order and its normative violence. This is done to preserve the collective and allow other modes of relation-making.

The last three chapters turn to cultural and artistic creativity in the Bahian hip-hop movement. An emergent *quilombo* also supplies a different cultural realm, in which Black people anchor themselves and thrive. In chapter 5, I show how Black Bahians take the abject Black body and produce a new aesthetics that gives it value, worth, and meaning without resorting to notions of redemption, transcendence, or recovery. I emphasize "artifice" as the emergent *quilombo* aesthetic resisting the "natural" and its essentialist ideas of Blackness. Artifice anchors Black people's bodies, styles, and fashions to different tastes, sensibilities, and affects that depart from the Brazilian rubric of beauty.

Because *quilombos* are also political, in chapter 6, I explore rap videos that convey and assert sovereignty with other marginalized Black people in the periphery and resist Brazilian necropolitics that target Black people. This ranges from protecting the periphery to providing for other Black people to practicing restorative justice. It must not be forgotten that *quilombos* historically created a space and refuge for Black people from the ravages of enslavement and colonial society, safe havens in which they could assert their humanity with dignity. The last chapter turns to graffiti murals of Iemanjá, a Candomblé *orixá*, as representations of ordinary Black women. These visual representations are the makings of a different genre of the human whose orientation is not based on Western white Man but rather his opposite: poor Black mothers in the Global South. It bestows "real women" with human dignity and offers a dialogical relationship for other Black people to assert their humanity.

1 | Racial Conditions

Follow me to Salvador da Bahia, the city that connects Brazil to Africa, its diaspora, and the rest of the global community. After a red-eye flight, you arrive at the Deputado Luís Eduardo Magalhães Airport, tired from having to connect internationally at the Guarulhos airport in São Paulo. The moment you see the bamboo-covered road leading out of the airport and into the city, you get excited. The salty ocean air breathes life into your sleep-deprived and jet-lagged body. You drop off your bags and race to Pelourinho, meeting me outside the Mercado Modelo that sits in front of the Bay of All Saints. The gorgeous body of water is picture-perfect, stretching across the Reconcâvo region; boats, ferries, and fishermen steadily pass to and fro. Walking inside the market, we weave through kiosks offering shot glasses, T-shirts, a mini berimbau (an instrument to play capoeira music), cachaça, and other souvenirs for friends and family.

We keep it moving, heading back outside, crossing the busy street, avoiding the buses, cars, and mototaxis whizzing by. We walk up to the majestic and towering Lacerda Elevator, the nineteenth-century elevator that connects the "lower city" with the "higher city." We are swimming in a sea of Black people of all different hues, hair types, and body sizes. Just beautiful. We pay our fifteen-centavo fare to the city employee and get in line to take the elevator ride up to Pelourinho. It does not take long to get to an elevator, and the woman on her chair presses the button to take us up top. Exiting, we walk shoulder-to-shoulder with our fellow visitors. I excitedly blurt out, "We must get ice cream from Cubana!" We do, ordering from the little stand nestled inside the top level of the elevator structure. I get *nata goiaba* and you *maracuja*. "Senhor, we would also like two *cafezinhos*!" We exit to the left to marvel at

Figure 1.1. SALVADOR: block letters in front of the Lacerda Elevator in Pelourinho; photo courtesy of Sedrick Miles (2022)

the water. You've never seen a body of water so blue, so we make our way over to the Fallen Cross Monument to take photos. Every angle. Some of you. Some of me. Some of both of us. Within five minutes, we've been clocked for the tourists we are. We no longer pass for locals. Street vendors come to us: Do we need a water? Do we want a *lembrança* bracelet? Do we want a tour? Do we need sunglasses? Do we ~~want~~ need an ice-cold beer? We politely say no to all but the ice-cold water—hey, and maybe a beer. We navigate our way through the tour guides, tourists, and tour buses to the street, where we take *even more* pictures in front of the "SALVADOR" blocks that sit in front of the Lacerda Elevator.

We put away our phones and venture deep into Pelourinho, the colonial neighborhood with its baroque architecture. Today, it is a UNESCO World Heritage Site. As so many of us have heard, Pelourinho is *the* center of Afro-Bahian culture, a combination of folkloric and mixed Blackness. Everyone also wants us to know that Afro-Bahian culture is the center of Afro-Brazilian culture. And Afro-Brazilian culture is the center of Brazilian culture.

Since I have been here numerous times, I am excited to show you *all* the places. First, we visit the Afro-Brazilian Museum, where you are amazed by Carybé's wood carvings of *orixás*, Afro-Brazilian deities. We then march down to the Olodum headquarters, the infamous Afro-bloc with Pan-African colors and percussion instruments booming onto the cobble-stoned streets. You get the classic Olodum T-shirt, a peace sign with a black outline and red, green, and yellow filling in the middle. We make our way to the Casa Fundação de Jorge Amado to learn more about Bahia's most famous literary figure, a revered Communist. As we tour the three-story building, I tell you that despite his notoriety, he had complicated and, to be honest, racist views about Black people, especially Black women.[1] You purchase a few of his books, including *Sea of Death* because I told you it's my favorite. And *Gabriela, Clove and Cinnamon* because it is his most famous. We have done a lot of walking, a lot of talking, and the tropical heat combined with the thick humidity in the air is winning a battle it can never lose and we could never win. We barely notice the dehydration because the sights and sounds of Africa in the Americas are all around us. We stop for some water as we walk back up to the main plaza. We grab a few shots of *cravinho*, a clove-infused spirit, and some cheap cold beer to wash it down. We must eat. Soon, a warm and smiling *baiana* hostess, wearing the traditional *baiana* dress,[2] in front of "a very authentic" Bahian restaurant pulls us in to eat *baiana comida* like *moqueca, mariscos,* and *vatapá*. There is so much palm oil and seafood that the African influence is unmistakable. As we leave, we see a *capoeira roda* form, Black Bahians and a few white foreigners playing the much-cherished Afro-Brazilian music-dance-fighting genre (Lewis, 1992).

Structures of Racial Exclusion

This vignette is an oft-repeated performance, exemplary of how dominant actors, agencies, and institutions imagine, enact, and assign meaning to Bahia as well as how they desire people to move and interact there. The local government, the white middle classes, Afro-cultural agencies, and corporate media all contribute to this ideological process, creating stages that seduce locals, national visitors, and international tourists into expected cultural scenarios that cut across ethnic difference. They exert tremendous amounts of energy to make Bahia appear as a premodern locale of African culturalisms, void of the racial prejudice that plagues other places around the African Diaspora. In these performances, both Black and non-Black Bahians have, together, turned their city into a racial paradise that preserves Black people's African heritage and makes it available for others, Black and non-Black, to experience and consume. These exchanges eventually produce interracial mixture, cultural syncretism, and acculturation, hallmarks of Brazil's racial democracy mythos.

This romantic depiction and performance of Salvador da Bahia as an exotic playground is key to the idea of Bahia (O. Pinho, 1999), a racially harmonious locale based on both folkloric and mixed Blackness. Dominant Bahian actors, agencies, and institutions use Pelourinho as a stage to produce a Bahian regional identity that is fundamental to national narratives of racial harmony (Paschel, 2009). In this imaginary, Blackness is seemingly made available for every Bahian, and so Salvador is void of ethnic conflict and class struggle (Armstrong, 2001). Yet Blackness here does not refer to Black people's particular ethnicities, lived realities, or material conditions (C. Smith, 2016a). And Black cultural visibility and commodification do not correspond to improved material conditions for Black people (Malveaux, 1992). The hypervisibility of folkloric Blackness in fact obfuscates Black Bahians' sociopolitical realities across a variety of racial conditions (K.-K. Perry, 2013).

Rather than focus on the Blacknesses widely accepted in Bahia, like the vignette in Pelourinho, I am more interested in the Blacknesses that are excluded, outside of the Bahian imaginary and its representations and subsequent performances. What would it mean to begin with Blackness as a racial condition, distinct from a white bourgeois middle-class reality? This shift does not abandon the cultural. Instead, it opens an approach to analyze the cultures that emerge from Black realities, contexts, and experiences. It does not fissure Black cultures from Black social and political realities, but instead *anchors* them within Black people's social, economic, and political realities.

The Bahian hip-hop movement approaches Blackness materially. For them, race is not reducible to nation or ethnicity. It is a sociopolitical reality that corresponds to a specific set of experiences, circumstances, and conditions, what Howard Winant describes as "racial conditions" (1994): the expected circumstances, opportunities (or lack thereof), life chances, social situations, access to citizenship, and general welfare that afflict racialized peoples. Black Bahian hip-hop artists' keen insights expose the fact that Bahia is not an exception to racism, as the dominant actors, agencies, and institutions would suggest, but is in fact deeply anchored in them. These artists do not see racism as an issue of individual prejudice or cultural exclusion; instead, racism is structural, a matter of how social, economic, and political power is distributed and maintained (S. Almeida, 2019). Bahian hip-hop artists and community members base their cultural lives, expressions, and ideologies on ordinary Black people's racial conditions. Black Bahians' racial conditions are also diasporic; their environments are structured in global gender and racial hierarchies that cross legal, cultural, economic, imperial, and social boundaries (T. R. Patterson and Kelley, 2000, p. 20). Put simply, Black Bahians live under racial conditions similar to those of Black people in Rio de Janeiro, São Paulo, New York City, Havana, London, Los Angeles, Chicago, and Kingston.

Today, the Brazilian constitution recognizes that *quilombos* have a distinct cultural identity but elides the country's history of political exclusion and racial discrimination that made them necessary (Bowen, 2016). That is, Black people created and create *quilombos* in response to their social conditions (B. Nascimento, 2018b). Beatriz Nascimento defines a *quilombo* as a group of socially excluded Black people and their cultures that are also not accepted (2018b). This extends past independence and abolition, folding over into the Brazilian Empire, republic, dictatorship, and democracy. For centuries, Black people have continued creating *quilombos* in response to the varying racial conditions that impede their never-ending search for freedom. This holds true today in the "afterlife of slavery" (Hartman, 2008), in which Black people continue to face skewed life chances, premature death, and an ongoing search for freedom. In the *quilombo* they create communes for other Black people fleeing their racial situations who also desire a different set of conditions not premised upon racial marginalization, subjugation, and violence.

Since a *quilombo* is defined first as a grouping of socially excluded Black people, this chapter focuses on the social forces that exclude them—specifically, displacement, economic precarity, and racial violence—putting my interviews and fieldwork alongside broader quantitative social science research that tackles racial conditions. *Displacement* focuses on how Black people are forced into lower-class neighborhoods and out of newly desirable neighborhoods targeted for development. A key feature is ensuring that undesirable Black people are kept away from the middle classes and tourists. This means they live in overcrowded communities, often without land rights, and are susceptible to state-enforced removal. *Economic precarity* describes Black people's place within and even outside the formal workforce (B. Nascimento, 2018a). One's presumed occupation and supposed income-earning ability assigns meanings to one's position in society. It also dictates one's quality of life: where one can live, what modes of transportation can be used, and what broader nourishment patterns are inherent in how one eats. Finally, I consider the racial condition of *violence*. Racial conditions are political, involving state and societal calculations regarding who has political rights. One's exposure or nonexposure to violence and subsequent inaction informs who can seek protection from and by the state. Violence also assigns meaning to who is human and thus has value worthy of the state's and society's protecting, saving, and even avenging them.

Displacement

Here, I focus on how Black Bahian hip-hop artists narrate this spatial displacement and peripheralization by refusing their own disposability, while critiquing Brazilian government agencies and nonprofits that wish to take over their communities. Even as Brazil works to include some Black people, even if just symbolically, in the national community, it also actively works to keep the majority out. This work is not just symbolic but also spatial. When local government and nonprofit agencies began to rehabilitate Pelourinho into the tourist destination it is today, it forcibly relocated thousands of poor and working-class Black Bahian residents to other periphery neighborhoods, like Sussuarana. Since the 1990s, residents have had to accept indemnifications ranging from US$200 to US$5,000 to move out of Pelourinho (J. F. Collins, 2015). The state and developers displaced Black people and subsequently an abject Blackness. They welcomed some Black people back, provided they were "redeemed": eschewing an abject Blackness, "cleaning" up one's self according to bourgeois standards of respectability, and conforming to a folkloric Blackness that valorizes African cultural purities but does not call attention to Black people's racial conditions. This fundamentally altered the racial dynamics of Pelourinho: who lived there, who belonged there, and what meanings circulate there. The state and society view the Black people they themselves exclude as disposable, easily discarded, without value, and better kept out of sight.

Just below Pelourinho sits the Ladeira da Preguiça (Lazy Slope) community, straddling the upper city and lower city, with the Lacerda Elevator standing just north of the small community. Whereas Pelourinho represents both folkloric and mixed Blackness, Ladeira de Preguiça is representative of an abject Blackness in the eyes of the state and civil society. Yet the residents and local hip-hop artists see this community as a refuge from the harsh realities in Salvador da Bahia. The intimate community is home to several key Black cultural institutions and a central meeting point for numerous organizations. It is adorned with graffiti murals by local artists. The "slope" was built by enslaved Black labor in the sixteenth century for rich whites who mocked Black people as "lazy." After the bourgeois elite abandoned the slope, Black people turned the neighborhood into a *quilombo* in the eighteenth and nineteenth centuries, using arts and culture as sites of resistance against Salvador's structures of racial domination. Throughout the twentieth and twenty-first centuries, the Ladeira "has not stopped developing and bringing together *quilombolas*" like capoeira grand masters, football players, samba schools, and Carnival blocs.[3]

Today, this periphery community defines itself as an urban *quilombo*. Since my research began in 2012, Ladeira da Preguiça has been an urban refuge for poor and working-class Black people around the city. It is also extremely protective against outsiders. In 2017, I awkwardly learned a lesson about how Black people can and cannot enter this *quilombo*. One day, I arrived before an interview and waited around for a local graffiti artist. I had been to this neighborhood many times with this person and others. They introduced me to several residents, and some even recognized me on subsequent visits to the neighborhood. That day, a small group of residents marked me as an outsider—that is, not a community resident. One older Black man approached me, looked me up and down, and asked who I was. Why was I there? I quickly became nervous, sweating through my T-shirt. I said I was a US researcher, there to do an interview with the local graffiti artist, whose name I certainly dropped to gain credibility. At that point, the elder also marked me as a foreigner and a researcher. That made my intrusion even worse. I said I had been to the Ladeira many times and worked with folks at the local community center. He said the graffiti artist should have accompanied me into the community. Even though I felt very comfortable in Salvador and moving in many hip-hop spaces, this was a moment when I had been an intruder, an unwelcome outsider who overstepped his boundaries. This example illustrates that visiting certain places does not guarantee unlimited access. I scurried out in shame and sadness, but also with respect for the way that the community is protective of those who enter and on what terms.[4]

The community's emphasis on protecting itself against outsiders also extends to the state. In May 2015, the National Historic and

Artistic Heritage Institute (IPHAN) designated a handful of buildings in Ladeira da Preguiça to be demolished. However, an accident occurred: a building collapsed, killed a man, and destroyed two other houses. Afterward, the owner of the remaining property was robbed several times because his home remained exposed. Soon, community residents constructed a wall to protect him and his belongings. However, on September 8, 2015, the Urban Municipal Secretary (SUCOM) ordered the community to demolish this wall because local residents had built it without the proper licensing and authorization by City Hall. But no one demolished the wall because it would have left the resident's home and belongings unprotected. Also, they knew the state would not protect this local resident. Finally, they were combating the long-term issue that the state was demolishing people's homes and expelling them from their neighborhood. Land grabs by the state, real estate developers, and banks are increasing, targeting Black communities that were previously undervalued and yet are close to highly desirable areas like the beach, financial districts, trendy neighborhoods, or historical centers (K.-K. Perry, 2013).

Later that year, the state entered Ladeira de Preguiça on October 2 to demolish the wall. The city government's goal was to build a cancer support center—part of further efforts to develop and expand the historic center. As the community intrinsically knew, this development also meant the state and developers would displace long-standing poor and working-class Black residents. Two artists from a local graffiti crew intervened and attempted to prevent the state from tearing down the wall. They wanted to preserve the resident's home and his ability to be safe from local thieves. After some arguing, municipal guards apprehended and attempted to arrest the two graffiti artists. At this point a fight ensued, and one of the graffiti artists broke a municipal officer's nose (*Prefeitura vai demolir três "cascas,"* 2015; G. Santos, 2015). News quickly broke out in the Bahian hip-hop movement. Many hip-hop community members saw the state's actions and heavy-handedness as part of continuing state-led efforts to displace Black people, usually without the residents' input, and develop social projects that would not benefit Black people.

Indeed, various state, business, nonprofit, and private agencies have sought to forcibly take the Ladeira de Preguiça and its prime location near Pelourinho from its predominantly poor and working-class Black population. The community document "Quilombo Urbano—Ladeira da Preguiça" addresses these issues: "In the 1990s, the community was totally abandoned by the public power, unleashing a racist process of expelling residents, known as 'Gentrification.' Residents are being seduced to sell their houses for very cheap, the public power degrades its residents by denying them basic rights like sanitation and paved roads, and the state violates residents' lives using its police force." Community members view displacement as a set of material racist strategies, like social abandonment, police violence, and economic pressures.

When the state, nonprofits, banks, and developers wish to get Black people out of suddenly desirable areas, they often use the language of "hygienification" and "cleaning up" to name their actions. They view areas like Ladeira de Preguiça as diseased and filthy. This is like the discourse of abject Blackness. In the nineteenth century, the medical ethnologist Raimundo Nina Rodrigues led a series of studies that presumed Black people were diseased in their bodies, filthy on their bodies, and a threat to public health (Otovo, 2016; Romo, 2010). These studies used biological notions of race to justify Black people's stigma and dismal racial conditions, construing them as childlike and unable to participate as reasonable and self-actualized citizens. This was why they naturally populated the lower rungs of society. Today, the association of Black bodies with dirtiness and thus an abject Blackness marks public discourse, the workplace, and media representations (P. Pinho, 2015). In Ladeira de Preguiça, community members pressed back against their ongoing degradation. They are not dirty because Black people are just dirty. They are dirty because the state denies Black communities basic sanitary services and even necessary infrastructure. Yet the state and dominant social actors view Blackness as something they must clean up from its inherent pathological state. They do this by civilizing and redeeming an abject Blackness and its social referents. They target Ladeira da Preguiça and other similar periphery communities for cleaning, meaning they wipe away undesirable Black elements.

If one looks not at Pelourinho but rather from Pelourinho, one will notice that Salvador's racial and classed inequalities are highly visible. In 2014, I met up with Carlos for an interview in his Plataforma apartment on the northern outskirts of the city. We went to the spare bedroom with yellow egg-crate foam bedding on the walls, a makeshift studio where he produced music and records rappers and singers. As I pulled out my recorder and a list of questions, the usually convivial and lighthearted MC became quite serious. Even his shoulder-length dreadlock hair stood still. When I asked him about the general struggles of living in Salvador as a Black man, he bowed his head as if he was struggling to think about where to begin. He went on to say:

> There exist real problems in Salvador. Problems of infrastructure. You got this historic shit that's happened right here and now it is so complicated to reverse this.... But it has this key question that revolves around Pelourinho but also what's next to it, all around it: it's all Black people. People start crowding to these neighborhoods next to Pelourinho and then to areas just outside the center. Salvador is one giant favela, right? Everywhere you look, you see a ghetto (*gueto*).... Salvador does not have an urban structure. Although it's an urban city, it does not have the structure for an urban city. It's the kind of place that was constructed crazy, right?

Carlos points out there is much more to Salvador than the dazzling spectacle of folkloric and mixed Blackness in Pelourinho. He urges us to go further to where Black people are, where they live, and their vantage point of Salvador da Bahia. I read Carlos' statement as identifying Blackness as more than just cultural attributes, one's origins, or one's national/ethnic marker. It is a material reality that shapes who is and is not included in society. Carlos's point is that Salvador is one giant favela, filled with Black people, by design. It is both historical, happening over centuries, and contemporary, shaping Black people's present realities. The state and other powerful institutions removed Black people from Pelourinho. Now many Black people have moved to communities, like Ladeira de Preguiça, that are close to Pelourinho. The state and their allies keep Black people out of Pelourinho or other "cleaned up" places because they believe the Black masses do not conform to a white bourgeois standard (Maia, 2019; Maia and Reiter, 2021) or some type of acceptable Blackness.

In Salvador, race and racism shape Black people's social realities, ranging from where they can and cannot live to where they go and how they get there, or to how they get treated and by whom. Carlos calls attention to the fact that Black people are more likely to live in lower-class communities composed of the poor, the working class, and the lower middle class. These periphery spaces are usually self-built, abandoned in part or wholesale by the state, and highly socially stigmatized (Pardue, 2008). Often, but not always, periphery residents do not have land rights. Many own their homes. Others rent. It is not uncommon for someone born and raised in a community to still live there. Many of their families may have lived there for generations. Yet without land rights, they are vulnerable to being displaced at any given moment (K.-K. Perry, 2013).

The strong racial prejudice that stigmatizes the periphery and its inhabitants is not insignificant. The state, middle-class society, and the media consider the periphery a dangerous neighborhood that runs on criminality, lawlessness, and backwardness (Pardue, 2008). Often, they socially construct peripheries as non-Brazilian spaces and part of the developing world, like in Africa, in contrast to middle-class and upper-class neighborhoods that are part of the overdeveloped world, like in Western Europe (M. A. Soares, 2012). They then blame the peripheries for hindering Brazil's progress toward modernity and utopic futures. The state, middle-class society, and the media portray periphery residents, especially Black people, as a dangerous social group who occupy social space (Campos, 2005). When Black people leave the periphery and go into public and consumer spaces of the middle classes and/or elites, the state and society meet them with suspicion, fear, interrogation, derogatory insults, physical harm, and police searches (Herschmann, 2005; O. Pinho, 2018). Their logic is that Black people are poor and automatically from the periphery; people from the periphery are also criminals, and criminals should be apprehended by the police and even ordinary citizens. Even if someone has not committed a crime, it is believed that a poor Black person from the periphery has at some point or will in the near future. The signifying chain from race and geography to criminality justifies police entering the periphery, treating everyone like criminals and indiscriminately shooting at residents (K.-K. Perry, 2012).

This shift in perspective that Carlos makes—moving from the Bahian imaginary to Black people's racial conditions—challenges Bahian society's beloved notion that Salvador is a class-based society influenced by color and culture (e.g., Azevedo, 1955; Pierson, 1944). Statistics back up Carlos's claim that peripheries are Black communities (I. Carvalho and Barreto, 2007). In a larger sense, the relations between the center and the periphery have a racial character. Blacks make up approximately 80 percent of Salvador's population, yet this is not reflected in residential neighborhoods across class profiles. Lower-class spaces are predominantly Black: Black people constitute 85 percent (60.9 percent *parda/o* and 23.3 percent *preta/o*) in lower-working-class neighborhoods and 85 percent (64.8 percent *parda/o* and 20.2 percent *preta/o*) of agricultural working-class areas. White people constitute only 13.7 percent and 12.6 percent, respectively, of the lower working class and the agricultural working class. The state, developers, and middle classes are driving Black people farther north into lower-middle-class, working-class, and lower-working-class neighborhoods. From 1991 to 2000, the Pelourinho historic center, Rio Vermelho, and the Brotas neighborhoods went from being middle class (*mídia*) to upper middle class (*mídia-superior*). Activists see this same process occurring with Ladeira de Preguiça: the state, the white middle class, and developers suddenly desire a neighborhood populated by poor and working-class people, and the change in a neighorhood's class profile also corresponds to a change in its racial profile. Middle-class spaces are mostly white with a small segment of "acculturated" Blacks (mostly lighter in complexion). Upper-class spaces are disproportionately white. In the 2000 census, whites constituted more than three-fifths of the upper-class areas and two-fifths of upper-middle-class neighborhoods. Conversely, Blacks (*preta/o* and *parda/o*) constituted just 34 percent of the upper-class areas (27.5 percent *parda/o* and 6.5 percent *preta/o*, respectively) and 58.6 percent of the upper-middle-class ones (44.3 percent and 14.3 percent, respectively). White people are concentrated in the southern tip/historical center of the city and around Itapuã, almost entirely upper-middle-class and upper-class neighborhoods. These dynamics continued in the 2010 census: white people constituted more than 50 percent of upper-class neighborhoods. White Bahians still lived in nicer neighborhoods on the Atlantic Ocean coastline, while Black people predominated in poorer neighborhoods at the periphery (I. Carvalho and Barreto, 2007; I. Carvalho and Pereira, 2015).

Brazil prides itself on having never codified racial segregation like the United States. The truth is it never needed to. The segregation between the big house (*casa-grande*) and the slave quarters (*senzala*) now plays out in the city landscape. Both the plantation and the city mimic a center-periphery model (I. Carvalho and Pereira, 2015). Although geographers typically use the model to describe the relations of power and exploitation between Europe and North America vis-à-vis Latin America, Africa, and Asia (Cardoso and Enzo, 1979; Cox, 1964; Rodney, 2018), they insist that it also works at the local level in Salvador. They argue that the center, which includes the downtown area and coastline neighborhoods, mirrors overdeveloped nations. The center's development depends on its ability to transfer resources from the periphery, keeping the latter impoverished and underdeveloped.

While the center and the periphery each rely on the other, both state and nonstate actors and institutions create and maintain them as two different worlds. These relations are fluid, as they expand "the center" by "cleaning up" neighborhoods. As a newly desirable neighborhood becomes part of the center, it is viewed as whiter, more civilized, and of a higher social standing.

Socioeconomic Exclusion

Racial conditions do not magically appear: state and nonstate entities produce them by ingraining gendered anti-Blackness throughout various social and political structures. Elevating whiteness and subjugating Blackness causes racial inequalities across various social, economic, and political indices (e.g., Telles, 2004). The state and civil society stitch these racial conditions into the very fabric of everyday worlds, into the most mundane and ordinary elements of people's lives. Individual actors maintain these systems through a variety of quotidian performances. Across Brazil's history, Black Brazilians, including contemporary Black Bahian hip-hop artists and activists, have created *quilombos* in response to these racial conditions, challenging their enslaved subjectivities *and* their socioeconomic exploitation in and exclusion from the workforce. They challenged and continue to challenge racial capitalism, a social order and economic system that fundamentally requires racial differentiation to benefit a dominant racial group and aggressively exploit and marginalize a subordinate racial group (e.g., Hudson, 2018; Jones, 2009; Makalani, 2014; Robinson, 2021).[5]

In 2013, I joined João, a thirty-nine-year-old MC, rap battle organizer, and record label owner, at a hip-hop festival at the Parque Boa Vista in Brotas. As the afternoon sun shined on us and he sat on the water fountain ledge, I asked him about the challenges of living in Salvador. As he looked up at me, his voice struck a note of frustration, a feeling presumably built up over years: "It's a challenge living here in Bahia, in Salvador. It's a huge challenge. The people here are the largest concentration of Black people outside of Africa and we also have the largest contingency of unemployed people who are Black. Salvador is considered a national capital: the Brazilian capital of unemployment" (cited in Henson, 2019, p. 466). João's insight about Black unemployment levels in Salvador challenges the "Bahian school of race relations" (Guimarães, 1999) that emphasizes Black cultural acceptance and individual success. Some social scientists, such as Thales Azevedo and Donald Pierson, argue that Salvador has harmonious race relations because Black and white Bahians freely interact with one another regardless of class, rank, or status. They go on to argue that since some Black people can join the upper social strata, there is no racial discrimination in Bahia. In this school of thought, Black people succeed due to individual exceptionalism, adopting a Eurocentric worldview, valorizing whiteness, and distancing themselves from the Black masses (Azevedo, 1955; Pierson, 1944). João disrupts the Bahian school of race relations by focusing on the systemic nature of racial discrimination, such as in unemployment, instead of individual aberrations. He connects the fact that Salvador has a large Black population with the fact that it also has a large unemployed population. João sees this as being by design, a structure that economically keeps Black people out of the workforce, creating a large unemployment pool. A few successful Black people do not offset the pervasive problems in the city. For example, Salvador has the highest income inequality in the nation (Mitchell-Walthour, 2017). And Black people are on the lower end of these scales. Even though Black people are hypervisible in cultural representation, this does not translate to improved employment opportunities for most Black people.

How Black people earn income or even obtain jobs shapes where they can and cannot live. Income is an important factor in the unequal distribution of wealth across race, class, and gender that disproportionately affects Black people, and especially Black women (S. Carneiro, 2019a). In addition to racial discrimination in the workforce, Black people face limited choices about where they can live, what they can buy, and how they can eat. In 2013, I met with Marisa, a local graffiti artist, at my friend's house in the Nazaré neighborhood. When I asked her about the challenges of living in Salvador, she stressed the high cost of living. The fast-talking Marisa touched on how working-class income affects home ownership, rental possibilities, and even food security:

> The question of renting here, it's expensive. Living in Salvador is also very expensive. And to buy your own house in Brazil, from a general standpoint, it's so difficult, you know? You stop looking to buy and go back to renting. And, again, it's so expensive, even out on the periphery here. You see absurd prices. It's not just renting and buying. There's also the problem of food prices. Food is pricey here. Even with just the basics, you can't spend less than R$200 to have decent food for two people, you know? And that's really complicated for a nation where

the monthly minimum salary is R$670 [in 2013], right? It's this. It's that. It's all of this.

Even though Salvador is cheaper than other large cities like Rio de Janeiro, São Paulo, and Brasilía, it does not offer equitable access to income, living spaces, and cost of living. Programs like Zero Hunger have reduced hunger among people in the lower classes (Ansell, 2014), but Marisa points out that it is still not enough. She does not even touch on utilities like electricity, propane gas, and internet service. Marisa's point is that rent and home costs eat up a large amount of one's salary. Employment constraints, rent, and food prices limit Black people's ability to purchase a home and achieve residential stability.

As Marisa notes, food prices strain poor Bahians' budgets, contributing to their conditions. She remarks that buying food can take up approximately one-third of a monthly minimal salary (MMS), the federal standard for a minimum wage. The situation was much more difficult in the years that followed my interview with Marisa in 2013. The MMS rose to R$1,000 in 2021, but Brazil entered an economic crisis, with the Brazilian real falling in value and inflation rapidly increasing. Food has steadily increased in price, doubling or tripling for basic staples like coffee, bread, pasta, rice, and beans. When I checked in with Black hip-hop artists in 2020 and 2021, they often mentioned hyperinflation and worsening homelessness and hunger.

It merits attention that Marisa's calculations are based on two people eating, not just one. I want to read her comment through a gendered lens to acknowledge several possible housing situations where multiple people rely on a single income. This could be a couple that lives together but only one partner has an income. Maybe a single parent, most likely a mother, must buy food for their child. Perhaps someone lives at home with an elderly relative, such as a parent, and must care for them as well. Almost always, it is a woman who must financially and domestically take care of their family members. Regardless of living arrangement, Marisa alludes to the fact that marginalized Black people often have to care for another person on limited funds intended for one person.

The cost of living includes the cost of mobility, even at the basic level of how one travels to work to earn income. Urban transportation is very expensive. Black Bahians spend a considerable amount on public transportation, which many of them depend on. In 2020, Salvador's mayor, Antônio Carlos Magalhães Neto, confirmed that local bus fare would reach R$4.20. It is now R$4.40. This may not sound like a lot, but if you take the bus twice a day for work, five times a week, and four weeks a month, then you are spending R$176 a month on bus fare alone, 16 percent of an MMS. While there are reduced or free fares for students, the elderly, young children, and disabled people, numerous people do not qualify for these public programs and thus are burdened by an expensive yet underserving public transportation system.

For most Black Bahians, owning a car is beyond their means. This is not to say that no one has a car, but rather that buying a car can be cost-prohibitive for most. Beyond the purchase cost, gas and maintenance are additional expenses that make it difficult to own a car. In 2020, gas was often around R$4/liter, or roughly R$15/gallon (based on US$2.83/gallon). In June 2022, it was R$8/liter. A car is an expensive commodity to have.

Beyond money, public transportation costs time, bleeding Bahians of the precious hours they have outside of work. Carlos once told me that going from the city center to his periphery neighborhood, whether by car or bus, is like sand going through an hourglass. Just like an hourglass, the streets in the center and in the periphery are wide with many lanes. But in between the center and the periphery, there is only one lane, where cars, buses, and motorcycles must slow down, merge, and trickle through the middle until they can spread out on the other side. I felt this in my soul. I would always leave my apartment in the city center two hours before an interview if it was on the periphery and during the day. A thirty-five-minute bus ride with no traffic can take two hours on the often-neglected bus system. Carlos's house was very difficult to reach because the bus would always slow down to a halt on Avenida Afrânio Peixoto. Almost always, I would leave the bus sweaty and musty after being crammed with dozens of fellow riders and no air-conditioning for two hours. Carlos's point about transportation is as important as João's point about Black unemployment and Marisa's about the expensive cost of living. Social and economic forces expel Black people from the city center, like Pelourinho or Ladeira de Preguiça, and move them to the periphery. Black people are kept on the periphery through slow-moving and frustrating public transportation that eats up their leisure hours. When many Black people get home from work, they often do not wish to endure this taxing journey to go back out again for leisure. Ever-increasing fares impose a substantial burden on the Black poor and working classes in traveling from the periphery to the center. Transportation problems maintain the center-periphery model in the city and shape Black Bahians' racial conditions.

Rent, everyday expenses, and transportation costs must be understood as part of the income inequalities stretched across race and gender. Income does not paint the entire picture of Black people's class dynamics and circumstances, but it does provide a material perspective on how race, gender, and class work together through capitalism to overwhelm and marginalize Black people. In the 2010 census, 80 percent of residents in the city of Salvador da Bahia were categorized as Black (those who are *preta/o* or *parda/o*). For a city with an overall population of 2,667,691, Blacks numbered 1,888,188 (IBGE, 2010). The income distribution in 2010 disproportionately disadvantaged Black people, even though they were a numerical majority, and benefited white people, who constituted less than 20 percent of the city's population.[6] Income distribution is not favorable to women either. Tables 1.1 and 1.2 illustrate how income is distributed using the monthly minimum salary (MMS) as the unit of measure, which was 510 reals in 2010, 788 in 2015, 1,045 in 2020, and 1,100 in 2021.

In the city of Salvador da Bahia, there is a racial disparity in income between Blacks and whites. Like many other American societies, there are three main classes in Salvador: the local bourgeoisie consisting of whites and some light-skin *parda/os* who are invested in national and international interests; a middle sector of some whites, many *parda/os*,

Table 1.1. Race and income distribution in Salvador

Monthly Minimum Salary (MMS)	Branca/os	Preta/os	Parda/os	Negra/os
Less than ¼ MMS	4,223	17,065	24,886	41,951
¼ to ½ MMS	6,317	23,112	33,876	56,988
½ to 1 MMS	71,793	192,428	287,063	479,491
1 to 2 MMS	64,596	112,891	191,859	304,750
2 to 3 MMS	30,464	30,625	63,052	93,677
3 to 5 MMS	39,350	23,189	56,283	79,472
5 to 10 MMS	47,098	13,717	43,958	57,675
10 to 15 MMS	12,592	2,037	8,743	10,780
15 to 20 MMS	11,418	1,185	6,168	7,353
20 to 30 MMS	6,451	512	3,127	3,639
More than 30 MMS	3,550	273	1,581	1,854
Nonreporting	143,752	245,872	468,767	714,639
Total	441,604	662,906	1,189,363	1,852,269

Table 1.2. Gender and income distribution in Salvador

Monthly Minimum Salary (MMS)	Men	Women
Less than ¼ MMS	11,449	35,586
¼ to ½ MMS	20,936	43,523
½ to 1 MMS	251,412	308,777
1 to 2 MMS	216,419	159,205
2 to 3 MMS	73,961	52,314
3 to 5 MMS	65,181	55,519
5 to 10 MMS	57,640	48,653
10 to 15 MMS	14,097	9,563
15 to 20 MMS	12,517	6,488
20 to 30 MMS	7,202	2,993
More than 30 MMS	4,083	1,369
Nonreporting	339,550	532,900
Total	1,074,447	1,206,890

and a few *preta/os*; and the working class, who are predominantly Black and in the least valued and least well-paid positions (Bacelar, 1997). The racial profiles of Salvador's three main classes help explain the following statistics in table 1: 31 percent of Black people (both *preta/o* and *parda/o*) earn up to one MMS or less, whereas only 18 percent of white people earn so little; Black people are more than one and a half times as likely to earn one MMS or less than are their white counterparts. On the other side of the spectrum of the MMS, 27 percent of white people earn at least three MMS, whereas only 8 percent of Black people do so. Thus, white people in Salvador are three times more likely to earn at least three MMS than are their Black counterparts. These differences are further exacerbated in the rate of those who earn more than 10 MMS. Of the more than 400,000 white people in Salvador, almost 8 percent earn more than 10 MMS, while for Blacks, this number is little more than 1 percent. At this level, white people are six times more likely to earn at least R$5,100 a month than their Black counterparts are.

Dissecting census information brings to light the differences in the Black community and their income earnings. Some may argue Salvador does not have a race problem because so many Black people earn more than five MMS, roughly a middle-class salary, and almost 5,500 earn more than twenty MMS, apparently on par with the number of whites. However, the number of Black people in those segments compared to other segments shows that Black people are not climbing up the income scale at the same rate as their white peers. And worse, Black people are more likely than whites to not report income to the census, perhaps because they are unemployed or are in the informal economy, working as street vendors, for example.

While the census does not organize income by race *and* gender, it does provide important information about gender and how income is distributed along gender lines in a city that is 53.3 percent female, according to the census. The polar extremes make table 2 quite germane here.

Women are more than two and a half times more likely to earn a quarter or less of an MMS and almost 75 percent more likely to earn between a quarter and half of an MMS. Between a half and a full MMS, men (23.4 percent) and women (24.6 percent) have roughly the same percentage of earning these wages. After one MMS, the percentages shift strongly in favor of men, who are 60 percent more likely to earn between and two MMS than are women. For those who earn more than two MMS overall, men are 55 percent more likely to earn at least R$1,020 a month. At the highest levels of income earning, men are more than twice as likely to earn between 15 and 20 MMS, almost three times as likely to earn between 20 and 30 MMS, and three and a half times more likely to earn more than 30 MMS. Looking at race and gender distribution of income, it would be safe to assume that Black women are disproportionately affected: they earn less, which as Marisa points out sends them to the periphery, and they struggle to pay for basic living expenses for themselves or others.

Economies of Violence

Black Bahians' racial conditions include political conditions that shape their relationship to life and death. As the state and civil society drive Black people out of urban centers, they also exclude Black people from the polis. Here, I use polis to refer to the governing, political, and cultural centers of a city. Outside of the political community, Black people do not possess legal, political, personal, or property rights like a (white) citizen would. The state and civil society view Black people as foreign threats, barbarians ruled by nature and violence. In response, the state and even civilians feel at liberty to violently engage and even kill Black people from these neighborhoods. The Brazilian community portrays poor and working-class Black communities as "internal enemies" (Campos, 2005) who must be violently persecuted. Just as Brazil's colonial administration waged war on *quilombos* (Kent, 1965), the state is engaged in a never-ending war with the peripheries, treating anyone who lives there or is associated with these spaces as enemies of the state. The state manufactures an economy of violence with Black premature death as its desired product, intensifying Black Bahians' racial conditions. The state creates this economy by managing how it produces and distributes psychic and physical harm toward target recipients, in this case Black people.

Bahian hip-hop artists frequently spoke about the pervasive violence that shapes their everyday circumstances. Let me refer to two examples from interviews. João became quite angry regarding state-sanctioned violence against Black people in Salvador: "My homie just took a bullet. And his cousin was just killed by the police, you know? Justice rarely sticks. [Society] gotta keep it steady for the police, so [the policeman] can stay strolling in the street.... People are going to question the report, but the police are only gonna say my people are good when they say we're good. That way police can use physical force [when they want to]" (quoted in Henson, 2019, p. 467). Black hip-hop artists reveal the gaps between justice as an ideal and justice as a political system. Merriam-Webster's dictionary defines "justice" as "the process or result of using laws to fairly judge and punish crimes and criminals." João believes justice would be the Brazilian courts holding the police accountable for shooting his homie's cousin. However, the Brazilian juridical apparatus will not challenge the police's own reporting of events, upholding it as objective truth. Black people see how Brazil lets police freely kill Black people and inhibit justice for injured parties and their families. For them, justice is contradictory; it is a political ideology and praxis always used against them and very rarely for them.

On one occasion, I interviewed Carla and Camila, two Black women MCs, in a periphery neighborhood following a hip-hop event. They touched on the contrast between the hypervisibility of African-derived cultures and the mundane experiences of anti-Black racism.

> **Carla:** Let's put it this way . . . : People from outside Bahia, they have this very romantic point of view, right? African culture . . . exotic black women . . . samba . . . capoeira . . . Candomblé . . . all that, right?
> **BH:** It seems like the world has a vision of Bahia as a paradise.
> **Carla:** We don't do that shit.

Camila: ... and like everything is much easier here in Bahia, right?
Carla: It is not.
Camila: If you are a Candomblé practitioner, I've heard it this week, someone saying that here it is a paradise for people in Candomblé.
Carla: They don't even know what the hell it is to be a Candomblé practitioner.
Camila: Exactly. We in Bahia also suffer, I don't know the percentage of Black people here in Salvador, but the amount of racism we endure in Bahia, there's no way to describe it in words, because every single day there's a Black man dying, every single day a young Black man dies in the slums.

Dominant state, nonstate, and media actors and agencies may portray Salvador da Bahia as a racial paradise. Carla and Camila see it differently: Salvador is a racial hell. Beyond Pelourinho and its staged celebrations of folkloric Blackness, Black people experience race in social and political terms, not simply cultural terms. Brazilian society accepts Black men dying every day; it is ordinary and expected. There is no outcry, no political or ethical crisis (Ferreira da Silva, 2001). The Brazilian state and civil society banish Black people out of the polis and into a position that is fundamentally at odds with the political community. This forced imposition is a "structural antagonism" (Wilderson, 2010) founded on fundamental anti-Black racism, sexism, homophobia, and class exploitation. It is not a conflict that a person can resolve.

Amnesty International has produced two damning reports regarding police violence in marginalized neighborhoods. The first, *Brazil: "They Come In Shooting": Policing Socially Excluded Communities* (2005), traces a history of police violence against periphery residents, who are mostly Black. Police violence, intimidation, and fear tactics have sowed distrust and revulsion among these communities. One resident noted that they cannot leave their community because the police will stop and inspect them (p. 17). Several point out that "[police] come [in] shooting" with "their guns unholstered and ready" (p. 32). The police search homes without warrants, violate human rights, use corrupt tactics, and kill favela residents indiscriminately. The judicial system aids the police by issuing community warrants, permitting poor police reporting, and allowing confessions made under torture (p. 58). Ten years later, Amnesty International produced the report *You Killed My Son: Homicides by Military Police in the City of Rio de Janeiro* (2015). Like the previous report, it highlights pervasive police violence and the criminalization of poor and Black communities. When police shoot innocent community members, they report it as "resistance followed by death," which paints the victim as the aggressor against the police, who have no choice but to take lethal action in self-defense. The police justify their actions by portraying the victims as immoral actors who fit the criminal profile: young, poor, Black, and from the periphery (p. 75). Civil society supports the police's actions because they often feel that the police are keeping "good" citizens safe and protected from criminals. A logic of being at war with the periphery is widespread and accepted. For that reason, there is rarely outrage for the premature/ untimely death of Black people at the hands of the state. This is why João says, "Justice rarely sticks." Even when people inquire about police misconduct, both the judicial system and civil society support the police and their actions.

The material violence in Salvador is grave and demonstrates that the former colonial capital is anything but a racially harmonious locale. It is difficult to obtain accurate information regarding state-sanctioned killings around race. The state of Bahia has been publicly criticized for its poor recordkeeping with respect to police lethality. According to the Brazilian Public Security Annual Report (ABSP), Salvador's police murdered 146 people in 2017 and 103 in 2018. The 249 deaths over this time were fourth only to Rio de Janeiro (1,058), São Paulo (853), and Goiânia (258). However, many Black victims of this violent economy are the result of informal death squads that consist of numerous off-duty police officers (C. Smith, 2016a). Thus, the number of deaths is likely much higher than 249. Of course, this cannot account for all the murders of Black people in Salvador. Still, in 2020, every single person killed at the hands of the police in Salvador was Black (Rede de Observatórios da Segurança, 2021, p. 11). In the state of Bahia, the percentage is 98 percent (p. 14). As the Security Observatory Network points out, "Black communities are under constant attack, targeted by authorities such as the police, but also by other agents encouraged by the proposal of permanent conflict" (p. 15).

While the state may not kill every Black person, it helps shape the conditions in which Black premature death occurs. Between 2002 and 2012, Salvador had 14,176 homicides, going from 585 in 2002 to 1,644 in 2012, and peaking at 1,883 in 2009 (Waiselfisz, 2014). For context, Philadelphia had the most homicides of any US city in 2021, with 521. The vast majority of homicides in Salvador are the result of handguns (Waiselfisz, 2015). Consider these astonishing statistics of Black homicide victims in Salvador: 1,727 in 2010, 1,517 in 2011, and 1,531 in 2012 (Waiselfisz, 2014, p. 165). During those years, Black people constituted 94 percent,

91 percent, and 93 percent of those homicides, respectively. The profile of those Black victims is overwhelming male: all but 118 of them in 2010 (94 percent), 133 (92 percent) in 2011, and 132 (92 percent) in 2012 (Waiselfisz, 2014, p. 51; 2015, p. 19). In addition to race and gender, age is also a factor. Those between ages 15 and 29 constitute most of the homicide victims: 1,272 (69 percent) in 2010, 1,080 (65 percent) in 2011, and 1,058 (64 percent) in 2012. Young Black men disproportionately suffer premature death. However, Black women experience its effects in their wake (Celeste, 2018; Sharpe, 2016; C. Smith, 2016b).

Considering Salvador's size, its economy of racial violence is extremely lethal compared to other large Brazilian cities. In the same 2002–2012 time period, São Paulo, with a population roughly four times larger, went from 5,575 annual homicides down to 1,752, numbering 30,957 in total. Rio de Janeiro also dropped considerably, going from 3,728 homicides down to 1,372, totaling 26,319. While Salvador witnessed a 181 percent increase in homicides, São Paulo and Rio de Janeiro saw their numbers drop 68.6 percent and 63.2 percent, respectively. Salvador's homicide rate is 60.6 per 100,000 people, while São Paulo's is 15.4 and Rio de Janeiro's is 21.5 (Waiselfisz, 2014). Yet Salvador's homicide rate is still only the fourth highest, behind Maceió (90), Fortaleza (76.8), and João Pessoa (76.5). The cities with the top six homicide rates are all in the Northeast, the Brazilian region with the greatest proportion of African-descended population. It also happens to be its poorest region. Between 2002 and 2012, 373,713 Black people were murdered in Brazil, equivalent to 67 percent of all victims in Brazil. The number has steadily increased from 29,656 in 2002 (60 percent of all homicides in 2002) to 41,127 (73 percent of all homicides in 2012). In that time, the homicide rates of white people went down 24.8 percent, while the rate for Black people increased 39.6 percent (Waiselfisz, 2014, p. 150).

How is this acceptable? Brazilian political discourse regularly depicts Black people as bandits and criminals (Terra, 2010). In everyday encounters, civil society and the state also treat poor and working-class Black people as criminals. The philosopher Lewis Gordon describes how the state and society criminalize Black people: "I am black. I have therefore committed a crime. I am black. I know what is the problem with my black body. It exists. I therefore 'am' a crime" (1995, p. 101). The criminalization of Black people extends back to the colonial plantation. Black people who escaped and fled the plantation committed crimes, and thus were criminals. Their biggest crime? Stealing their lives, taking them back from the slave owner. Over time, the police and society find the congregation of Black people without white supervision suspicious and indicative of criminal activity. Police officers and civilians can often murder Black people with impunity because Black people do not have the same rights as a citizen in the polis. The Brazilian saying "A good bandit is a dead bandit" symbolizes how killing Black people is considered a social good for Brazilian society.

If Black people are a threat to national security and public safety, then the solution is policing as a repressive state apparatus that can kill with impunity. Black mothers feel the brunt of this, experiencing trauma after the state murders their sons (C. Smith, 2016b). To justify the police's actions, politicians, the media, and citizens attack Black women as unable to conform to social norms and a racial moral order. For example, former Rio de Janeiro governor Sérgio Cabral infamously described the periphery as "a factory producing criminal people" (quoted in M. A. Soares, 2012, p. 86). His comments have multiple significations. One, he demonizes Black women as "bad mothers" who are unfit to raise children. Two, he portrays Black women as social deviants who are reckless in their sexual behavior, having too many children with too many men and without enough money to properly raise them. Three, Cabral represents Black women as fundamental to a broader pathology in the periphery that normalizes banditry and socially reproduces it with each subsequent generation. Cabral is far from an exception. Brazilian citizens see Black women as threats who should be punished, sterilized, or even "exterminated" as a public safety measure to protect Brazilian civilization and its citizens (M. A. Soares, 2012).

Of course, police do not treat white residents in middle-class and upper-class neighborhoods like this. There, law, order, and political rights are part of Brazilian civilization. The relationship between the periphery and the center mirrors Fanon's observation that the colonial world is fissured into two zones, one for the colonizer and another for the colonized (2004). In this case, poor and working-class Black communities occupy the zone of the (still) colonized.

The state also opens up Black communities to more violence on the periphery, just in less spectacular ways. The state often neglects providing social services, building infrastructure, developing sanitation services, and creating economic opportunities for these communities (Amnesty International, 2005). On a larger scale, this diminishes the residents' quality of living, not to mention their life expectancy. Worse, the police refuse to protect these communities because they see periphery residents as criminals already and therefore their enemies. In Brazil, criminal factions and drug traffickers take advantage of the absence of state protection and inclusion into Brazilian civil society. They commonly engage in turf wars to expand their own territories, with many periphery residents caught in the crosshairs between warring factions. When police refuse to protect periphery residents, they help expand the economy of violence by attracting nonstate actors to also participate in the production and distribution of violence against periphery residents. This permanent war exposes countless Black people to gratuitous violence and premature death.

Quilombo Formations

What does it mean to be Black in a nation that narrates itself as a racial democracy? Beatriz Nascimento (2018c) argues that to "be Black is to confront a history of almost 500 years of resistance to pain, to physical and moral suffering, to a sensation of not existing, to a practice of still not belonging to a society" (pp. 51–52). She describes a Black identity as a sociopolitical category of resistance against erasure and outrageous racial conditions that fundamentally produce social exclusion, economic marginalization, and political precarity against Black people.

Black people's conditions today are no better than when the first Black people arrived as chattel property in the early parts of the sixteenth century (roughly a decade before 1619). Black people then and now occupy a sociopolitical position within a structure of antagonisms where Brazilian state and nonstate actors displace, exploit, underserve, and violently harm them.

No wonder *quilombos* are still emerging today. Just like in the colonial era, Black people are still drawn to rebellion, actively undermining and dismantling a system that is grounded in their suffering. They do not want to resolve racism by seeking inclusion in a reformed system that is fundamentally barbaric, grotesque, morally bankrupt, and ethically loose—a system that is inherently corrupt. And Black people still want more than just liberty from an oppressive system: they want human dignity within a new system. *Quilombos* assured Black people's existence as human beings, not as criminals, slaves, or abject beasts. Black people could secure their humanity by escaping the plantation and their spaces of captivity, producing their own free societies on Brazilian territory (A. Nascimento, 1980).

Colonial administrations have long painted resistive Black people as unruly, bellicose, and a threat. The first documentation of Africans in Brazil dates to 1552 (Kent, 1965). Some suggest it dates even earlier, to sometime between 1511 (Skidmore, 2009) and 1531 (Pierson, 1944). Contrary to Freyre's romanticization of Brazilian colonialism, slavery was extremely violent and abhorrent (Boxer, 1962; Calógeras, 1933; O. Pinho, 2008).

Quilombos were under constant attack by Portuguese and Dutch colonial forces. Brazilian colonial forces destroyed seven of the ten largest *quilombos* within two years (Kent, 1965, p. 162). During the colonial era, the 1740 Ultramarine Counsel defined a *quilombo* as "all habitations of Black fugitives in groups of more than five, even if destitute or lacking buildings, tools or cultivation" (B. Nascimento, 2021, p. 300). When caught, many fugitives were branded with the letter F for *fujão* and had their ear slashed (Ramos, 1951). Colonial society described these Black fugitives as "internal enemies" (E. Carneiro, 1947) and "enemies within our doors" (B. Nascimento, 2018h, p. 106).

Deeply afraid, white colonizers deemed enslaved Black people a dangerous population who posed a threat to the safety of their masters (Calógeras, 1933). This held true as Brazil gained independence from Portugal and became an empire. In 1835, the Penal Code defined a *quilombo* as "a refuge for bandits" (B. Nascimento, 2021, p. 302) who were a threat to the Empire's stability and integrity. This is no different from criminalizing Black people in peripheries under the name of security and public safety. The punishment for being in a *quilombo* was the same as that for any other revolutionary act: beheading. White elites feared Black people and hundreds of years of their insurrections, rebellions, riots, and *aquilombamento* because Black fugitives destabilized not only the political economy but also a racialized moral order and human hierarchy.

Today, the history of *quilombos* still matters, teaching Black people that freedom means liberation from the oppressive racial conditions that mold their circumstances, experiences, situations, and chances. The folkloric Blackness, like in the opening vignette, can be described as "Afro-kitsch" (Diawara, 1992): the celebration of African cultural ancestry without attending to ordinary Black people's material conditions and everyday lived experiences. Black Bahians did not keep creating emergent *quilombos* because they desired recognition by and inclusion into Brazilian society. For them, any new *quilombo* must situate Black diasporic cultures within Black people's material conditions and provide alternative systems that resist against Brazil.

2 | Hip-Hop *Aquilombamento*

"Negro Fugido" (Black fugitive) is the third track on rap group Quilombo Vivo's sophomore album, *Negro Original 100 + ou −* (Black original 100 + or −). Produced by the group's own DJ Bandido, the song has a slow-paced, gritty beat with piano notes rising victoriously out of the depths of the low bass. It is a metaphor for Black life, the Black fugitive fleeing Brazilian society. Where Brazil's racialized structures bring Black people to their lowest point, Black people find a way to get out. We can find joy, hope, and even rebirth. Our conditions do not define us. The song acknowledges both Black people's racial conditions and their pursuit of liberation outside of the nation.

Beyond its sound, the lyrics wade through the tension between Blackness as a site of derision and a site of endless radical possibility. The group's MCs, Nego Juno and Preto Jacó, depict Black life in Salvador's peripheries, out of the purview of most Brazilians and tourists. In their lyrics, they convey how Black suffering is ubiquitous. Shoeless feet cut up from rocks on the street. Raw flesh burning under the blistering sun. Bodies fighting off the periphery's rancidity due to a lack of sanitation services. Hands that are both calloused and bleeding. Laboring just to get by and yet still being called lazy.

Quilombo Vivo does not reduce Black people to their racial conditions. Their song lyrics remind their audience, other Black people from the periphery, that they are not descendants of slaves; rather, they are descendants of Africans who have endured colonialism, slavery, and their violent afterlives. Quilombo Vivo's rhymes show their listeners that Africa is already present within Brazil, in the form of Candomblé, among others. Black people have rich ancestral histories that connect them with their homeland. Black people do not need to return to Africa to have access to their ancestral knowledges and cultures because Black people have already cultivated an African sense of being in Brazil. The song centers on how Black people have created Black life in Brazil through African heritage to protect themselves against Brazil's symbolic and material degradation of their abject Blackness.

Black people's search for freedom, especially on their own terms, away from the racialized stigma in Brazil and toward a dignified existence, is filled with peril. Nego Juno explains why. He raps that Black people should not pay for their manumission; they should simply take it. At the same time, he emphasizes that Black people's political actions are met with resistance. He foresees how Brazilian actors, agencies, and institutions will label these radical Black people and their actions as disobedient, rebellious, and threatening. Nego Juno's point is that when Black people pursue freedom outside of national boundaries, they are disrupting symbolic, ideological, and material systems that depend upon the subjugation of Black people. Quilombo Vivo expresses that Black freedom, the assertion of bodily sovereignty, is a dangerous proposition, just as when enslaved Black people took their freedom by stealing the slave owners' property: their own bodies. The song is a reminder that the Brazilian community will describe and treat Black people's actions taken to obtain their freedom, not just emancipation, as criminal acts. The Brazilian community will then deride, stigmatize, and harm Black people for their freedom dreams with impunity.

Quilombo Vivo identifies Bahian hip-hop as an emergent *quilombo* where Black people can take refuge and resist with one another. Formed in 1998, their group name translates to "living maroon." Nego Juno, Preto Jacó, and DJ Bandido chose the name to connect *quilombos* and hip-hop as Black cultural and political forms of resistance that stretch across Brazilian history. On their SoundCloud page, writing sometimes in the third person, they define their work as "strong, bold, and political," using "urban language as their own characteristic style" to create a literary poetic consciousness for the racially excluded. While Afro-Bahian cultures are "the principal reference and musical influence on its members," rap music serves as "engaged discourses with all of the music that comes from the ghetto." In other words, rap music is the anthem that blends Afro-diasporic cultures and the sociopolitical realities of Blackness in Brazilian society. The group's goal is "denouncing the various forming of everyday violence, police violence and social inequalities, preaching self-esteem, and valorizing the Black person." The members view the tension between Black people's racial conditions and pursuit of freedom today as a continuation of their historic struggle. On their SoundCloud page, they write that they "understand that the QUILOMBO, which was Palmares in the past, remains ALIVE today in every favela with the same resistance, precarity, and forms of organization and survival" (Quilombo Vivo, 2020). The relationship between the *quilombo* and the Brazilian colony now emerges as the relationship between the periphery and the Brazilian nation.

In Bahia, the members of Quilombo Vivo are not the only people who connect *quilombos* and hip-hop; Áurea Semiseria's "Áurea Abolicionista" (Abolitionist Áurea) and Rapaziada da Baixa Fria's "Negros Fujões" (Black runaways) are also examples. They are part of a major cultural movement. In the 1990s, hip-hop exploded in Salvador da Bahia and the Reconcâvo region more broadly. Black Bahians went from being hip-hop consumers and audiences to hip-hop performers and producers (Ferreira Bastos, 2009). Artists, groups, posses, networks, workshops, and events popped up everywhere. Like their counterparts in the diaspora, many Black Bahian performers worked in one or more hip-hop elements: rapping (poetically speaking over music), DJing (making and mixing a beat on turntables and speakers), breakdancing (a kind of street dancing), and graffiti (spray painting murals on public walls). Since then, Black community leaders, activists, and artists have put hip-hop into the service of a broader political movement aimed at supplying Black people with a network to critique their racial conditions, socially organize, and work toward freedom on their own terms. While hip-hop culture and the hip-hop movement are not synonymous, they are inextricably linked to one another. The latter depends on the former but is strongly politically conscious and social justice–minded (Costa Lima, 2006). Today, there are hundreds if not thousands of artists in the hip-hop movement, not to mention many more who participate as fans, supporters, community members, intellectuals, educators, and activists.

As hip-hop has gained popularity in Salvador, Black Bahian artists have utilized its power and potential as an ideological adhesive to bring Black people together into an emergent *quilombo*. Black people join a *quilombo* because its members exalt certain values, practices, and ideals that are meaningful to them. Some include racial pride, diasporic connections, ancestral rituals, and the collective over the individual. Bahian hip-hop artists express these *quilombo* values, practices, and ideals in their work and everyday interactions, drawing the Black masses into their *aquilombamento*. In their street philosophies and practices, artists use hip-hop's cultural expressions and political currency to expand a critical consciousness among the Black masses that challenges Brazilian colonial logics and structural antagonisms that shape Black people's conditions, experiences, and ways of being. This critical consciousness consists of three elements: knowledge and awareness, racial self-affirmation, and a collective political struggle. Black Bahian hip-hop artists express these elements through three themes: negritude, *ancestralidade* (ancestrality), and transforming reality. Negritude is acceptance of and pride in one's Blackness. "Ancestrality" is not an English word, but I favor this translation over *ancestry* or *ancestral knowledge* because it conveys an Africanized quality and a state, not just a lineage and epistemology. Through these three themes, Bahian hip-hop artists contend that Black people cannot be reduced to their racial condition, whether that is slavery in the past or marginalization and poverty in a periphery today. They also assert that Black people can transform themselves by valorizing their racial background, ancestral cultures, and impoverished communities. Finally, these artists convey that individual change leads to social change; that Black people must fight together for their collective freedom, hell-bent on abolishing all forms of injustice and seeking liberation for everyone, not just exceptional individuals.

Bahian hip-hop artists use available media, popular culture, and technology to develop an informal education curriculum that operates outside the school building and labors with love to raise a racial consciousness among Black people on the margins. Hip-hop, as a politically inflected ideological weapon, is a tool against Brazilian nationalism that uses *mestiçagem*, or interracial mixture, to portray itself as racially tolerant and exceptional, a safe haven for Black people unlike other locales in the diaspora.

Hip-Hop Cultures and Black *Conscientização*

When Black people *aquilombar-se*, they are going beyond refusing, escaping, taking flight, and finding refuge with one another. They are creating an ideological structure for Black people to join and participate in, providing symbolic, discursive, and social alternatives for the construction of Black life beyond abjection, a folkloric past, and interracial mixture. The *quilombo* as an alternative mode of Blackness and Black community intervenes in Brazilian dominant discourses that reduce Blackness to misery and poverty and then propose that redemption can be achieved only through the nation. Black people's *aquilombamento* practices refuse the ideology that the very system built to subjugate Black people is the system that will redeem them, bestow citizenship, and ultimately recognize their humanity. Before a person can take flight and then *aquilombar-se*, they must know that there are alternatives to the ones presented and forcibly imposed on them. They may do that on their own. Or other people might inform them about a world of freedom Black people in Brazil thought would be impossible.

Once we have escaped, where do we go? Quilombo Vivo would direct us to the periphery, where Black people continue to build *quilombos* in the contemporary moment. This is where the alternatives exist. Drawing on the history of *quilombos*, the message behind Quilombo Vivo's music is that Black people must become fugitives and band together today against the Brazilian nation. Like many other Bahian hip-hop artists, Quilombo Vivo is invested in creating Black communion and cultural conviviality where Black people can take refuge and be nourished. To do that, Quilombo Vivo and other Black Bahian hip-hop artists foment a Black *conscientização* through hip-hop cultures to reach the Black masses. In his book *Pedagogy of the Oppressed* (2000), Paulo Freire made the term *conscientização* popular, commonly translated as "(critical) consciousness." Borrowing from Frantz Fanon's coinage of the term *conscienciser* in *Black Skin, White Masks* (2008), Freire describes *conscientização* as the process of raising marginalized people's critical analytical frameworks, developing their political awareness, calling out injustices around the world, and working with others toward a better tomorrow. As Fanon (2004) argues, "One cannot divorce the combat for culture from the people's struggle for liberation" (p. 168). Bahian hip-hop artists know that they must first create a culture for their communities where Black people can strengthen their imaginations to reinvent themselves, how they create community, and how they take political action. This begins with transforming one's consciousness. Black Bahian hip-hop artists contribute to a Black *conscientização* by using hip-hop as an informal educational tool to stress the political importance of *aquilombar-se*, particularly as a form of radical Black self-affirmation, knowledge production, and collectivization. Various other artists have influenced them in some fashion, and now they want to reach others, further expanding the *aquilombamento*.

Changing Black people's consciousness is an important site of social change, the first step in getting Black people to understand themselves, relate to one another, and assemble in different ways. Black Bahian hip-hop artists use hip-hop to reach and develop Black people's consciousness as part of their *aquilombamento* efforts. For example, Quilombo Vivo deems their work "Afrohiphop resistance," signaling that hip-hop is the ideological umbrella that binds Black people together in this specific emergent *quilombo*. In the Bahian hip-hop movement, Black artists draw on US Black popular culture, African cultural heritage, Caribbean music, and Afro-Francophone literary theory. They use a Black *conscientização* to critique structural racism and urge their fellow hip-hop members to come together as a diasporic community.

Bahian Hip-Hop's Beginnings

As *quilombos* have taken different forms in Brazil's history, Black people have revamped their ideological tool kits to express a Black *consientização* that manifests differently depending on genre and transmission, ensuring that they reach the Black masses and respond to a given conjuncture. Before Black people can achieve collective freedom, they must first mentally transform their own and others' consciousness.

Hip-hop first came to Salvador da Bahia in the 1980s when DJs played it at *bailes black* (Black dances) in the Periperi periphery (Sobral Freire, 2018). In Bahia, hip-hop is a cultural product of Black youths on the periphery of Salvador da Bahia (Costa Lima, 2006). Sergio, a thirty-two-year-old graffiti artist, recollects Bahian hip-hop's origins: "It is hard to pinpoint the exact beginning, but it is a periphery thing, having a periphery attitude, existing in different places. Castelo Branco was doing it, Amaralina was doing it, Boca do Rio was doing it, São Caetano was doing it, and eventually they migrated down to the center where everyone met up together. . . . Hip-hop in its foundation is rooted in the peripheries." Hip-hop artists, activists, intellectuals, and fans might not know about hip-hop's origins in Periperi in the *bailes black* or when exactly it began, but they know it is a culture from the racialized margins. Bahian hip-hop traces the histories, conditions, and experiences of being poor, Black, and on the periphery that it has in common with other large Brazilian cities and cities in the United States (Sobral Freire, 2018).

These *bailes black* were already intense spaces of diasporic sonic intimacy. In the 1970s, Black people procured and played soul and funk music in the periphery in Salvador and other large capital cities. The crowds danced to James Brown, shouted "blaque pau" (Black Power), and donned various "Afro" aesthetics on the body and in fashion. Brazilian elites deemed soul and funk a threat to a Brazilian nationalism predicated on (Eurocentric) national unity, not racial pride (Hanchard, 1994). Soon after soul and funk arrived, Brazilian DJs brought hip-hop to these *bailes*, providing a different lexicon, style, visuality, and sound for Black Brazilians to engage the African Diaspora culturally and politically. Across Brazil, these *bailes* were important in forming a sense of Black identity, pride, consciousness, and community, at a time when Brazilian society regularly denigrated and stigmatized anything associated with Africa or Blackness.

In the 1980s and 1990s, Black Bahians moved beyond being audiences only; they also became hip-hop artists. Bahian hip-hop combines the emphasis on Black cultural pride and African heritage of previous cultural genres with a critique of Black people's social experiences and material conditions of racism (Hanchard, 1994; O. Pinho, 2005). It also strengthens Black Bahians' connections with US Black people, who confront similar histories of colonialism, slavery, and racialization as well as experiences of racial prejudice, violence, and segregation (J. L. Santos, 2016; A. L. S. Souza, 2011; Teperman, 2015). Finding these connections, Black Bahian hip-hop members criticize Brazil as a racial purgatory, not a racial paradise.

Like other locations in the African Diaspora, the Bahian hip-hop movement has a fifth element besides rapping, DJ'ing, breakdancing, and graffiti: knowledge. Its members view knowledge and information as fundamental to a Black *conscientização* that critiques Brazilian anti-Black racism, sexism, and classism. They also use it for self-affirmation and as a foundation for alternative Black social, cultural, and political systems. Hip-hop artists, activists, and fans challenge Eurocentric ways of knowing and institutions still grounded in coloniality, the social and cultural practices of the white middle and elite classes: "the system" (Pardue, 2008). The system also encompasses structural forces like police brutality and corruption; scarcity of resources like schools, libraries, etc.; and symbolic processes that naturalize racism in a plethora of ways. Hip-hop members point out as well how people marginalized by the system are also upholding it. Yet they also welcome former custodians of oppression who have developed a Black *conscientização* and now wish to work against the system.

Hip-Hop Negritude

In *quilombos*, members encourage one another and those who might join them to take pride in their negritude as a social reality rather than just a cultural affinity. This is the first step of self-affirmation, key to hip-hop's own *aquilombamento*. In Brazil, negritude translates to Blackness; this is different from *africanidade*, which translates to Africanity. It is also the name of the Black aesthetics movement (*négritude* in French) led by Afro-Francophone intellectuals and activists, who were part of a broader political movement against French colonialism in Africa and the Caribbean (Sharpley-Whiting, 2002). This Francophone *négritude* movement also influenced and shaped Black Brazilian thought (Munanga, 2009). In Brazil, Black people use negritude in cultural expressions to instill racial awareness and pride as a mode of political identification (Sterling, 2012). Dominant Brazilian actors and institutions attach meanings of abject Blackness to the Black masses. At the same time, they decry when Black people veer toward racial identifications, politics, and activism because the dominant classes see this as divisive, challenging the beloved racial democracy mythos that no one is Black, everyone is racially/ethnically mixed, and there is no racism in Brazil. Yet the social realities of being Black stand in stark contrast to being Brazilian (Gonzalez, 1988a).

The Bahian hip-hop movement uses various tools, like documentaries, to reach the Black masses and foster a Black *conscientização*. In 2003, the Rede Aiyê Hip-Hop network released the *Hip-Hop e Educação Popular* (Hip-hop and popular education) documentary highlighting the critical pedagogical labor that hip-hop art educators are doing in Salvador. The documentary features the premier artists of that time: Jorge Hilton, Ananias Break, Thina Break, and Denis Sena. It reinforces the assertion that hip-hop is an educational tool not just in informal classrooms but also in media (Dimitriadis, 2009; Hill, 2009). A Bahian hip-hop education takes shape in a variety of cultural texts, like music and graffiti, and in a multitude of spaces, like workshops and after-school programs. Hip-hop artists are invested in using hip-hop as a site of informal education for their communities, meant to supplement the blind spots of the Brazilian education system as well as the media (Andrade, 1999; Henson, 2016b; Messias, 2015; Ribeiro, 2016). Only seventeen minutes in length, the documentary follows Bahian hip-hop artists and their workshops in classrooms, community centers, public squares, and studios. Their students are youths who wish to know more about hip-hop as a culture and a practice. In the documentary, the hip-hop artists educate the students by giving them Black history lessons, raising their self-esteem, elevating racial pride, and critiquing Brazilian national narratives that make claims of racial egalitarianism. The students express the impact hip-hop has already had on their own lives. For many Black Bahian youth, hip-hop is the first place where they learned to love their Blackness, or negritude. They may have learned to love Blackness in Brazilian culture like samba and capoeira, but they may not have loved their own Blackness as a social feature in terms of skin tone, hair, phenotypes, ancestry, family composition, or social practices.

The negritude movement is most known for its Francophone origins among Black (male) intellectuals including Aimé Césaire, Léon Damas, and Léopold Senghor. Suzanne Lacascade, Jane and Paulette Nardal, Suzanne Roussy-Césaire, and other Black women were also leaders and key thinkers in the Francophone *négritude* movement (Sharpley-Whiting, 2002). Across the African Diaspora, negritude accepts and embraces Blackness as embodiment, a distinct social reality, and a cultural formation. In Brazil, negritude has a long history that also values Blackness and African cultural roots (e.g., Munanga, 2009). In Brazil, negritude simply signifies an acceptance of being Black, in contrast to being Brazilian, which negates Blackness. It also refuses and critiques Brazilian racial democracy ideologies of *mestiçagem* and whitening (Sterling, 2012). It holds that Black people do not need to distance themselves from their Blackness through Eurocentric cultural values, (non-Black) mixed race identifications, or trying to whiten themselves or their children with a lighter partner.

Negritude is a consistent theme in the Bahian hip-hop movement. João taught me that every MC has "roots in negritude, in African ancestrality. It's this rap consciousness that is a vehicle of communication, an artistic vehicle for the people to carry our message, you know?" Artists like João embrace hip-hop because it is a powerful and effective tool to communicate a Black *conscientização* to the Black masses and change their political thinking, diasporic awareness, and racial self-making.

João described to me the intersection between hip-hop and negritude: "People have a [militant] side here that is very strong, where the negritude in rap is a little more politicized. The rap that is trash, the people are not only going to do rap to create a fun environment, even though we need that at times. But [rap] is ultimately preoccupied with social causes, you know? ... I believe that these things, they arise naturally for rap crews that have a [political] commitment and observe [society]." For João, every hip-hop MC must commit themselves to becoming an educator who raises a Black *conscientização* and acts against racialized social inequalities. They must labor to save themselves and others from a system that may grant Black cultural citizenship but demands that Black people adopt a Eurocentric consciousness, white-*mestiço* social practices, and anti-Black political systems. Instead, MCs strategize how to expand the Bahian hip-hop movement by making it a cultural refuge for marginalized Black people. To do that, they must speak to Black people's conditions, realities, and thought processes in ways that are based in negritude rather than internalizing anti-Blackness.

In Bahia, Black people join the hip-hip movement for reasons beyond the pleasures of producing, performing, and consuming rapping, DJ'ing, graffiti, and breakdancing. Many hip-hop artists point out how US hip-hop gave them a style of Black cultural resistance. Here, Black Bahians saw other Black people in the diaspora walking with pride, confidence, and even attitude. They found this very political. Dominant Brazilian actors, agencies, and institutions produce a representation of Bahia as a space of racial cordiality. However, many Black Bahians view Bahia as a space of racial submission. White and white-*mestiço* elites expect Black Bahians to be deferential to them. And Black Bahians are always vulnerable to ridicule, shame, and even punishment for overstepping social norms (Pierson, 1944). In response, Black Bahians turned to hip-hop as a Black culture that values negritude as a social reality distinct from a white-*mestiço* reality that shapes the Brazilian consciousness. In addition, Black Bahians use this distinct racial reality as a point of political identification, to call attention to the invisible racial injustices Black people face in Brazil.

In Brazil, school textbooks and dominant discourses represent Black people's history as starting with slavery (da Costa, 2014). They represent Black people as only descendants of "slaves" who are today locked in pathological cycles of misery, poverty, and ill repute (O. Pinho, 2021). This historical omission ignores Black people's African histories, which overflow with great civilizations, technological advancements, philosophy, cosmologies, conquest, and agricultural mastery. Dominant educational discourses reproduce the idea that Africa is a geography without history and culture, sitting idle while the world marches forward. Hip-hop develops a Black *conscientização* by connecting Black people's negritude back to Africa, bringing it into the present, and critiquing Brazilian history's erasure of their legacies and contributions.

In the 1990s, Brazilian rappers rose in popularity and prominence, becoming the voice of urban Black youth resistance. The greatest example is Racionais MCs featuring Mano Brown, Edi Rock, Ice Blue, and DJ KL Jay (O. Pinho and Rocha, 2011). They rap about Black people's racial conditions like living in a periphery, living in poverty, not having good social infrastructure, the poor education they receive, social stigmatization, and police violence (J. Nascimento, 2011). Their lyrics also advocate for social justice. Black urban youths identified with their critiques and demands. Other prominent Brazilian rappers include Sabotage, MV Bill, and Central Facção. In Salvador, groups like Nova Era and Rap Etnia are similarly important. Carla details the influence São Paulo rapper Criolo had on her: "He's critical and brings this perspective that makes you dream. It doesn't make you say, 'I'm a miserable person, born poor for this, and born Black [*preto*] for this.' No, he brings [to our attention] that Blacks [*pretos*] were born robbed, that this and this and this happened, but the Black person can, is, and must [be something different]." Rap music gave Carla and others a history lesson not taught in schools and the media, a different history of the present that explains Black people's conditions in Brazil as part of a hemispheric phenomenon.

Through rap music, Black Bahians learn that their histories of colonialism and slavery and contemporary racial conditions are similar to those of other Black people in the Americas, from the United States to the Caribbean to Colombia. For poor and working-class Black people from the periphery, like Carla, these history lessons are invaluable. When she told me "this and this and this happened," I interpreted it to mean Brazilian hip-hop teaches that white people robbed Black people—from Africa, during Brazilian history, and even today through colonialism, slavery, and now racial capitalism. Criolo teaches Carla that their histories begin in Africa, not with slavery, and that Black people are displaced Africans in the Americas. And now Carla teaches others. This history lesson also points to a set of structures put in place that reproduce Black people's racial conditions. It disrupts how Brazilian the middle and elite classes justify racial inequalities by blaming

Black individuals for moral failure stemming from Black people's deviant community values. Black Bahians engage hip-hop to critique the system and valorize their negritude in ways the Brazilian nation-state does not. This is how negritude intervenes: by teaching Black people that they do not have to be ashamed of themselves or attempt to find comfort in subservient roles in the nation. Even as Brazil marginalizes Black people and stigmatizes their Blackness, Black Bahian youths participate in hip-hop to affirm their negritude and refuse dominant ideologies that Black people must conform to nationally permissible performances of Blackness.

Carla and Camila take hip-hop as a critical institution of education and apply its teachings in their own lives. A Black *conscientização* is not just imaginary. It is useful in everyday experiences. When I asked them about racism and sexism in Brazil, they said this:

> **Carla:** Homie, that's daily. That's a daily struggle. From the moment you get onto a bus.
> **Camila:** Jesus, you don't even need to enter the bus. You just need to put your foot outside the house.
> **Carla:** I remembered that time that you said when we got onto the bus and you said, "That idiot was giving me back my change and he stroked my hand. Like this guy is at work [on the bus], he's giving back some change and he feels himself in the right to stroke my hand." So that's no different...
> **Camila:** From any other place, right? But then you have this question, that thinking a Black woman [*negra*] is attractive.... This is a historic question, that people think they can do whatever they want with women, especially Black women [*negras*]. People have only been fighting that for a century now.

Carla and Camila express how Black women are constantly exposed to unwanted attention, harassment, and even assault. This vulnerability to unwanted sexual attention, harassment, and assault mirrors Black women's life on the plantation, where they were unable to defend themselves and assert bodily sovereignty. Hip-hop has taught Black women like Camila and Carla that a Black *conscientização* is also gendered by critiquing the hypersexualization of Black women in Brazilian society (e.g., Gonzalez, 2021). Often, Brazilian society values Black women only for their physical appearance, associating them hypersexuality and sexual availability. The bus driver who strokes Camila's hand believes that Camila wants this attention or doesn't care if she wants it or not. Carla remembers this and is also upset about it. The person attracted to a Black woman thinks they can, as Camila says, "do whatever they want with women, especially Black women," but Black women do not have to be attractive to be valorized. Their Blackness is enough on its own.

Black women in the hip-hop movement work tirelessly to intertwine Black *conscientização* with Black feminism, pointing out that sexism is central to structures of racial oppression. Unsurprisingly, the Bahian hip-hop movement features and privileges Black men as its leaders. The ratio of men and boys to women and girls is imbalanced. Sure, one can name Áurea Semiseria as an important Black woman MC in the Bahian hip-hop movement. Yet it does not change the fact that the Bahian hip-hop movement valorizes some Black people's negritude and not others. I often ask men in the movement why there are not that many women artists in Bahian hip-hop. It seems they are always shocked that another Black man would ask such a question. Some say something like women prefer to be R&B singers. Most fumble (and this is putting it lightly) with a half-thought-out response that women are not serious about hip-hop because they have family duties. Others give an "I don't know/I never really thought about that" response. Mostly, they do not think women are well suited for the hip-hop movement's demands. This is a patriarchal standard, where men are leaders, authoritative, and equipped to be workers outside the home (hooks, 2004). The broader issue here goes beyond women to patriarchy, which organizes gender relations that center masculinity and represses femininity (Sobral Freire, 2018). This is not just a hip-hop problem but a Brazilian problem and a global problem as well.

To say the least, Black women's absence in the Bahian hip-hop movement is concerning because the movement purports to be invested in developing a Black *conscientização*. At the same time, the movement creates its own centers and peripheries within its spaces, re-creating a microcosm of the world they supposedly wish to eradicate. Too often, hip-hop community members reduce women to being a mother, a lover, a Black woman warrior, or a vulgar object (Matsunaga, 2006, 2008). Black men don a persona, usually through US gangsta rap personalities, such as those of Tupac, 50 Cent, and Snoop Dogg, that subjugates and denigrates Black women (Jackson II, 2006). Many Bahian hip-hoppers vehemently reject gangsta rap and its association with criminality, but they still like the language of "courage, combat, and war" (Messias, 2015, p. 150). But this performance of masculinity, even while it rejects gang factions and criminality, also embraces misogyny, sexism, and patriarchy.

Despite these patriarchal limitations, hip-hop is a modality of Black self-realization that can change a Black person's whole life. Many Black hip-hop aficionados and artists describe how hip-hop saved them from falling deeper into the system (D. F. Gomes da Silva, 2019). This is a redemption that reaches not for national inclusion but for a diasporic connection. João recounts how hip-hop saved him from a life of drug trafficking and conspicuous consumption:

> Hip-hop saves people, feel me? When I began to be a teenager, the necessity to have fresh sneakers, really dope clothes, and to date around also arrived, you know? ... Shit homie, the money is scarce and your friends over there have money in their pocket, but through illicit activities. Like ... I thought of becoming a trafficker, bro, right? And my idea was to become a boss, you know? Like, I'm not gonna stay as a lookout [*boca*], stay selling as a cornerboy, no. Like, bro, I'm going to do this plan, you know? We gonna calculate this thing here [to become a boss]. Like, you need intelligent people, to arrive with a plan. And I'm the boss, right? Gonna pay the whole world, legit. Thank God, I encountered hip-hop, I encountered rap. It's like I was telling you earlier, [rap] has those negritude roots that I can see, that I can understand how that plan [to become a trafficker] was part of the system, you know? To destroy the people.

João points out that in general Black people are not able to meet their basic needs. Being Black sucks. Being poor sucks. Being from the periphery sucks. Being Black, poor, and from the periphery: all these troubles compound one another, each one worsening the next exponentially. João believed he could counter these cascading stigmas by turning to illicit activities to provide discretionary income for life's joys, pleasures, and leisure activities. But hip-hop showed him this would lead him along a path that would destroy him and his community. When he says a part of the system is "to destroy the people," I take that to mean Black people would increase violence in their communities, contribute to premature death, and contribute to drug addiction in the Black community. When João turned to hip-hop, he could escape the destructive route he was on and value his existence as a Black man.

While negritude is often associated with the fine arts, poetry, and literature, the Bahian hip-hop movement demonstrates the centrality of media and popular culture, like rap music, to raising Black people's critical consciousness to resonate with and be meaningful to those most marginalized. In Salvador da Bahia, hip-hop furnishes Black youth a cultural conduit to community with other Black people around the African Diaspora. It dignifies poor and working-class Black people's existence without requiring moral redemption or national allegiance to a racialized death machine. Through hip-hop, Black Bahians discover they are not alone in their racial conditions; they are instead part of a diasporic community that opposes systems of anti-Black nationalism and racial capitalism. They find commonalities with other Black people in the Americas and are able to imagine cultural and political alliances that can have transnational implications for collective liberation (Gonzalez, 2018a).

Ancestrality

As part of their hip-hop *aquilombamento*, Bahian hip-hop artists also foreground *ancestralidade* as fundamental to a Black *conscientização*. Once Black people take pride in their Blackness, they can also take pride in their African ancestrality. When Black Bahian hip-hop artists conceive of ancestrality, they are gesturing toward something grander than simply African ancestral cultures and knowledges. They point to ancestrality as an Africanized quality one has and/or a state of being. When Black people embrace ancestrality, they are fundamentally changing their metaphysical being and way of life, seeing themselves as displaced Africans in Brazil.

The first Bahian hip-hop group was called Posse Orí, acknowledging the importance of Candomblé *orixás* (Miranda, 2006). For centuries, Candomblé has been a means of changing the way that Black people view themselves and each other (Braga, 1992). In Candomblé, the Orí signifies the head, which is central to one's spiritual intuition and destiny. Bahian hip-hop artists frequently celebrate African roots in their expression. Many hip-hop artists already have an education in African-derived epistemologies through Candomblé. Carlos once told me: "Here, you also have this connection with Candomblé. . . . A good part of MCs that I know are Candomblé practitioners or have some kind of connection to Candomblé. And that's the majority of the people, in Black resistance, you know?" Zeze Olukemí and DJ Nai Kiese are exemplars of this. Hip-hop artists see themselves as custodians of ancestral knowledges, not as gatekeepers to a timeless past. Carlos points out that many Black Bahian hip-hop artists engage ancestrality as a network of rhizomatic knowledges that mobilize the past through a set of representative, social, and lived practices to articulate a political vision (Sterling, 2012). Black Bahians do not see hip-hop and Candomblé as antithetical; they can and do work in tandem.

Some Bahian hip-hop groups and artists are very explicit about ancestrality. Opanijé, consisting of Lázaro Erê, Chiba D, and Rone DumDum, is evidence of this. The group formed in 2005. Generally, *opanijé* is a Candomblé song and dance for the Afro-Brazilian deity Omulu to bring health and longevity. The group's name is also an acronym, meaning Organização Popular Africana Negros Invertendo O Jogo Excludente (Popular organization for African Blacks inverting the exclusion game). Opanijé use ancestral knowledge in Candomblé musical rituals in their own rap songs and music videos to disrupt the system that marginalizes the Black popular masses. *Oganpazan* writer Carlim describes Opanijé as follows: "The Candomblé rhythms mark the group's sonority, giving them an identity that is so unreachable for the majority of rap groups. Opanijé stands out by uniting the organic metrics of rap rhymes to the rhythms and beats of Candomblé" (2015). As with negritude, Black hip-hop artists transmit ancestrality through rap music, using it as a vehicle that takes its listeners on a road toward affirmation and Black *conscientização*.

In Bahian hip-hop, artists, musicians, and dance meld Candomblé with other musical influences, blooming in new and exciting ways. Numerous artists will combine various genres under the rap umbrella, showing off Black artists' genius, intellect, and sheer creative magnitude. João put it this way to me:

> Being here in Salvador, you can see that this is a plural city, you know? It is a city where you can hear various musical rhythms, various cultures that are circulating in the streets, that it's an environment that is a global cauldron here, you know? You're taking a little from each. That can leave hip-hop with an identity here, too.... It's because it is rap, it [also] can globalize other rhythms, you know? You can take samba, you can take bossa nova, you can take forró that you are

listening to at the base and the thing stays being rap, you know? It makes it so much richer.

João is describing the expansive nature of Bahian hip-hop while also making a subtle critique. Too often, the state, the mainstream media, and the upper classes overrepresent African culturalisms in Bahia, keeping Salvador in a colonial past and out of the modern world. For that reason, one might think that Candomblé would be the only local cultural form that Black people would insert into rap music, as a globally circulating cultural form around the African Diaspora. João explains that Salvador is indeed a *global* city, part of the modern world that includes samba, bossa nova, and *forró*. Jamaican dancehall has influenced his own work. Also, artists like Tícia and Fall Clássico regularly blend hip-hop, reggae, and sound system cultures. Years after our interview, João's music started to take on more jazz influences as well. Like many African-derived cultural expressions, Bahian hip-hop has an internal logic that emphasizes repetition, sampling, layering, circularity, and difference. It is not a rigid cultural form; it can incorporate multiple cultural influences. When João calls Salvador a global cauldron, he is positioning the city as a key diasporic producer and receiver of both African ancestral and Black popular cultures.

Over the past decade, one of my favorite questions to ask people is what makes Bahian hip-hop unique. One reason is that I just love listening to these street intellectuals spit knowledge. The sheer genius of their artistic philosophy is jaw-dropping. I also like inquiring because I want to know how Black Bahian hip-hop artists understand and articulate Black cultures beyond an African cultural purity or even Brazilian cultural hybridity. Carlos philosophized about Black music more broadly, placing hip-hop within a current rendition of a long-standing tradition:

> In only twenty years from now, people are going to say, "Oh, how I miss the Black music in 2014!" And it's because they don't live in the present, you know? You said that people always believe that the past was better, only for a certain type of person. It is [better] through changes, when you actualize a radical change in a generation, always appearing in new generations.... It's no different than Black culture in Bahia, no? The things we're mixing together, it's the *atabaques* [African drums] that were from the Candomblé *terreiros* [worship grounds]

that are on stage. They become something else, a style of music.... But the roots remain permanent, feel me? You're going to see fruit up there on top, but you're going to be able to see it and see where it began, you know? Just like that, you see a *tambor* drum in the *axé* band, you're going to see the *tambor* and going to remember it naturally from Candomblé.

Rather than romanticizing and valorizing the past, Carlos argues for an understanding of Black culture as always evolving and making something new and innovative that responds to the present. Black Bahian hip-hop artists demonstrate that ancestrality is not the recuperation and maintenance of a premodern cultural lifeway. There is no going back to a mythical Africa. Instead, these artists show how ancestrality is flexible and innovative; they transmit it through different genres, expressions, and media. They operationalize ancestrality as an energy force that connects Black people to an African homeland and cultural knowledges which then contribute to emergent modes of consciousness, communal creation, and creative activity. While many Brazilians refer to Candomblé as a site of ancestrality, Black Bahian hip-hop artists mediate and express ancestrality in their everyday perspectives, practices, and representations, drawing on its cosmologies to assemble emergent *quilombos* among themselves and their communities. Black cultures are not static, timeless, or homogenous.

Similarly, Carlos critiques the folkloricism of African-derived cultures in Bahia. Like he says, the African roots remain, but the tree keeps growing and blossoming. The roots are African ancestral knowledges and philosophies that Black people brought with them via the Middle Passage. These roots created atabaque drums, Candomblé, *tambor*, and *terreiros* hundreds of years ago. Hip-hop extends, rather than replaces, those roots; it builds off them, creating new products, or what Carlos calls fruit. In Bahian hip-hop, the African ancestral roots are there, but the plants sprout up, stretch out, and give us new fruit every year. And the fruit can be taken by artists and combined with other foodstuffs to create proverbial meals that nourish our bodies and souls. The metaphorical fruit, even separated from the tree, is part of ancestrality's routes to new spaces. Each time Black people transmit ancestrality with different materials and modes of transmission, its expression is going to appear to be different.

Many hip-hop artists looked back fondly on their first encounter with hip-hop. Most Bahian hip-hop artists told me that they discovered hip-hop in their adolescence. Many would smile and their eyes glitter, as if thinking back on their first romantic crush. For many, finding hip-hop was like finding themselves in a world that labors tirelessly to obscure and obfuscate their limitless potentiality. Carla said: "It's just that different reasons, I've always been interested in research, looking for knowledge and whatnot, even on cassette tapes, there weren't even CDs then. I listened to RBF [Rapaziada da Baixa Fria], a Bahian group ... that came onto the scene around the question of ancestrality, talking about negritude, and this caught my attention. Because of that, I started researching more people here.... Those people made me graduate, let's say." The twenty-five-year-old Black woman MC saw hip-hop as a mobile school, educating through sonic and oral traditions. Instead of books, she has cassette tapes and eventually CDs that convey Black *conscientização*, where she can imagine herself as part of a broader collective critiquing and taking refuge from Brazilian anti-Black racism, sexism, and classism. Groups like Rapaziada da Baixa Fria are her educators who teach her about African history (ancestrality) and Black diasporic social movements (negritude). And rappers like Criolo teach her about a Brazilian history of racialized violence, theft, extraction, and dispossession that is not in elementary and secondary school textbooks.

The Bahian hip-hop movement is politically staunch, yet culturally promiscuous. Even though the movement is committed to a Black *conscientização*, Black artists will draw upon Brazilian cultural influences, decoding cultural texts in oppositional ways that give them new meanings and purposes based on a *quilombo* conceptual map.[1] As Carla tells it, she first engaged with hip-hop through the São Paulo group Expressão Ativa and then Racionais MCs. Still, a key reference for her is Elza Soares, the ninety-year-old carioca samba singer who passed away in early 2022: "I listened to her since I was a little girl, you know? Since I was a really little girl because she plays samba and people at home like it, she's really good and I listened to her a lot. So, musically, my first reference to say like 'Damn, I will listen just to create a song' it's her, my goddess." Shortly after, she recollects that her family listened to Raul Seixas, the "father of Brazilian rock," quite a bit and that he also influences her work. After referencing Soares, Carla goes on to say, almost in the same breath, that she is also influenced by Ludmilla, Rael, Emicida, and Criolo. Referring to Rael and Emicida, she notes, "Emicida, he brings the chaos and he brings the problem, and how to solve it. Rael brings the problem, and he brings how to solve that problem." On the flip side, Camila stresses the importance of more established rappers and posses in Salvador, like Dark MC, Simples Rap'ortagem, and Rapaziada da Baixa Fria. Both Carla and Camila give concrete examples of how African-derived cultures continue to emerge, transform, and circulate among Black hip-hop artists, developing a Black racial *conscientização* through ancestral cosmologies and intertwining contemporary Black and Brazilian cultural influences.

Transforming Reality

Within a hip-hop *aquilombamento*, Black *conscientização* also demands a political commitment to others and forging a better world. Many Black Bahian hip-hop artists frequently talk about transforming reality, changing how people see themselves and other Black people, how they live their own lives, and how they want to change the lives of others at both individual and systemic levels. They want to bring Black people into their *quilombo* spaces of refuge and renewal. For them, hip-hop is a social movement, a type of informal social work (Miranda, 2006). One thing I have heard many times in the movement is that "Rap is what you do. Hip-hop is what you live." Bahian hip-hop artists are deeply invested in various social movements and political activism. Admittedly, it has not yet changed the structures, but they are tirelessly working to bring forth a better and more just world. This pursuit of liberty is prevalent across rap songs. For example, Carla told me that "we know that liberation is constant, liberation is daily, so we try to bring that perspective within our songs, all the time." The movement's most active and militant members arduously labor to understand, critique, *and* dismantle the proverbial "system."

The Bahian hip-hop movement's quest for liberation on Black people's terms follows the *quilombo* model. Artists understand their work must extend beyond producing and performing their cultural expressions and raising awareness. There must be action. Carla told me that "you won't change your community because people talk about it in songs, right? That's the question of community and lived experiences, but if you don't have money, you don't have ways to change this reality." In Salvador, the Bahian hip-hop movement is unique because it begins with Black people's material realities, not ideas of a mythical past or national belonging. Artists anchor a Black *conscientização* in Black people's racial conditions, distributing a conceptual map to help Black people understand and critique their lot in this world as well as understand their metaphysical being beyond hegemonic narratives and representations.

Numerous Black Bahian hip-hop artists proudly claim the Bahian hip-hop movement is *the most* militant movement in all of Brazil, even more so than in Rio de Janeiro or São Paulo. In her groundbreaking book *Hip-hop feminista? Convenções de gênero e feminismos no movimento Hip-hop soteropolitano*, Rebeca Sobral Freire (2018) demonstrates how Black Bahian hip-hop artists practiced their political activism: "The first generation of the Bahian movement, the change in social participation and organization by Black Bahian youth in the Hip-Hop movement was extremely rich, coming back initially to concerns with their community and understanding issues of their identity and history, and subsequently, for the expansion of its field of action in the city, the involvement with the discussion about committed public policies with Black community development" (p. 86). These artists are not just cultural producers; they turned themselves into social agents and political activists who worked with and on behalf of their communities to improve Black people's realities.

Hip-hop artists model changed behaviors and pursue social work, broadly defined, in various ways. Over the past decade, I have witnessed hip-hop art educators participate in various social movements and forms of political activism. Some are directly related to Black people. For example, many are involved in the *movimento negro* (the Black Movement), an umbrella term for various Black social movements.[2] Others are involved with organizations like *reaja ou seja morto!* (React or be killed!) that contest police violence.[3] Even those not involved in more formal organizations show up to political demonstrations, protesting state-sanctioned violence against Black youths. Others are involved with causes that intersect with racial justice, oppression, and inequalities: feminism, LGBTQ+ rights, veganism, youth education, land rights, antigentrification, and anarchy. They even take up national politics. Many were upset former president Luiz Inácio Lula da Silva of the Workers' Party was unable to run for president in 2018.[4] He was extremely popular during his two presidencies from 2003 to 2010. After his successor, Dilma Rousseff, Brazil's first woman president, was impeached in 2016, Lula sought to run for election again in 2018 and maintain the Workers' Party's reign in the presidential office. Numerous right-wing politicians and elected officials attempted to implicate Lula in a bribery scandal. With very little evidence of corruption, Judge Sergio Mora unjustly imprisoned Lula, which barred the former president from running. As a result, Fernando Haddad, former São Paulo mayor, stepped in late as the Workers' Party candidate. While many in the hip-hop movement were not thrilled about Haddad, they publicly advocated for him and mobilized their communities to support him against the ultra-far-right candidate Jair Bolsonaro. Haddad eventually lost to Bolsonaro in the presidential runoff.[5] Bahian hip-hop artists see themselves as community leaders who must step up and labor to create a better world.

In his book *Bahia com H de Hip-Hop* (2014), the first historical treatment of Bahian hip-hop, Jorge Hilton (who also goes by Jorge Hilton de Assis Miranda), an MC in the Salvador-based group Simples Rap'ortagem, details the local movement's history through the five elements, its political actions, and its role as a "hip-hop university." To capture the movement's political and cultural specificity, Hilton describes the Bahian hip-hop movement in this manifesto-style description:

> The Culture is in the Movement,
> but the Movement is not always in the Culture.
>
> In the Culture, there are artists;
> in the Movement there are art-educators.
>
> The Culture works the professional side;
> the Movement works the militant side.
>
> The Culture is global (worldwide);
> the Movement is local (regional).
>
> The Culture is susceptible to becoming fashionable;
> the Movement, never.
>
> The objective of the Culture is to spread Hip-Hop;
> the Movement's is, through hip-hop, to transform reality.
>
> The Culture is instrumental to the Movement;
> the Movement is the son of the Culture.
>
> In the Culture, there are four elements:
> Rap, Street Dance, Graffiti and DJ'ing;

in the Movement there are these four and also a 5th:
the Knowledge/Militancy (in the Movement everyone is a militant).

In the Culture the "battle" is between artists;
in the Movement the battle is against injustices.

The Culture mobilizes;
the Movement articulates.

The Culture with the Movement is partially blind;
the Movement without the Culture is crippled. (pp. 15–16; emphasis removed)

Hilton illuminates the connections between the culture and the movement. Artists use hip-hop culture as the building blocks for a cultural community. When artists become art educators, they are moving into a militant political movement that fights to transform people's politics and their realities. They are carrying on a *quilombo* legacy that creates alternative social, cultural, and political systems for Black people (Freitas, 2016; A. Nascimento, 1980; B. Nascimento, 2021).

Quilombo Values in the Contemporary Conjuncture

In "Historiografia do quilombo" (The *quilombo* historiography), Beatriz Nascimento (2018b) argues that Black people built the *quilombo* as "an instrument of self-affirmation" (p. 131). On the plantation, the planter class reduced Black people to slaves, chattel property with neither social privileges nor political rights. When Black people fled the plantation and formed *quilombo* communities on the hillsides, they recognized one another as African people, inherently valued and worthy of a dignified existence. They could practice their African-derived cultures, blending them together into a syncretic totality. They did not need to be ashamed of their Blackness; they could take pride in their Blackness. Finally, they sought to contribute to other Black people's freedom, seeing liberation as a collective journey, not an individual pursuit.

Elsewhere, Beatriz Nascimento (2018g) writes that *quilombos* serve as a model for Black social change. Today, Black Bahian hip-hop artists do that by developing other Black people's critical consciousness and working to transform marginalized people's realities. They do not shy away from how Brazilian society labels them as "marginal" subjects, a shorthand for poor Black people from the periphery who are prone to criminality (Pardue, 2008; D. Santos, 2002). Many Black hip-hop youths express that they are marginalized but they are not marginal subjects (Roth-Gordon, 2009): that is, they understand how the system marginalizes them, but they refuse to accept the subjectivities the hegemonic classes wish to impose upon them. The Bahian hip-hop movement metaphorically and socially takes "marginal" subjects and ties them to negritude and *ancestralidade*, defining a social and cultural Blackness that exceeds the Brazilian nation. Black artists and activists draw from, further develop, and spread a Black *conscientização* as instruments of Black self-affirmation. More importantly, they carry on the *quilombo* legacy by taking political action and working toward social change.

3 | Black Spaces of Culture

An array of global Black artists have introduced Salvador da Bahia to large segments of the African Diaspora, usually featuring Pelourinho, the city's historic center. For example, Michael Jackson's 1996 music video "They Don't Care About Us" showcases both Salvador's Pelourinho and the Dona Marta periphery in Rio de Janeiro. The Salvador scenes are primarily in front of the Casa Fundação de Jorge Amado. The video, directed by Spike Lee, prominently features Olodum, an Afro-bloc group that dates back to Bahia's reafricanization era in the 1970s. Before the King of Pop sings, we hear a child say, "Michael, they don't care about us" in Portuguese. Michael then walks out of the civil police station in Pelourinho rocking a white Olodum T-shirt. Later, he appears on a window balcony overlooking the cobblestone street. Down below, dozens of Olodum drummers masterfully play their steel pan drums while Neguinho do Samba, Olodum's founder, conducts his large ensemble for Jackson. All the Olodum drummers are men and almost all are Black. Their chiseled bodies are adorned with some combination of Pan-African colors (red, yellow, and green) or are shirtless. Today in Pelourinho, buildings still display cut-outs of Michael Jackson, reminding visitors that *this* is the place where the King of Pop shot his music video. In 2017, São Paulo rapper Emicida filmed his music video "Baiana" mostly in Pelourinho. The video follows a Black woman from São Paulo as she visits her lover, also a Black woman, in Salvador and they dance, drink, and parade around Pelourinho. "Baiana" also features Filhas de Gandhi, an all-women Afro-bloc group. In the video, the audience views Pelourinho as a romantic environment in which Black love has no boundaries, especially not heteronormative ones.[1] Emicida describes the music video as romantic, "but we wanted to venture into another form of love, a more plural one perhaps. A thousand memories and dreams arise, infinite, beautiful and pure possibilities" (Menezes, 2017). Right before COVID ruptured our worlds, the carioca pop singer Anitta shot her music video "Me Gusta" with the US Afro-Latina rapper Cardi B and Afro–Puerto Rican rapper Myke Towers in the same public square where Jackson's video was set. Whereas Jackson features Olodum in his music video, Anitta enlists the services of Didá, another all-women Afro-bloc started by Neguinho do Samba, Viviam Caroline de Jesus Queiros, Adriana Pereira Portela, and Deborah de Souza.

These three music videos all symbolically tie Salvador, Pelourinho, and Blackness together, connecting race, culture, and space into a unified whole. Each one represents Pelourinho as a space where Black people can enter, discover African culturalisms, be in community with other Black people, and be unbothered by the problems of the world. Black people have no care in Pelourinho. The historic center appears like an exotic playground where Black people can safely be themselves with African music, fashion, and festivals; it is seemingly cut off from the rest of the world. It should be noted that none of these artists are Bahian but come from the United States, the Caribbean, and other Brazilian cities. Yet they all see Pelourinho as a cultural refuge from their given locations in the Americas. These televisual representations portray Pelourinho in particular, and Salvador more broadly, as their own *quilombo*, where they safely flee their own spaces and escape to a locale where they can supposedly be free from the racial animosity and conditions that shape their own geographical locations. On the flip side, it merits asking if Pelourinho is a *quilombo* for Black Bahians who live in Salvador. Do they also go to Pelourinho? Or do they form their own *quilombos* elsewhere? This chapter transitions from where Black people in the diaspora wish to *aquilombar-se* in Salvador to the spaces where Black Bahian hip-hop artists *aquilombar-se* around the city.

Race, Space, and Culture

When Black people *aquilombar-se*, they are searching for a space where they can secure relief from their racial conditions and continue to expand a Black *conscientização* through various cultural expressions and communities. For them, a *quilombo* is a refuge where they can hide from the morally corrupt system that violently exploits them

(B. Nascimento, 2018g). It is a material place. Black people can *aquilombar-se* in a variety of places as long as they can assemble with one another in safety. Black Bahian hip-hop artists, activists, and fans find Pelourinho to be very different from how Michael Jackson, Emicida, and Anitta represent it. The members of the Bahian hip-hop movement view Pelourinho as a space of Black culture, but to them it is not a Black space for local and ordinary Black people and their own cultures (Maca, 2013).

Black Bahian hip-hop artists challenge us to understand the difference between "Black spaces of culture" and "spaces of Black culture." Black Bahian hip-hop artists are more interested in Black spaces, the places that are made for and by Black people and the cultures that emerge from them. They demonstrate this interest through praxis, putting theories into action when and how they flock to particular geographies that are out of the purview of most Brazilians. They congregate in Black communities like the periphery or events made for Black people, not just in places of Black culture. These are all space-making practices, in which they produce spaces, assign them meaning, create boundaries for them, locate them within systems of power, and determine who belongs and does not belong within them. Their everyday discourse, community organizing, and representations also reveal how space is dynamic, which partly means that it is susceptible to a series of forces, objects, movements, and relations (M. Santos, 2021). And their space is also social, made in relation to other spaces (Massey, 1994).

Black Bahian hip-hop artists assemble their *quilombo* spaces in contrast to Brazilian spaces. Their space-making practices echo the colonial era, when Black people fled the plantation and constructed the *quilombo* in a material place to congregate, rejuvenate, commune, and find safety from the racialized terror in Brazilian spaces. The *quilombo* could be as grand as Palmares or just a few days of refuge, renewal, and religious rituals (Price, 1996). Bahian hip-hop members execute these space-making practices where they contend that the periphery is an urban *quilombo* or create soirees for Black people to congregate for just one night.

When Black people participate in space-making practices, they are engendering relations of power that delve into questions of authority and meaning. In Brazil, the dominant classes believe they reserve the right to define and organize space, determining which spaces are valuable, how they are valuable, which are private or public, what can or cannot happen in certain spaces, who belongs to certain spaces, when spaces are accessible, and why this is part of the moral order. They mark Black spaces as "philosophically undeveloped," which justifies dispossession, and Black people in these Black spaces as "ungeographic" (McKittrick, 2006). Yet Black people's *aquilombamento* reveals their philosophical sophistication and alternative geographical belonging in opposition to Brazilian spatial relations and logics.

When people create, maintain, and define space, they insert racial and cultural meanings into these social processes of geographical boundary-making. In the United States, the dominant white classes and their allies invest in a "white spatial imaginary" that privileges purity, homogeneity, and a stable environment with predictable patterns, behaviors, and movements. They also work to eliminate social problems, especially from groups they deem as "impure" and dangerous (Lipsitz, 2011). In Salvador, the white spatial imaginary manifests differently; it is not a majority white place with a dominant Euroamerican culture. Salvador is a majority Black city in which the dominant social, economic, and political classes are white (and usually men). In Bahia's capital city, the state, nongovernmental entities, cultural agencies, tourism industries, and the middle and elite classes mold Pelourinho according to a Bahian imaginary, which is also a white spatial imaginary. For decades, the state has displaced Black people from Pelourinho in the name of "cleaning up" the neighborhood, meaning removing dangerous groups, and making it alluring to the white middle and elite classes (J. F. Collins, 2015). State and nonstate actors, agencies, and institutions permit folkloric Black cultures to enter because they are the pure Africanisms that signal Salvador as a majority Black city where Black people do not face cultural prejudice. In addition, these white dominant classes foster an environment where white people can safely experience, perform, and consume folkloric cultures.

A confusing element is that Black people from around the African Diaspora also travel to Salvador and go to Pelourinho to consume and experience this folkloric Blackness. US African Americans in particular are a significant client base for "roots tourism" (P. Pinho, 2018). Numerous Black Brazilians also come to Salvador to experience folkloric Blackness there. Whether from Brazil or abroad, they often regurgitate the dominant Bahian ideologies of Pelourinho: a city of exotic African culturalisms where Black travelers can freely recover the cultural roots they believe their ancestors lost during slavery and meet local Black people who have been practicing these African cultures for centuries. They can have the diasporic cultural encounters they so desperately desire. These Black visitors may imagine this to be a *quilombo*, but they are missing a critical element: the socially excluded Black people and their stigmatized cultures. The dominant white Bahian classes across government, nongovernmental organizations, and cultural agencies facilitate this diasporic exchange because it links Black people through ancestry and culture, not racial struggle, and praises Brazil as a racial paradise, not a racial hell.

Black hip-hop artists do not seek inclusion into white spaces in Salvador like Pelourinho. Rather, they look to mold Black spaces for Black people. As the history of *quilombos* illustrates, Black people generate their own geographies that address Black people's needs, expressions, and knowledges in opposition to white spaces, even those that include some exceptional forms of Blackness. They contest the white racial domination that determines which Black cultures and people are exceptional and valuable, and can be a part of white spaces and serve white purposes.

Taking Flight to Black Spaces of Culture

As a white space, Pelourinho celebrates folkloric Blackness by featuring African culturalisms that hark back to a premodern African past that is both pure and unaltered. In contrast, Black Bahian hip-hop artists see their Blackness as first a racial condition that determines which spaces they can and cannot enter, occupy, and belong to. This flows over to their Black *conscientização*, by which they navigate the tensions between the diasporic cultures in their *aquilombamentos* and both folkloric and mixed Blackness in Bahian society.

Tucked away on the backside of Pelourinho is the Sankofa Bar on Ladeira de São Miguel. Established in 2006 by Ghanian-born Justine Lloyd Ankai Macaido (also known as DJ Sankofa), the bar became a well-known spot where Black activists, artists, intellectuals, community organizers, and musicians could congregate, break bread, organize, and make community. In an interview with the local newspaper *Correio*, DJ Sankofa said he created the bar to establish diasporic links between Brazil and *current* Africa. He recalled his address to the crowd at his first performance in 2005: "Good evening, folks. My name is DJ Sankofa, I come from Africa, and this is my music. Isn't Salvador Africa?" To the journalist, he added, "There's so many Black people here, and playing things in the streets. The people began to clap their hands and the success started there" (Trabazo and Lahiri, 2013). DJ Sankofa saw the African influences in many local diasporic cultures in Salvador, his new home, and he wanted to build a space strengthening cultural and social links between Black Brazilians and other diasporic populations.

In Pelourinho, the Sankofa Bar was unique. While Pelourinho has catered to white and Black diasporic tourists from the middle and elite classes, the Sankofa Bar catered to Black Bahians, especially from the periphery. The state does not advertise Black people from the periphery in their representations of Pelourinho. And Sankofa was a *closed* space for Black people, an internal venue closed off from the streets. In Brazil, many white Brazilians consider the streets to be Black spaces because this is usually where Black people sing, dance, eat, drink, and listen to music. Indeed, Black people find the streets to offer a reprieve from small and overcrowded homes in periphery neighborhoods. White Brazilians also believe that the streets are democratic because they can freely join Black people and their cultures. This perspective ignores that Black people do not have access to private property where they can limit who can enter their spaces in the same way that white people do. And this perspective misses that Black cultures are performed by Black people but aimed at a white target audience. The headquarters for Olodum is not in the street, but it is a semi-outside space, closed off from the street but still in the open air. Whites, tourists, and other outsiders can pay an exorbitant fee to enter these cultural spaces and feel safe. Olodum's headquarters re-create the idea of the streets but in a "safe" and predictable environment that protects its patrons from the undesirable Black people who could join them on the public streets. Olodum's combination of high admission prices and semi-closed spaces reestablishes the association of whiteness with private space, status, and higher class standing even as the organization uses the appeal of the street as a space of cross-cultural conviviality. Sankofa often had cover charges, but they were more reasonable for the average Black Bahians than the fees to get into other clubs, sometimes as low as R$10. For these reasons, many Black Bahians cherished the Sankofa Bar.

Sankofa was more than just a bar. The nondescript building that DJ Sankofa rented became a *quilombo*, a space for Black people marginalized by Bahian society and Brazilians in general. The Sankofa Bar was part of a "Black spatial imaginary" that fosters Black creativity and community making, charting "new democratic imaginations and aspirations" (Lipsitz, 2011, pp. 53, 57). Black people could find refuge there from the brutal machinations of everyday Brazilian society and also partake in a variety of social and political activities that are otherwise heavily policed in Salvador.

During my preliminary dissertation research in 2013, several friends told me that the Sankofa Bar would be a good place to connect with hip-hop activists. Specifically, a "soiree" called Sarau Bem Black, an open mic night every week, attracted numerous hip-hop artists. Local intellectual, poet, and university professor Nelson Maca organized the soiree every Wednesday. He was part of a larger collective called Blackitude, a diasporic linguistic play on the English word "Black"; "attitude," or *atitude* in Portuguese (Messias, 2015); the Portuguese word *negritude*, which in Brazil denotes a refusal of European/white cultural values and emphasizes Black identity, fidelity to the African homeland, and solidarity with other Black people (Munanga, 2009); and the French political philosophy of *négritude*. My first night there was June 19, 2013. I walked from my friend's apartment and found the nondescript building. Inside were approximately fifty Black people, dressed in urban fashion and sporting a variety of hairstyles like dreadlocks, fades, twists, and Afros. I tried to enter without calling attention to myself and found a place to sit in the middle of the room. Awkward, shy, and with limited Portuguese, I planned initially to observe, be seen, and meet one or two people; I would then come back the next Wednesday for, I hoped, deeper conversations. From 7 to 9 p.m., the host called up various folks to come play music, sing, or recite their poetry. As 9 p.m. struck, many folks rushed out to catch their buses home, especially if they lived on the periphery and could expect a ride home of more than an hour. As I left with them, I encountered a skinny Black man with brown tanned skin, long dreads, a thick beard, and baggie clothes; he gave me a dap and a hug. I did my best to say the Portuguese sentences I had practiced all morning: "Hi, I'm Bryce. I'm a researcher from the United States. I'm interested in the hip-hop movement and connecting with Black artists." Already nervously sweating, I was *so* ready to just duck out quickly. However, the tall brotha' flashed a wide smile and said in Portuguese "Yo, that's dope, man. My name is João and I'm a rapper. I just released a CD last week. Here, take one." We later connected on Facebook, setting up several meetings and informal conversations at Sankofa, his apartment, and cultural events.

During that month-long homework research trip, I went to the Sankofa Bar about a half-dozen times. Many times, I thought to myself how ironic it was to be in Pelourinho, this great space of African heritage, only to escape to an obscure building with a Sankofa bird sign swinging in the wind to be among rappers, punks, skaters, activists, and other Black people *not* associated with a typical Bahian Blackness. This irony was not lost on the Bahian hip-hop community either. They frequently talked about their own social worlds that stand in stark contrast to Brazilian society, even outside in the Pelourinho streets. A few weeks after my first visit, an artist delivered a poem, with the crowd repeating his words, about the German Complex in Rio de Janeiro, a sizable periphery neighborhood in Rio de Janeiro's North Zone that the Brazilian state and society both stigmatize. The irony, as the poet pointed out, is there are no Germans there. Just Black people. Brazil was then preparing for the 2014 World Cup and the 2016 Summer Olympics, and the state developed the Police Pacification Unit to militaristically occupy Black spaces in the name of public safety and security (Franco, 2014). The state marked the German Complex as a community to invade. The poet's point was to make clear that the state sees communities composed of Black people differently than they would a community of white people, for example, Germans.

In that same meeting, Maca opened up the soiree to speak about political protests that had recently begun over a recent increase in public transportation fares. Brazilians in general were upset that the government had invested so much money in global sporting events but were underfunding public services. The outrage at bus fares quickly spilled over into inflation, poor housing, a shaky public health-care system, and substandard education. At the Sankofa Bar, the patrons expressed their support for the protests and generally were concerned with the same socioeconomic issues. Yet they also conveyed concern about how Black people's particular issues were generally ignored in the protest's political discourse. The protests welcomed Black people's participation: they could join in the popular resistance and be part of "the people" (*o povo*). But where was the uproar over police violence against Black male youth? Where was the uproar over sexual harassment and violence against Black women? Where was the uproar over everyday transgressions against Black people? Where was the uproar over Black people's displacement? They felt that Black people could be a part of a Brazilian community only if they did not show up as Black people.

For centuries, white Brazilians have become afraid when Black people congregate by themselves without white people present (Calógeras, 1933). They have targeted these Black assemblies and the spaces they occupy for harassment, punishment, and violence. One example is Candomblé *terreiros* (worship compounds) that the state outlawed because it associated Candomblé with witchcraft. Another is the first Afro-bloc Carnival groups in the late nineteenth century (K. D. Butler, 1998). During that time, the Eurocentric white Bahian elites viewed Black people's actions during Carnival as a blight on the city's reputation. The government banned "African clubs" from 1905 until 1914 (K. D. Butler, 2017); however, this did not stop Black people from participating in Carnival groups in whatever spaces they could (E. Carneiro, 1974).

After the Haitian Revolution,[2] many white elites feared that Bahia would become the next Haiti. Black people were revolting every few years in the early nineteenth century (J. Reis, 1995). The authorities detained, whipped, and executed many of the Black rebels. They even repatriated some back to Africa. The white disdain for and the state's repression of Black spaces sought and still seeks to neutralize a dangerous group's ability to disrupt the racial moral order. This also applies to the Sankofa Bar. For years, police harassed and pressured DJ Sankofa to shut down this sacred space. DJ Sankofa fought for many years to preserve this *quilombo* hidden in Pelourinho.

Despite valiant efforts, the Sankofa Bar met its fate on August 9, 2013. That night, five military police officers who were working with Superintendence for Municipal Control and Land Use Planning (SUCOM) employees on excessive noise complaints and lack of permits barged into the bar, terrifying the occupants inside. Two more officers stood outside the door, preventing others from entering the establishment (Zulu Inform@, 2013). Directed by SUCOM employees, the police confiscated the collective's sound equipment. A local lawyer inside the building advised the bar patrons how to handle the situation. Those inside complained about police heavy-handedness and quickly moved to create an inventory of items being removed.

Black activists, artists, and communities reacted strongly and swiftly. They immediately called attention to the absurdity of the claim itself: that Sankofa Bar's music was too loud and neighbors made noise complaints. The bar is just down the street from Bar do Fua with equally "excessive" noise (Zulu Inform@, 2013). Fewer and fewer people even live in Pelourinho these days. If anything, there are hostels for tourists. DJ Sankofa pointed out the sheer ridiculousness of the claim, and its history: "Pelourinho has always been a place of entertainment. This is not the first time that the police came here to provoke me. A few years back, the police entered the bar wanting to shut down the party. I got in front

Figure 3.1. Document posted on the internet supporting the Sankofa Bar after a police raid (2013)

of them and said that they were only doing it because of their uniform. I despise this. [And] I was arrested" (Trabazo and Lahiri, 2013). Even if there was some credibility to the charge of noise complaints and volume problems, it does not justify the presence of heavily armed military police. The locale was not known as a violent one.

On August 19, Sankofa Bar supporters protested in front of the bar to denounce the state's actions. On social media, supporters created the "Campaign against the criminalization of Black spaces of culture." They circulated the hashtag #iamagainstthecriminalizationofblackspace circulated on social media, that is, Facebook and Instagram. Many hip-hop artists used this hashtag and posted photos of themselves or memorable events at Sankofa Bar. On Facebook, they described how much the Sankofa Bar meant to them and to their hip-hop community. Black artists, activists, and organizers made a common critique against the state: Black people at Sankofa did not commit any criminal act, including noise violations. Instead, they pointed out that this was another instance of the state criminalizing Black people and their spaces. The state associated this community with an abject Blackness that made its members dangerous enemies. This was why SUCOM requested police assistance; it assumed that Black people at Sankofa would become violent, and so its officers brought in the police to quell the expected violence. As Black people were familiar with these state tactics and discourses, they were able to identify and critique the evening's events.

Despite various in-person and online protests, the state eventually forced the Sankofa Bar to shut down in November of that year. Nelson Maca puts Sankofa in a longer Black sociohistorical context, reflecting in *Correio*, the state newspaper, on its seven years as a cultural point of "independent action": "Happy Old Year, Sankofa" (*Feliz Ano Velho, Sankofa*). He identifies Sankofa's fate as another instance of conflict between Black community leaders and the state, especially the governor and the State Council of Culture. Maca persuasively frames Sankofa as a "Black space of culture" rather than a "space of Black culture," calling attention to how space and race are connected, pointing out that Black cultural appreciation does not eradicate anti-Black racism. I take this distinction to mean that people see white spaces as normative and thus do not characterize them racially. So white space becomes just space. On the other hand, they consider nonwhite spaces to be deviant, a racial marking distinguishing them from white spaces. Black spaces are different from white spaces *and* pose a threat to them. Therefore, the state can justify punishing a Black space to protect whiteness in the name of public safety, signifying white spaces as superior and dismissing Black spaces as inferior.

Maca brings another valuable point to light: the Black cultures in Black spaces differ from those in white or supposedly mixed spaces. Racial difference shapes the cultural meanings of a given space. From a Brazilian perspective, a Black space has no extraordinary culture; geographically, Black culture does not belong anywhere. Many Brazilians do not see the need to qualify the culture in a Black space as Black because there is no meaningful culture there. For Black Bahian hip-hop artists, Black spaces already produce a Black culture, so there is no need to qualify both space and culture as Black. If a space is Black, then the Black people in it are going to produce Black cultures. Black people in Black spaces are participating in Black culture. A space of Black culture retains its white racialization but calls attention to the Black cultures in it so that it can remain exceptional and superior to a Black culture in a Black space. Maca points out how the state appropriates African-derived cultures and represents them as evidence of racial exceptionalism and capitalist exploitation: "A foundation or publicly financed project can promote [Afro-Bahian] cultural events, but every day their people still have to pass the majority of the Bahian population who live in pockets of misery, in a society that is adverse to Black skin" (Maca, 2013). Like many other Black artist intellectuals, Maca critiques how the state and nonstate agencies, actors, and institutions appropriate Black culture, only to strip away its political currency, social community, and the racial conditions that it came from (Hanchard, 1994). Yet they stigmatize poor Black people and the conditions in which they live, like houselessness. Celebrating Black culture is not antiracist work when foundations and the state stigmatize Black people and do nothing about their social, economic, and political conditions. The state's repeated attempts to close the Sankofa Bar through intimidation, citations, and violent attacks demonstrate how race shapes and is shaped by space and subsequently by culture.

For Maca and many others in the Bahian hip-hop movement, Black spaces are first and foremost social assemblies of Black people who are not accepted by Brazil. Their Blackness is social and political before it is cultural. The cultural aspect of Black spaces includes the ideals, creative activities, and ways of living that blossom from Blackness as a social lived reality and political identification; Blackness here is not based on a claim to homeland cultures or heritage. In the same *Correio* opinion piece, Maca links the Sankofa Bar with other Black spaces of culture, explicitly naming them as *quilombos*: "This persecution has passed historically through Lundu, capoeira, samba, maracatu, Afro-blocs, Black carnival, Candomblé, Rio funk parties, Bahian pagodé.... They are cultural *quilombos* that fight against law that create and re-create mechanisms that impede our human trajectory" (Maca, 2013). For Maca, the Sankofa Bar was a *quilombo* because it provided refuge for Black people, thus making it a Black space, where Black people could socially gather and perform their cultures without white people supervising them and/or commodifying their cultures for economic exchange. Spaces like the Sankofa Bar are racial and stand in relation to and against white spaces in Salvador. Beatriz Nascimento once wrote, "Is it not possible that we [as Black people] have our own characteristics, not just in 'cultural' and social terms, but in human terms? As individuals? I believe so" (2018e, p. 44). As a Black space, the Sankofa Bar was composed of individuals, objects, and actions that uplifted Black people's humanity, giving them a dignified existence. These characteristics differed from those of most Pelourinho spaces and Bahia more generally because humanity begins with Black people, not with a white patriarchal authority determining which Black people do and do not have human value.

Spaces do not operate in isolation from one another. Social agents, forces, and institutions create and materialize them with and against other spaces, intertextually informing boundaries between us and them, belonging and nonbelonging, humans and nonhumans. These spatial logics and boundary-making are intensely racial (R. D. G. Kelley, 1998). In Salvador, white and Black spaces may share common cultures, but not common peoples. State and nonstate actors and agencies assign cultural meanings to a space as they also assign racial meanings. They create "imaginative geographies" (Said, 1978) that dictate in people's minds which spaces are for "us," that is, white people, and which foreign and distant spaces are for "them," that is, Black people. State and nonstate actors and agencies imagine Pelourinho as a white space where white and Black people can freely mix with one another, where African culturalisms are shared among all and racial harmony is ubiquitous. They imagine Black spaces, like the Sankofa Bar, as where dangerous Black people assemble, without the oversight of white people, and as posing a threat to racial conviviality in Bahian civil society. The relation between white and Black spaces mirrors the relation between the romanticized colonial plantation and the threatening *quilombo*. This relation between white and Black spaces also reproduces the Manichean divide between the settlers' zone and the natives' zone in colonies in the Caribbean and Africa (Fanon, 2004). Pelourinho is like the settlers' zone in that it has infrastructure, is spacious, and is joyous, with delicious food and an easygoing atmosphere. It is filled with white people, foreigners, and tourists. Black spaces, on the other hand, mirror the "natives' zone," where the white spatial imaginary assigns it meanings of a dangerous primitivism, what Fanon calls "a place of ill fame, peopled by men of evil repute" (p. 39). It is a crowded space, riddled with hunger and filth, where no one cares how people are born but do wonder how they die (p. 39).

Whitening Black Spaces

Today, the state, tourism agencies, cultural groups, and nonprofit institutions have taken over Pelourinho, realizing their vision of Bahian civil society. It is now a white space made for the Baumanian "tourist" (1997), the elite mobile subject whose movements around the world are effortless and valuable as they search for excitement and the exotic outside of their "home." The state, tourism agencies, cultural groups, and nonprofit institutions privilege the tourist's "wandering interests, his shifting attention and the mobile angle of view" (p. 91), providing him access to African heritage, interracial mixture, and cultural hybridity without asking him to stay and remain rooted. They must also protect the "tourist" from the "vagabond," Bauman's metaphor for the stigmatized and disposable poor. Whereas the tourist travels to Pelourinho out of desire, vagabonds must travel out of Pelourinho as the state forces them out.

Today, the Bahian imaginary celebrates Pelourinho as a (white) space where the white-*mestiço* patriarch has determined which African cultures, heritages, and actors may join him in producing Brazilian civilization. Visitors usually do not know that Pelourinho is also a white space of immense racial terror and violence that asserts whiteness as superior to Blackness within the moral order. The name itself echoes this history: Pelourinho translates to "little pillory," the wooden post to which white people and their appointed overseers tied unruly Black people for a public flogging. White people would punish Black people when they resisted colonial violence and took action, like revolts, rebellions, and flight, that would lead to their liberation (J. Reis, 1995; Schwartz, 1995). When they flogged Black people, they did so publicly to affirm whiteness as superior, authoritative, and physically dominant and to warn other Black people against transgressing the racial moral order. In Pelourinho, whiteness represents masculine power that can use phallic weapons, like a whip, to violently subjugate Black people, reducing them to subordinate and inferior positions (C. Smith, 2016a). Black people have also participated in this, wishing to perform their aspirational whiteness and thirst for masculine power through the act of subjugating another Black person to abject Blackness.

Black Bahian artists have not forgotten the local history of racial terror in plantocratic society. Nelson Maca's book *Gramática da ira* includes a poem titled "Díaspora" (2015) that describes how these floggings from the colonial era left a socio-psychological scar inside of Black people long after the exterior physical wound had healed. For him, Black people share these scars with one another, knowing that the white elites and their accomplices can also flog them. They also pass down these internal scars, reminding subsequent generations that white people can brutally violate them and cause incalculable harm to their bodies and their psyches. The title of the poem signals that the diaspora connects Black people who have endured countless acts of racial violence and procured cosmological forms of resistance, often through culture and politics, that challenge their inferior status. For Maca, the diaspora is both historical and contemporary. Instead of an overseer with a whip who flogs Black people, white people now have police officers with firearms who can arrest, beat, and even kill Black people to maintain the racial order of whiteness dominating Blackness.

By the mid-twentieth century, Pelourinho was anything but a tourist attraction. It was sketchy and seedy. The buildings were decrepit after decades of state neglect. For the city's (and even national) elite, Pelourinho was a blight on the city, more evidence that Salvador was stuck in Brazil's colonial past (Albuquerque, 1999). Pelourinho's reputation was no doubt tied to the numerous poor and working-class Black people living there. Sex work, criminal activity, and drug use were rampant, giving white people "proof" that Black people were backward and pathological (J. F. Collins, 2015). Across the country, Brazilian elites viewed Black Brazilians as unfit for the modern world of industrialization, urban life, and capitalism (Fernandes, 1969). In Salvador, local elites believed the city was unable to compete economically and politically with Rio de Janeiro, São Paulo, and other Southern cities with larger white populations.

Still, white Bahians valued Blackness if it was already diluted through interracial mixture and cultural hybridity. At the least, they could argue that their city (Salvador) and region (Bahia and the Northeast in general) were culturally significant even if they had little political and economic influence. Even though mixed Blackness was accepted, African culturalisms were not. Bahian elites still associated Africanisms with an abject Blackness, chaining Black people to the most deprecating stereotypes like savages, beasts, and devil worshippers.

In the 1970s and 1980s, Black artists, intellectuals, and activists transformed Pelourinho into a Black space to contest their marginalization. They sought to valorize African cultural styles, genres, materials, texts, rituals, and belief systems. People refer to this as "reafricanization" (Paschel, 2009), a cultural and political movement that embraced African cultural productions and, more importantly, the Black masses who did not conform to mixed Blackness. These Black Bahian agents connected their local struggles to other diasporic political and cultural movements such as US Black Power, Rastafarianism, and African decolonization efforts (Armstrong, 1999). Afro-blocs such as Ilê Aiyê and Olodum formed, recruiting Black masses who desired Black cultural organizations they could join. *Afoxés*, Carnival groups that play Candomblé music, also proliferated in the city. Black Bahians drew on global and local networks to interrupt the hegemonic meanings of abject Blackness (O. Pinho, 2005). Black people in Bahia, Brazil, and around the globe came to appreciate Pelourinho as a space where they and others could embrace and celebrate African culturalisms.

Modes of resistance are prone to incorporation (Hall, 1981), and soon after, in the 1980s, the state sought to rebrand Pelourinho as a commercial space that would facilitate "roots tourism" (Clarke, 2006; P. Pinho, 2018). With the help of cultural agencies and nonprofit organizations, the state advertised Pelourinho as a space where local, national, and diasporic Black people could learn about their African roots. They attributed Bahia's African cultural "preservation" to its long trade history with West Africa, conveniently omitting information about Black political resistance. The state sought to appropriate, commodify, and assert control over Black spaces and cultures (Paschel, 2009). State agencies rehabilitated many old buildings. In 1985, UNESCO declared the Pelourinho neighborhood a World Heritage site, and its website notes Pelourinho's significance. It emphasizes the following features. Salvador in 1558 had the first slave auction market in the Americas. It was Brazil's main port for the slave trade, sugar industry, and trade with Africa and the Far East. Finally, Pelourinho is dotted with brightly colored stucco houses, baroque palaces, grand public plazas, and colonial buildings, influenced by the Renaissance. Even though Pelourinho is a space of African-derived cultures, UNESCO praises the "blending" of African, Indigenous, and European peoples (UNESCO, 2020). The website uses a lusotropical framework, holding that, because the Portuguese came from a warmer European climate and were already familiar with other cultures, they were benign, friendly, and more humane colonizers who adapted easily to tropical climates (e.g., Freyre, 1986). As UNESCO mobilizes this framework, it represents Bahia as first a spatial incubator of African culturalisms and then a lusotropical cauldron that mixes different races and cultures together. Pelourinho is a modern example of how Black spaces of culture can become spaces of Black culture.

Diasporic Connections

Black people establish *quilombos* to foster Black space and diasporic intimacies that encourage interethnic sharing, bonding, and communal creation. During the colonial era, Black people from varying African ethnic groups came together to create *quilombos*, and such diasporic cultural exchanges are just as important to Black spaces of culture today. There is also a shift from bringing together people from different places in the same space to imagining a space as connected to people in different places. Today, Black Bahian hip-hop artists see their Black spaces and diasporic exchange as connected to other communities in the African Diaspora with a similar set of racial conditions, space-making practices, and diasporic cultural syncretism. *Quilombos* are not bound by nation-state boundaries. Black Bahian hip-hop artists view the *quilombo* as a multisited and transnational entity that can be reterritorialized across locations in the Americas. Across the Americas, there is trafficking of cultural symbols between these *quilombos*. In each *quilombo*, Black people can take refuge, whether it is in Salvador or abroad.

Black Bahians see Salvador in Brooklyn and Brooklyn in Salvador. These diasporic connections are a two-way street. Having taken a bus up to the Tancredo Neves neighborhood, I was greeted by DJ Larissa, a Black woman in her early twenties, and Tharles, a young Black man who raps. When I stepped off the crowded 1211 bus line, Tharles held his arms wide, smiled, and said, "Welcome homie! This is the Brooklyn of Salvador!" I asked him why this is the Brooklyn of Salvador. For him, they are both Black spaces with strong cultures of resistance that embrace Black people. I eventually told DJ Larissa and Tharles that Brooklyn is gentrifying rapidly like Pelourinho, that it's wildly expensive, and that the state and real estate developers were displacing longtime community residents. By the disappointment on their faces, you would have thought I killed their puppy. Still, Tharles cared less about the material reality in Brooklyn; he was more concerned with representations of Brooklyn that were meaningful to him and could be applied to his own community as a similar Black haven. As we walked through his periphery neighborhood, Tharles noted the importance of "Beiru" (not Beirut), the Black nickname for Tancredo Neves, for its strong Black artistic community and its influence on the Black Bahian cultural scene. For artists like DJ Larissa and Tharles, Brooklyn is an important imaginary that they use to connect their Black spaces to others in the diaspora.

Jorge, a Black graffiti artist in his early forties, took the opportunity to move to Brooklyn, New York, in the 2000s. From the periphery himself, he was interested in finding a similar Black space. In his mind, Brooklyn would be the borough where he would feel most at home. In the Bahian hip-hop movement, and among Black Brazilians in general, Brooklyn holds an enormous symbolic currency as a Black space, a refuge where Black people can assemble and exchange diasporic cultures. This can be attributed to the Notorious B.I.G., Spike Lee films, Jay-Z, and the television show *Everybody Hates Chris*, which is *extremely* popular among Black Brazilians (Miles, 2021). Another important consideration for Jorge is that he has dreadlocks. He wanted to be around Black people who embraced Black bodily aesthetics, like hair, not a Black bourgeois community that attempts to change their hair, clothes, and look to be more palatable to white society. The large Afro-Caribbean population gave him some assurance of that. Brooklyn was not only a hip-hop space but also a diasporic one that would make a Black Bahian feel at home.

Outside of racial composition and cultural affinities, Brooklyn had another familiar feel for him as well. In our 2015 interview, he recounted his first night in Brooklyn: "They shut the whole, the whole square [down] and had like a gun shootout happen[ing] between the cops and a whole building. I'm like, I'm home." As he said this, Jorge's face expressed a mix of what I took as bewilderment, amusement, and almost comfort. When Jorge says, "I'm home," he is calling attention to the transnational linkages between state antagonisms against Black people and spaces. His surprise is probably that this occurred on his first night there, but his smirk is because it reminded him of home and oddly relieved him of some homesickness. Jorge also saw a familiar difference between how the state treats Black people versus white people: "So, this is the big difference like, the white people have more rights, for sure, than the Black people." By that, he means the big difference is *between* white people and Black people, a dynamic that is consistent in both Brooklyn and Salvador. In Brooklyn, he saw that white people have cleaner areas and newer construction projects, while Black people are getting kicked out of theirs, as happened in Pelourinho, because they can't afford to live there. Jorge points out how Salvador and Brooklyn are intimately tied to one another, influenced not just by Black cultural heritage and exchange but also by similar social conditions anchored in racial hierarchies and violence. For Jorge, Brooklyn has both familiar and distinctive local conditions of anti-Black racism; ironically, the familiar/distinctive local conditions of racism were part of finding refuge, community, and even resistance.

Jorge, Larissa, and Tharles all illustrate that they create Black spaces in relation to other Black spaces in the African Diaspora. They imagine Black spaces through the criteria of similarity to one another and sociopolitical difference from white spaces in their respective locales. While some Black Bahians only look back through time and space to a mythical African homeland, hip-hop artists are looking across space in the same time at other Black people, especially in the Americas, as points of solidarity and identification. Larissa, Tharles, and Jorge show Black spatial dynamics through physical mobility, as with Jorge, and through the symbolic trafficking between the United States and Brazil, as with Tharles. Black Bahian hip-hop artists understand, create, and search for Black spaces. This is central to their *aquilombamento* and subsequent spatial practices. They also heed the lesson of Pelourinho: they often refuse state and private institutional support because it usually requires a paternalistic relationship, opting instead for partnerships or even self-management (Freitas, 2016). Rather than attempting to redeem and reform their Blackness and be inserted into a fundamentally anti-Black system, these artists lean further into the diaspora as a radical modality of Blackness.

Hip-Hop Educational Spaces

When hip-hop arts educators develop a Black *conscientização* through negritude and ancestrality, they are building other knowledge systems to grate against the coloniality in Brazilian educational institutions (A. E. da Costa, 2014). Often, they are educating their students informally, through Black popular culture in music and on the internet, social media, streaming platforms, and television. The downside is that it is a linear transmission, only from the artist to the audience. In response, Black Bahian hip-hop artists also take up physical space at material locations where they and Black educators and intellectuals can meet with their pupils face-to-face and learn from one another. This is a dialogical model, where knowledge is social.

The Bahian hip-hop movement has its own flavor compared to its counterparts, especially in Rio de Janeiro and São Paulo. The Bahian hip-hop movement brings Candomblé, Brazilian rap, reggae, dancehall, and Brazilian popular music (MPB) into its cauldron. At the same time, Bahian hip-hop artists are also very aware of US hip-hop music, artists, and trends. In this moment, trap music, a Southern version of hip-hop music characterized by hi-hat patterns, kick drums, and synthesizers with themes around drug dealing, is quite popular. Rap artists have created a new genre that they call "soteropagotrap." "Sotero" derives from *soteropolitano*, or a person from Salvador; "pago" references *pagodé*, a fast-paced samba-reggae music with sexually explicit lyrics (see Lima, 2016); and "trap" is for trap music. Black Bahian hip-hop artists are using US hip-hop and Black popular culture symbols, icons, and images to empower Black Bahians. US hip-hop and Black popular cultures not only empower but also help Black Bahians. They challenge the dominant representations, discourses, and conceptual maps that signify them as bandits, criminals, childlike, athletes, or sexual objects.

Marisa explained the importance of US Black women rappers and their imagery to her own work as a graffiti artist. She uses them to contest dominant racial and gender stereotypes of Black Brazilian women as the hypersexual *mulata*, Mama Africa, the exploited domestic worker, or the bad mother (Gonzalez, 2021) that are hypervisible and in frequent rotation. She turned to them early on:

> I began to draw more feminine figures of Black women, who are always the most prominent women in Brazilian society. [Society makes them] prominent in order to popularize them in culture, right? ... In my case, I use Black Brazilian women figures. Other times, I'll venture out [outside of Brazil]. I've done Lauryn Hill twice, Erykah Badu, Black women that are really ... how do I say this? I would have to say they're really fuckin' dope! [laughter]. They are though! They really are. They're women. They're Black. And they communicate! How do you not revere this?!?

She intends for her murals of US and Brazilian Black women to be alternative templates to and for Black Brazilian women. Black women may be prominent in Brazilian society and popular representations, but their prominent positions are not inherently good, positive, or empowering. Instead, they reduce Black women to objects. This is why Marisa says Black women "are always the most prominent women in Brazilian society." The most prominent representation of Black women and their existence in Brazilian civil society is the *mulata* who is shown dancing to samba during Carnaval. She is the interracial product of the colonial plantation, of the white slave owner and the enslaved Black woman. Bahian author Jorge Amado once deemed the *mulata* "Brazil's greatest export" (Ramos Bennett, 2001) because she represents Brazil's interracial mixture, cultural hybridity, sensuous passion, and sexual freedom. Yet the *mulata* bears the brunt of this trope. She must always be sexually available, always desiring and always desirable, ready to fornicate at a moment's notice. In Brazil, there is a common adage that a white woman is there to marry, a *mulata* to have sex with, and a (darker) Black woman to work. The *mulata* is desirable enough for sexual fantasy, but not respectable enough for marriage and the social and political benefits and obligations (good and bad) that come with it. She is the racial *and* sexual fantasy that holds Brazil together and the single most important image that represents the nation to itself and around the world. Marisa makes the critique that, yes, representations matter, and not all representations are productive or disrupt human hierarchies.

Marisa wants representations that intervene and disrupt rather than solidify Black women's place in the racial moral order. And she produces her own in her graffiti, spray-painting murals of Black women to interrupt these prominent representations and call into existence a different set of meanings that they and especially Black girls attach to themselves. Marisa draws inspiration from US Black women rappers for her graffiti. Artists like Erykah Badu and Lauryn Hill are powerful Black women who deserve reverence because they provide different representations to Black Brazilian women. Graffiti murals like Marisa's create a visual "re-existence" (I. A. Reis, 2020), a visual text that represents marginalized people with different cultural meanings from the ones society normalizes. Marisa crosses hip-hop genres by using graffiti to depict rappers, who use a vocal-musical medium, as a "re-existence" of Black women in Brazil. What is so important about these two US Black women MCs? They "communicate"—they speak! Marisa almost jumped out of her seat when she said that. Not only do they speak, but they are "really fucking dope." In Brazil, Black women are usually objects with few opportunities to speak and narrate their own stories. Marisa uses Badu and Hill as models so other Black Brazilian women and girls can know that they can do more than just be seen. Black women can also be subjects who are active rather than passive. They can speak and communicate their ideas as subjects who narrate their own histories, experiences, and social relations (hooks, 1989).

Marisa's graffiti murals highlight the importance of women, gender, and sexuality in the hip-hop movement as well as the Black Movement and the feminist movement. Hip-hop feminists call attention to and critique misogyny and sexism in hip-hop communities and the nation in general (Sobral Freire, 2018). Hip-hop feminists name the gender dynamics between masculinity and femininity, noting that patriarchy positions men and masculinity as authoritative, physically strong, dominant, and emotionally distant (hooks, 2004), and women and femininity as subordinate, passive, and docile. Masculinity's goal is to conquer femininity in order to demonstrate dominance. In response, hip-hop feminists do more than show Black women speaking. Cintia Savoli and her 2015 album *Bruta Flor* (Brutal flower) is representative of this intervention. Hip-hop feminists like her do not see feminism as a mechanism for becoming "surrogate men" (hooks, 2014). Instead, they want to normalize femininity as strong, powerful, and knowledgeable through love, emotional connection, and community.

Social movements are not without their own perils. No march toward justice is linear (Clark Hine, 2014). Marisa is committed to using her graffiti as a pedagogical tool to open Black women's subjectivities that move past sexual objects, domestic servants, or failed matriarchs. Yet she is not immune from these discourses. She told me that her visual activism has put her in uncomfortable and even dangerous positions in Black spaces:

> It's not okay for a woman to be in the street alone painting. Then, I realized, that as a matter of safety, I had to stop painting. However, the original idea was always to draw a woman. I have this preoccupation with a woman in the street. This was my initial idea. Always a very feminine figure with phrases, captions, and where they express feelings that are always connected to sexuality.... I began doing this but then I had problems in the movement. Guys thought that just because I would speak and draw about sexuality that I was there to... I was there... ready to have sex with everyone and that was not the case. A possibility, sure, but it wasn't that way. I just wanted to talk about the body of woman, about the resolve of woman.... Then I had to stop because I became limited by safety concerns. Then, it was difficult for me to come back to these places because people were eyeing me as if I came there as a whore or a prostitute or a slut.

In the Bahian hip-hop movement, not everyone gets to occupy Black spaces equally. Marisa is laboring to value femininity when and where it is often undervalued. One goal was to show Black women as having their own sexual desires, needs, and interests separate from what men want from them. Marisa's attempts to depict women as sexual subjects were met with unwanted sexual advances by men. They saw her as being sexually available. Suddenly, Marisa became the vulgar object she was trying to disrupt. She acknowledges she is a sexual being and does not want to be inhibited. However, this does not mean she will sleep with just anyone. This is the paradox for Bahian hip-hop feminists: being hailed as the subjects they are trying to interrupt. For Marisa, this is the conflict between dominant meanings of race, class, gender, and sexuality in the lived domain, especially in Black spaces, and subverting these meanings at the level of representation. Artistic interventions such as Marisa's do not exist in a vacuum sealed off from already existing social relations and ways of thinking and imagining. While graffiti is a subversive tool, female hip-hop artists must still navigate social constructions of race, gender, class, and sexuality in their communities. Hip-hop's mobile classrooms have their own internal hierarchies, especially when Black men view Black women the same way white men do.

Many Black artists, activists, and educators are highly aware of patriarchy shaping masculinity and femininity in hip-hop, Black communities, and Brazilian society. On my second fieldwork trip in 2014, I attended an educational workshop on the periphery in Surburbana that demonstrates the friction between global hip-hop, diasporic connections, and local meanings. US hip-hop cultures do not settle well within Brazilian Portuguese and its linguistic hierarchies of race, gender, and class. That day, a US Black professor of global hip-hop gave a workshop on hip-hop as a diasporic force for global change. Through her translator, she linked hip-hop histories back to the griots (West African storytellers) and African oral traditions. Oddly, her Brazilian hip-hop references were limited to ones related to São Paulo and Rio de Janeiro, omitting Bahia, which caused some consternation among the attendees that day. Her references suggested that she reified the tired trope of Bahia as connected to an African past and Rio and São Paulo as connected to a modern African Diaspora. During the discussion portion of the lecture, a Black woman teacher, herself a hip-hop fan, provided important insight on issues of translation. For her, global hip-hop, especially from the United States, can reinforce gender hierarchies and patriarchy in Brazil. She praised hip-hop for giving Black youth a voice, a sense of empowerment, and a Black *conscientização*. However, she also criticized hip-hop's overtly hypermasculine performances. She described how young Black boys use hip-hop's lexicon to challenge racial hierarchies yet reinforce gender hierarchies. Seeing successful and entrepreneurial artists such as Jay-Z is indeed empowering, she noted. Many Bahian youths emulate Jay-Z and other male hip-hop moguls, saying things like "I am the boss." In Portuguese, this is "eu sou padrão." *Padrão* shares etymological roots with patriarchy. This adopts a gendered language that subjugates femininity and women. US hip-hop discourses can be subversive in a gender-neutral way in English but in Portuguese they reify existing gender hierarchies. The teacher's concern was that the word *padrão* amplifies Brazil's reliance on patriarchy as a mode of social organizing and dominance. US rap music can animate colonial logics in a space intended to be liberatory. When Black boys exclaim "I am the boss" in Brazil, they are assuming a masculinist position of power and authority that, within the Portuguese language, asserts its dominance over femininity. Even as Bahian hip-hop artists and fans alike engage with US hip-hop, they must note how it translates into local meanings and discourses that are differently structured.

The Black teacher is not alone in recognizing the gendered hierarchies within the Bahian hip-hop movement and Brazil more generally, where men leave out women, and especially Black women, as active participants in their community. Many Bahian hip-hop feminists have identified this problem and labor to address it (Sobral Freire, 2018). They do not participate as a mother/lover, a woman warrior, or a vulgar (sexual) object (Matsunaga, 2008). When Black men contribute to Black women's problems with racism and sexism, they are contradicting the movement's mission to confront social injustices and transform reality. If Bahian hip-hop feminists wish to address this power imbalance, then they know they must pique young girls' interest in hip-hop and nurture them as artists.

Hip-Hop Feminist Space-Making

When Black people refused slavery as a way of life and a condition, they were fleeing their racial and classed positions within plantation society, a plantocracy where the colonial planters were the dominant class. Key to the colonial apparatus, these enslaving planters built the plantation as a site of racial terror, dehumanization, and class exploitation, laying the foundation for what we now know as "racial capitalism" (Robinson, 2021). They also created the plantation as a gendered space through the division of labor, racial terror, and sexual violence (Aidoo, 2018; Davis, 1998; Spillers, 1987). Hip-hop feminists therefore ensure that their *quilombo* spatial practices are providing Black women and girls a safe haven from the agony of patriarchy, sexism, and misogyny inside and outside of the hip-hop movement. They are creating communal spaces where Black women and girls can express their gender in more expansive ways than what Brazil and even the Bahian hip-hop movement permits them.

In early 2015, a group of five hip-hop feminist artists created a collective to mentor and develop technical skills for poor and working-class (and predominantly Black) female youths. Every Sunday, the group met in front of the Lacerda Elevator in Pelourinho and then walked down to Ladeira de Preguiça for a workshop at a local community cultural center. Many of the founders and participants lived in various peripheries across the city, and Ladeira de Perguiça was a convenient space for them to meet. Each workshop would have a history lesson on a hip-hop element, teach basic principles of a particular skill, and then provide a chance for people to practice those skills. One day, I was one of only two men there; the other was a local rapper who was photographing the event. About ten minutes into the history lesson, one of the organizers politely came up to me and told me to move to the back of the room. She did not want me in the photos, and she also wanted me to give more space to the women and girls there. I understood and made my way to the back with the local rapper.

Graffiti was that week's subject. The instructor for the day addressed graffiti within the larger scope of hip-hop: detailing graffiti's role in hip-hop's birth in New York, specifically in the Bronx; the role and significance of tagging, attaching one's artistic name onto public spaces; and graffiti's purpose as a visual aesthetic practice that takes up space in ways that Black people cannot do with their bodies. She incorporated a lesson on graffiti in São Paulo, well known around the world for its own graffiti scene. She then turned to Bahian graffiti, teaching her pupils about local graffiti artists and the various approaches, styles, and meanings they bring with them. Her audience of young women sat in this makeshift classroom, lit mostly by the sun shining in through the windows, asking questions and engaging with the day's materials.

After the graffiti history lesson, the collective left the community center and walked back up the hill to a large cobblestone wall. I walked a few meters behind, chatting with the photographer. To show my gratitude for the invitation to accompany the feminist collective without intruding on their space, I helped carry equipment, several large cans of paint and smaller spray-paint cans, for the next task in the day's lesson. The graffiti instructor gave a technical lesson on how to use paint. This included how to use paint on a darker wall to brighten it up so that the mural itself will "pop," that is, stand out and be more noticeable. She also carefully pulled out and showed how different spray-paint caps provide different types of lines and, ultimately, styles. Different artists use different caps depending on what they wish to spray that day. Then

Figure 3.2. Hip-hop feminist collective mural in Ladeira de Preguiça; photo by the author (2015)

she explained how to graffiti "inside-out," meaning painting the body of the letters first and then the outline of the letters last to get the crispest lines.

Then the collective designed and painted a large mural on a stone wall. Against a light-purple backdrop, they graffitied the words "Risca Mina, Rima Mina," emphasizing a spray-paint can as the "i" in "Risca" and a microphone as the "i" in "Rima." This slogan is an important proclamation within the context of Salvador's racial and gender hierarchies, but it is punning and polysemic and requires multiple translations to convey its importance. The mural masterfully connects women's place in hip-hop, ownership over their art, and the value of their work. In Brazil, "mina" is a shortened version of "menina," which translates to "girl." Brazilians commonly refer to both girls and women as "mina." However, this term can also be condescending if a person, especially a man, uses it to diminish a woman's social position, opinion, or actions. One dominant meaning of the mural is "Girl Streak, Girl Rhythm," which means "girls" are hip-hop artists in their "streaks" of paint and their rhythmic flows on the mic. The mural can also mean "My Streak, My Rhythm," in which "mina" is a shortened version of "minha," the feminine conjugation of "mine" as in "my own." It should be noted that "mina" literally translates to "mine," as in the gold mines in the nation. The three interpretations (and translations) are not in conflict with one another. For them, women can have ownership over hip-hop spaces, they can be feminine and feminists in hip-hop spaces, and their place is valued. Thus, hip-hop feminists convey demands that the Bahian hip-hop movement see, hear, and include women as women.

The "Mina Risca, Mina Rima" mural addresses the same concerns Marisa expressed about Black women's place in the Bahian hip-hop movement and Brazilian society. Just as Marisa turned to Lauryn Hill and Erykah Badu as fuckin' dope Black women who speak, the feminist collective locates the paint can and the microphone as media that Black women use to speak. The collective hails Black women and girls as subjects who narrate their own stories through graffiti murals and rap songs rather than being narrated as objects. They are disrupting what a "woman's place" is, disputing that it is only in the kitchen or serving as their artist-boyfriend's manager (Sobral Freire, 2018). They can also occupy a "man's place" without becoming surrogate men. Instead, they create their own narratives about a woman's place in the Bahian hip-hop movement: hence the linguistic play on "mina" that can mean "mine" (possession), "mine" (a place of extraction for valuable resources), and "girl" (as something other than masculine). The hip-hop feminist collective takes ownership of the wall and public space, challenging their supposed domestic position and location. There, women communicate their voices and by extension their own subjugated knowledges, histories, and street philosophies. The hip-hop feminist collective shows that women and girls can enter hip-hop as "girls" rather than surrogate men. Long after the collective leaves, the mural stays on the walls, a public classroom where other women walking by can engage with its meanings and feel empowered to speak, to draw, to communicate, and to have ownership of their voices in spaces that properly value Black women's knowledges.

Hip-hop feminists also turn to rap music to make a difference in the Bahian hip-hop movement. They want to see more Black women as MCs and inspire more young Black women and girls to follow in their steps. This is what Carla had to say about her impact on other women: "The thing I can talk about is that women rapping here in Bahia is strong. And that brings references to new people, we realized. Right after us, we could see many women arriving [on the scene], speaking and rapping, beginning to sing. We began to see that we're also becoming references to these women." Black women use hip-hop to speak from the periphery and make their own spaces of refuge, disrupting hip-hop as a masculine space that continues to marginalize and subjugate Black women. Hip-hop feminists push the movement to create spaces for women as women. They are not waiting for others to make it for them. They have taken it upon themselves. In the Bahian hip-hop movement, men invest little in carving out spaces for women and feminist critiques. There are some male hip-hop artists who understand the value of feminism and support hip-hop feminists (shout-out to Jorge Hilton, who has long been an advocate for women in the movement). The feminist hip-hop collective, like much of the Bahian hip-hop movement, questions who gets to speak for Black spaces as *quilombo* geographies. They also create an educational space so that women can step into authoritative positions as graffiti artists and MCs, becoming agents who have the right to name, define, and describe their lives, their communities, and the world around them.

The hip-hop feminist collective's mission has important implications because it educates and trains young women to become artists who have the right to represent their own identities. However, increased representations do not correlate with improved conditions and experiences (Malveaux, 1992). The collective's real impact is that they are training young Black women to be critical thinkers and participants in political practices (Sobral Freire, 2018). Hip-hop feminists execute these political practices through youth workshops and community building. They build spaces where more women enter the Bahian hip-hop movement as *women*. Black women do not have to negate the fact that they are women to fit in. The hip-hop feminist collective wants to develop girls and young women as Black feminist artists-intellectuals-activists who challenge intersectional forms of oppression in society, even those that creep into the Bahian hip-hop movement.

The Periphery as an Urban *Quilombo*

In June 2015, I ventured out via mototaxi to Jorge's home in the Vila Canaria *subúrbio*, about fifteen kilometers north from Pelourinho. When I arrived, we walked around his neighborhood while he showed me various murals, introduced me to his community, and pointed out various Candomblé places of worship where the community practiced Afro-Brazilian religious rituals. We went on the same route that he normally takes when he gives graffiti tours for US tourists, but he added a few extra stops for me. As we walked around on that muggy June day, he casually noted, "See, it's like our own little *quilombo* up here." That comment has always stuck with me even if it has taken me a while to come to terms with what he meant. Jorge is forging multiple connections between the *quilombo* and the periphery. That is, they are both Black spaces, illustrating how Black people come to utilize alternative logics and systems for assembly. It mirrors Beatriz Nascimento's own insights that the periphery is a Black collective space, just like a *historical quilombo* (B. Nascimento, 2018f).

Black hip-hop artists exert considerable energy turning the periphery into urban *quilombos*. An "urban *quilombo*" (Pereira, 2015) is a majority Black community that confronts urban segregation as well as racial and economic exclusion. At the same time, an urban *quilombo* provides new forms of belonging and community otherwise unavailable to Black people in Brazil (B. Nascimento, 2018f). Beatriz Nascimento argues that a *quilombo* is a "multi-sited material and symbolic territorialization of Black space" (C. Smith, 2016c, p. 79). The Bahian hip-hop movement reterritorializes the *quilombo* onto the periphery. Today, the periphery occupies a spatial relationship to the Brazilian nation-state similar to that of historical *quilombos* to the colony (Campos, 2005). In the eyes of Brazil, both the *quilombo* and the periphery are threats to Brazilian society. However, in the eyes of Black people, the *quilombo* and the periphery are Black spaces where Black people can be the agents of their own liberation (Pereira, 2015).

It is not just academics and intellectuals who see the connections between the historical *quilombo* and the periphery. Hip-hop artists on the ground see this as well. They use hip-hop cultures to signify the periphery as a Black space of cultural and political resistance. Like historical *quilombos*, Black people in the Bahian hip-hop movement are participating in an urban revolt against Brazilian structural racism (Amorim, 1997). Bahian hip-hop artists take *quilombo* symbols, images, and narratives and extend them to their own realities, linking slavery, racial discrimination, and Black resistance as ongoing themes that unfold as Black people's contemporary imaginaries and material conditions (Carril, 2005). They use the symbolism of *quilombos* such as Palmares and *quilombo* leaders such as Zumbí and Dandara in their community spaces, creating historical links between the past and the present (Pardue, 2008).

One key parallel that Bahian hip-hop artists make is the geographical relationship between the historical *quilombo* and the urban *quilombo*. Both are hard-to-reach spaces atop hillsides; both function as a parallel society. Most maroon communities in the Americas share this geographical feature (Carril, 2005). In Brazilian colonialism, Black people formed historical *quilombos* as alternatives to Brazilian society (J. J. Reis and Gomes, 2016). Today, Black people still form collective spaces of refuge as an alternative to Brazilian society. For them, the periphery is the most logical space to form an urban *quilombo*. In fact, many peripheries today began as *quilombos* hundreds of years ago (Campos, 2005). The historical *quilombo* community eventually grew over time, through the arrival of more fugitives and simple biological reproduction. As cities expanded, especially after abolition, *quilombos* like Salvador's Cabula became part of the urban landscape. Even though Brazilians started to call these spaces the periphery, many politically minded Black Brazilians see the historical correlation. Both the periphery as an urban *quilombo* and the historical *quilombo* in rural areas are a Blackness that is "out of place" (Walcott, 2015) in the Western order. In the Bahian hip-hop movement, the periphery, like the historical *quilombo*, is a spatial beacon of liberation and a refuge from Brazilian society where Black people can congregate by themselves and for themselves.

4 | Intimacy

But you know, you would do the same for me if we were in the United States.

—CARLOS

In Pelourinho, between the Lacerda Elevator and Largo Terreiro de Jesus, dozens of people stand in front of a historic monument to one of most heroic Black leaders of political resistance in the Western Hemisphere: Zumbí, the fearless leader of the Palmares *quilombo*. The statue is important to Black Brazilian history, drawing locals, tourists, activists, artists, intellectuals, and curious bystanders who stand in awe. Created by Marcia Magno, it stands over seven feet tall (2.2 meters); the figure is alert, looking to his left, to the east, back to Africa. He is shirtless, showing off his muscular build, a sculpted body that is literally stone-chiseled. Zumbí's statue alludes to his agility. One foot stands firm on the ground while the other is balanced on his calf, as if he is ready to spring into action at a moment's notice. At his waist is a long knife. Finally, he stands with his long spear, always ready to defend the Black fugitive community. The statue is quite imposing, a representation of Black masculinity as powerful, mighty, agile, and fearless.

At the base of the statue, four plaques narrate the life of this great Black warrior, describing how he defended Palmares against Portuguese and Dutch colonial troops.[1] One plaque details his life from his birth in 1655 to his death on November 20, 1695. At the bottom, it reads: "After 300 years, the date of the Black resistance leader's death was memorialized, by the Black Movement, as the National Day of Black Consciousness." Another side addresses the construction of the bronze statue, noting that it "symbolizes the multiple faces of the spirits from Africa" and was erected on May 30, 2008. A third side pays homage to Zumbí as the leader of the "first democratic experience in the country"[2] and "the symbol of resistance of the Black Brazilian

Figure 4.1. Zumbí statue in Pelourinho; photo by the author (2018)

masses, their historical memory, and their fight and conquest for the exercise of liberty by strengthening Black consciousness." The final plaque has lyrics from Gilberto Gil's song "Zumbí (The Warrior of Happiness)" that refer to Ogum, the Candomblé god of war, linking Black happiness with the pursuit of war, valorizing *quilombos* in the far-off sierra, and heralding Zumbí as a leader of Black consciousness even today.

The history of Zumbí is also the history of Palmares, both of which merit further attention. Palmares was not the first *quilombo* in Brazil, but it is the most important. Most *quilombos* did not last more than two years during the colonial era (Kent, 1965). The fact that Palmares lasted almost one hundred years illuminates its exceptionalism and importance for Black political resistance. Historians generally agree that Palmares was founded at the beginning of the seventeenth century, no later than 1605, and existed until November 20, 1695, when Portuguese colonial forces killed Zumbí.[3] Palmares began on the Serra da Barria mountain range in the captaincy of Pernambuco, what is now the state of Alagoas.[4] It is likely that it actually consisted of numerous small *quilombos* that were legally and politically interconnected with one another (Green, Langland, and Schwarcz, 2019, p. 79). Some speculate that Palmares held more than 100,000 people, but it is more likely the range was between 10,000 and 20,000. These inhabitants were Africans, Brazilian-born Blacks, mixed-race Black people, and Indigenous people. Many Africans already had war experience fighting against colonial forces back on the African continent (F. dos S. Gomes, 2011). The community even included some poor whites; even then, the *quilombo* did not discriminate. But Palmares became the largest maroon community in the Americas. Born in 1655, Zumbí was not Palmares's first leader. His revered uncle, Ganga-Zumba, ruled Palmares for dozens of years. Ganga-Zumba occupied his own royal palace, which was Palmares's political and administrative center overseeing its various interconnected *quilombos*.

Quilombos exist neither in cultural nor spatial autonomy (F. dos S. Gomes and Reis, 2016). Palmares was no exception. In some ways, colonial troops respected and feared Palmares for its members' fighting and farming capabilities. In the late seventeenth century, Governor Pedro de Almeida of Pernambuco wrote that in Palmares, "they make bows and arrows, but steal and purchase firearms. Our assaults have made them wary and experienced. They do not all live in the same place, so that one defeat will not wipe them out.... There are great workers who plant all the land's vegetables, and prudently store fruits for the winter and at times of war" (2019, p. 81). But the grand maroon community created fear among Portuguese and Dutch colonizers, and so these colonial forces sought to destroy it (Kent, 1965).[5] In 1597, the Jesuit priest Pero Rodrigues described the "revolted Negroes" as "the foremost enemies of the colonizer" because of their attacks on plantocratic society, comparing *quilombo* warriors to "their relatives on the island of São Thomé" (quoted in Kent, 1965, p. 164).[6] Colonial forces saw the destruction of *quilombos* as necessary (F. dos S. Gomes, 2011): one, it negated an immediate and material threat to the existing racial order; two, it served as a deterrent to enslaved Black people who might be considering revolt, riots, rebellions, or flight.

The Dutch tried twice and the Portuguese tried fifteen times to destroy "a piece of Africa transplanted to the Brazilian Northeast" (E. Carneiro, 1958, p. 30). Ganga-Zumba fended off many of these attacks. In the 1670s, Portuguese forces ramped up their efforts to destroy Palmares (Kent, 1965), presumably to quash Black revolt and dissidence. In 1680, the Pernambuco governor offered a peace treaty that Ganga-Zumba seriously considered: in exchange for recognition of their autonomy, Palmares would be under the jurisdiction of the colonial government and could accept no new fugitives (F. dos S. Gomes, 2011, p. 22). Ultimately, Zumbí despised these conditions. In 1687, Zumbí killed his uncle and took over as the sovereign head of Palmares (Fagan, 1993). Immediately, Zumbí and Palmares reestablished the more aggressive stance toward Portuguese colonialism: they would fight for their and other Black people's freedom and the right to govern themselves. And so they did. They met Portuguese forces in battle almost every year. The last battle, which would kill Zumbí and destroy Palmares, required six thousand troops, consisting of *bandeirantes* and Portuguese forces, and lasted forty-two days (Kent, 1965). The Portuguese troops murdered Zumbí; some argue that they beheaded him, while others contend they pushed him off a cliff. Nonetheless, the Portuguese believed they had destroyed Palmares once and for all.

Zumbí may have died on that fateful day, but Black people have kept his memory alive, reinventing his story for various cultural and political purposes. Colonial authorities remained afraid of Palmares all the way into the nineteenth century. Yet various segments, Black and non-Black alike, have incorporated Zumbí into Brazil's national identity as an exemplar of a supposedly just society, one that is fair and committed to unity and equality (B. Nascimento, 2018d). Some Black people have used Zumbí's story to argue for national inclusion (Hanchard, 2008), while for others he remains a symbol of Black racial pride, African cultural valorization, and political militancy (F. dos S. Gomes, 2011). Though there are no physical descriptions of him (F. dos S. Gomes, 2011), he is always praised for his physical capabilities and shows of force.

Often, society praises men for their ability to embrace a heteropatriarchal masculinity that is based on dominance, social isolation, and being emotionless. The statue of Zumbí represents those very features, and he became a template for a Black masculinity, serving as the basis for many Black men's social relationships with women, with friends, with their children, and with their community. Many times, I have wondered what kind of man he was outside of those overemphasized characteristic traits. How was he as a husband to Dandará? How did he interact with his friends? How did he treat elders, the newly arrived, and the weak? To my knowledge, we do not have direct answers to these questions. *Quilombolas* did nourish the weak, the wounded, and the vulnerable until they were able to contribute to maroon society. My concern here is filling in those gaps and urging that we understand that Black people fled to the *quilombo* to socially connect with one another in ways that were denied to them on the plantation. While we do not have proof that Black men related in alternative ways, that is, beyond being warriors and farmers, we also do not have proof that they did not. So, what if they did? What if the *quilombo* was also a refuge for Black men from heteropatriarchal masculinity and a means to feel, experience, and express love with one another in more expansive ways beyond Western norms? What would they gain? What would it entail? And how would it lead to both survival and liberation? My interest here is in how Black men are developing social connections based on intimacy; in how they are able to feel close and emotionally connected to, and supported by, those around them.

Complicated Black (Un)genderings

On the plantation, Black people could not reasonably expect to keep their families, friends, and community together for extensive periods of time, not as long as slave owners could sell them as property. Black people did stay together when they could. They saw the *quilombo* as an opportunity to establish and maintain their social and emotional connections with one another, taking care of one another as they embarked on a new life in a new community in a new social environment. Beatriz Nascimento (2018g) writes that *quilombos* were about peace, not war. *Quilombo* men engaged in war only to protect vulnerable people inside, namely women, the elderly, the disabled, and children, as well as other recent refugees who were not yet ready to go to war. The goal was not to assert physical dominance but to preserve and nourish the collective. The maroon community nursed a space where Black life, with its socialities that were impossible in economies of political death, could blossom. Black people could foster a society that did not depend upon coloniality and dehumanization, valorizing their own group-defined social subjectivities. This is how Black people performed their "rehumanization" (Funari and de Carvalho, 2016) as they escaped the plantation and regrouped in the *quilombo*.

Yet today, many Black men have sought to rehumanize themselves and other Black people by subscribing to and instilling colonial logics around gender into their community formations. Under a "plantation patriarchy" (hooks, 2003), white people and their accomplices operationalized the colonial regime of power to impose systems of violence that "ungendered" (Spillers, 1987) Black people from dominant scripts of femininity and masculinity. In practice, this meant that the dominant white class worked tirelessly to ensure that Black people's genders did not embody masculine and feminine ideals. In Brazil, barbaric white colonists, slave owners, and overseers grotesquely emasculated Black men, uninhibitedly and gleefully using violence, incarceration, fetishization, sodomization, castration, and sexual exploitation to signify them as without masculine power or rights (O. Pinho, 2008). This ungendering set a racial order of whiteness over Blackness while embedding masculinity in white heteropatriarchal power.

Ever since, when countless Black men have developed racial pride and valorized their African cultures, they have uncritically adopted a white dominator model of gender norms from the colonial plantation. They exert considerable energy to make their families and communities "whole" again, which they believe will reverse the ravaging effects of slavery, colonialism, and racialism. Black men believe they need to become "benevolent patriarchs" (hooks, 2003, p. 3) to obtain freedom by providing for and protecting their families. They, as well as Black women and children, labor to "recreate a patriarchal past in which men were men and women knew their respective place" (Ransby and Matthews, 1993, p. 59). This is evident in the symbolic and physical violence many Black men believe are at their rightful disposal for dominating Black women, children, and even Black men who are not "properly" masculine enough according to racialized patriarchal standards.

The issue at hand is not masculinity itself. The issue is patriarchy and people, especially Black men, who perceive heteropatriarchal masculinity as the only modality of masculinity that is worthy and valuable, and the only one that stands as evidence of freedom. Many Black men are unwilling to disavow patriarchal power and thus change their conception and practices of masculinity (hooks, 2004). I have personally seen Black men perpetuating misogyny, homophobia, and transphobia in various freestyle battles and informal conversations and on social media. At the same time, this is all much broader than Black men, who find themselves in a world that valorizes Black masculinity for being strong, dominant, in control, emotionless (with the exceptions of rage and anger), socially disconnected, and independent. Black men's attitudes toward women, LGBTQ communities, and violence reflect society's values. Brazil is regularly among the nations with the highest levels of domestic violence (Hautzinger, 2007). We can find similar levels of misogyny at Brazilian festivals, in mainstream media, on the radio, and in everyday behaviors. The Brazilian media have been especially complicit in this: they all too often represent the Black man as an undesirable *neguinho*, asexual, childlike, and subservient; a *negão*, an overpowering hypersexual beast; or an urban warrior (J. J. Carvalho, 1996). The problem is simple, yet the solution is complex. Society values Black men for their physical capabilities, especially in pursuit of dominance, and rarely values them for emotional connection, feeling close to others, and giving and receiving support.

The Zumbí statue is a representation of this Black masculinity, as is the Black male rapper from the periphery. Both stress racial pride, cultural empowerment, and Western modes of gender. But we cannot simply take the stereotypes used against us, call them positive, and believe that we are combating white supremacy, because these tactics still maintain "the coloniality of gender" (Lugones, 2007; Oyěwùmí, 1997), the belief that the European patriarchal system is the superior gender order by which all gender systems must be evaluated and ordered. Throughout Brazilian hip-hop, Black youths see the "gangsta" as the model for masculinity and the use of violence to make a new system (Pardue, 2008, p. 135). In Bahia, many reject the "gangsta" trope, yet they are still drawn to notions of courage, combat, and war (Messias, 2015). In hip-hop, feminists have long noted how a heteropatriarchal hypermasculinity subjugates Black women, girls, and youths (Durham, 2014; Matsunaga, 2008; I. Perry, 2004; T. Rose, 1994; Sobral Freire, 2018). These critiques are sites of racial accountability, asking Black men to do better if they are serious about liberation.

Heeding Black and decolonial feminists, rejecting heteropatriarchal masculinity is not enough to do better. Where might we look for another model? What if we turned to "illegible" (Neal, 2013) Black masculinities, unnoticed in most societies, that produce alternative relations, logics, and systems? What if we demand that we recognize and value Black men for their emotional, affective, and mental capacities? By illegible, I am referring to certain social and cultural practices that are commonplace, but to which people do not assign any special meaning or importance. In particular, I am interested in lifting up/finding out how Black men are already creating intimacy with one another through "interbeing" and "interdependency" (hooks, 2004), acknowledging that their racial empowerment thrives when they mutually build up, care for, and protect one another as a community effort. Many Black men exhibit intimacy with one another, yet their actions are often illegible because they do not conform to diasporic or hip-hop or Brazilian ideologies of masculinity. I want to read how some hip-hop artists push the Bahian hip-hop movement to further develop the *quilombo* model by allowing Black men a different gendered and raced sociality not dependent upon heteropatriarchy. Just as *quilombos* exposed the breaks in the plantocratic system (B. Nascimento, 2021), some Black male hip-hop artists are exposing the breaks in our racialized gender systems and contributing to alternative modes of connection that preserve the collective instead of fracturing it. This is not a new intervention but the claiming of a different legacy: these illegible intimacies are fundamental to the *quilombo* model, the belief that Black people should be protected at all costs, gender norms be damned. The *quilombo* model dials into a frequency of connection and intimacy not available in the Western world.

Escaping Hip-Hop Masculinities

In the Bahian hip-hop movement, Black men and boys are invested in a specific type of masculinity based on heteropatriarchy. They have learned this gender model from their families, their communities, their society, media, and one another. Even as Black men and boys turn to the hip-hop movement in search of community, hip-hop cultures can be a barrier to that intimacy, instead leaving Black men and boys with loneliness and isolation. It is not that Black men do not want intimacy. Rather, their pursuit of patriarchal power and a hip-hop masculinity based on racial empowerment and gender recuperation—and the social pressures that accompany that quest—prevents them from obtaining the very things they so desperately desire: social connection and closeness. Some Black men are refusing this quest and escaping the hegemonic masculinity in hip-hop cultures based on a white dominator model. Here, I focus on two songs by Vandal de Verdade (hereafter, Vandal) and Baco Exu do Blues (hereafter, Baco). They both express the inadequacies and even dysfunctionality of diasporic and local rap music scenes that depend upon patriarchy, violence, hypersexuality, misogyny, and social disconnection.

In Brazil, hip-hop's reputation as a community that is simply grounded in cultures of violence (Messias, 2015) parallels how colonial archives describe the *quilombo* almost entirely as a warrior society. Of course, violence is a tool for decolonization (Fanon, 2004). Yet we must be mindful of what new systems we will build on the other side of oppression, suffering, and precarity. I am reminded of a remark by James Baldwin: "I imagine one of the reasons people cling to their hates so stubbornly is because they sense, once hate is gone, they will be forced to deal with pain" (Baldwin, 2021, p. 148). What exists on the other side of anger, violence, and hurt as emergent *quilombos* construct safe havens of rest, protection, care, refuge, and rejuvenation? What must we give up, what do we gain, and how do we find different modes of relating and being outside colonial systems?

Vandal depicts the social inadequacies of rap music, pointing out that it does not permit Black men a conduit to further knowledge of self and connection with others. In the Bahian hip-hop movement, Vandal has made a name for himself as a leading street philosopher: he speaks to both Black cultural styles and aesthetics and Black people's realities. His Genius.com webpage bio accurately describes him as such: "A Salvador MC, Vandal is known not only for his strong lyrics but also his innate charisma and unique manner of writing that always places an H at the end of words as well as great repetition of consonants. Debuting in Bahian rap with the mixtape 'TIPOLAZVEGAZH' and hits like 'BALLAH IH FOGOH,' the MC manages to combine his favela origins and appeal to be one of the most sought-after artists in the Bahian capital" (Genius.com, 2019). The Bahian rapper reflects on Black people's creative genius, cultural worlds, and experiences of state-sanctioned violence, urban segregation, and anti-Black racism.

Vandal expresses vulnerability, doubt, and self-awareness in his lyrics. This is most unusual in Bahian hip-hop. The fifth track of *TIPOLAZVEGAZH* (roughly, LASVEGASTYPE) is "EMOCIONADUH," which translates to "EMOTIONAL" (gendered as masculine).[7] The song is a nuanced interrogation of the pitfalls rappers fall into when they see hip-hop as a vehicle for personal gain and material benefit, rather than for social change. "EMOCIONADUH" narrates a future possibility where Vandal sells out to become rich and famous, excitedly imagining the lifestyle of money, women, and sexual conquests. Vandal rhymes that he ends up obtaining these supposed goals: he dates better women, which presumably in his mind most likely means more Eurocentric in appearance and attitude than the ones from his periphery origins. Now he has a big record-label contract. He goes on tour where his memorabilia sells out. He has big-budget music videos. He has international fame because he raps in English and is popular in the US market. With the fame comes the money that he uses to spend big in VIP lounges where he is popping champagne corks, taking drugs, and performing ridiculous escapades. But at what cost?

Vandal proceeds to rap that the success costs much more than what one might expect. In the song, he describes that he is emotional because he "made it": he has material gain, sexual dominance, and crossover appeal. Yet this supposed success steals the very things that Vandal wants for himself in the song: nourishing social connections. He wants a healthy romantic relationship, but he raps that he cannot trust his partner, portraying her as a "gold digger" who wants him only for his money. On the track, Vandal feels guilty because he had to sell out to become famous. Through a meta-analysis of himself, he raps about rapping about topics he does not believe in and that are detrimental to his community's well-being just to obtain wider appeal. Vandal has betrayed his impetus for becoming a rapper and now he regrets it. His new social world does not bring him happiness. On the track, he feels alone and isolated, surrounded by people he doesn't want to be around, in places he doesn't want to be in, and also becoming a person he doesn't like. Vandal's emotional response to success is not joy or happiness, but rather fear, isolation, and paranoia.

Let's step back from the lyrics themselves and contextualize the song. As a whole, the Bahian hip-hop movement is committed to social justice and political transformation. Yet it does not exist in a vacuum;

there are other globally circulating Black cultures that cross Brazilian borders. Like all hip-hop audiences in Brazil, Bahian hip-hop community members regularly receive visual and musical representations of US Black men rappers at the club, which show them wearing high-end, expensive clothing, spending lots of money, having women at their sexual disposal, and having wild and taboo sex. In the United States, rappers consider having money, beautiful women, and sex as indicators of success, power, and respect. They write and perform a hip-hop script of masculinity that an empowered Black man is a sexually charged urban warrior (Jackson II, 2006).

Vandal's song represents to its audiences an "illegible" Black masculinity not often found in hip-hop, whether in Bahia or around the world. Vandal expresses emotions outside the permissible boundaries of Black patriarchal hypermasculinity. He is realizing that patriarchal modality alienates him from his own being as well as from forming deep and meaningful bonds with others in his social circles (hooks, 2004). He calls into question the supposed positive representations of Black masculinity. It might seem like a victory to see someone on television who looks like us and comes from where we are from, with beautiful women and lots of money, touring the world and living the good life. But Vandal shows that his ascent is not necessarily positive. Instead, he has become part of the "native bourgeoisie" (R. Kelley, 2000, p. xiv), a "junior partner" who maintains structures of colonialism, racism, and sexism. He points out that it is far from the victory he wants, or that any Black man should want. The same representations that Vandal uses to ascend to fame and success are the very stereotypes that society, the state, and the media use to portray Black men as bandits, criminals, and suspicious figures (Terra, 2010). He is simply taking a negative attribute and resignifying it as an inherently positive attribute, but he does not subvert the association of Black men with violence, aggression, and physical power.

Yet in this imagined scenario the thing he wanted for so long, commercial success, disconnects him from his partner, his community, and most importantly himself. Vandal's dissatisfaction with a hip-hop masculinity, one that privileges domination, isolation, and disconnection, gestures toward a break from the gender norms in a heteropatriarchal system. Feminists have been pointing out how patriarchy is detrimental to women, children, and nonmasculine men. However, patriarchy is also detrimental to cisheterosexual Black men who are looking for their humanity rather than power. For Black men like Vandal, heteropatriarchal and capitalist success in hip-hop severs them from the very things they desire: deeper and more meaningful relationships with themselves, partners, and community (hooks, 2004). For Vandal, patriarchal power is antithetical to his pursuit of his own humanity and the social bonds he so desperately desires.

In the song, Vandal demonstrates a type of refusal of the heteropatriarchal masculinity that white dominant society has attempted to naturalize among Black as well as other minoritized communities. The song leaves his audience at an impasse. If Black men are refusing this type of masculinity so prevalent in hip-hop, then how do they establish alternative relationships with romantic partners, other Black men, and even his own masculinity? Put differently, we see him refusing, but we have no idea where he is fleeing to. Transitioning to Baco, we see the refusal, the flight, and the new position within hip-hop circles he is taking in his own masculinity as it relates to himself and other Black men. Baco has skyrocketed in the Brazilian hip-hop game since his 2016 single with Diomedes Chinaski, "Sulicídio." I focus here on his 2018 song "Desculpa Me Jay-Z" (Forgive me Jay-Z) from his award-winning sophomore album *Bluesman*.[8]

First, let's deconstruct Baco's full rap name as part of a broader Black *conscientização* in the Bahian hip-hop movement. His name references both Candomblé and the global Black arts when he connects "Exú" and the "Blues," reestablishing Bahian hip-hop's emphases on negritude and ancestrality. In Candomblé, Exú is one of the most important orixás, the African deities who take human form, guide human creation, and distribute energy forces. Orixás are embodied messengers of *axé*, the spiritual ability to make things happen (Thompson, 1984). Many Brazilians who condemn Candomblé as witchcraft consider Exú to be the devil because he is a "trickster" and his colors are red and black. However, Exú is the *orixá* of communication, mediation, interpretation, and the crossroads between the metaphysical and the physical worlds; he is also associated with potentiality. Exú can lead his followers to new places, new understandings, and new energy. Exú is the messenger of the gods who guards the gateways. Many of his followers place an altar for him near the door of their homes. In Candomblé *terreiros*, his "house" is by the entrance so that a practitioner gives *axé* to him first when they enter (Sterling, 2012). On his first album, *Esú*, Baco juxtaposes Exú with Jesus rather than the devil, situating the *orixá* as a caring and cherished figure, not a stigmatized one.

Baco also incorporates the Blues into his rap persona, evoking its philosophies, themes, and structures of feeling. His second album, *Bluesman*, is a reflection on his own success following his freshman album, thinking with, through, and against Jay-Z, Kanye West, Van Gogh, and BB King. He expresses commonalities between the US South and the Brazilian Northeast: their histories of colonialism, plantations, and remoteness from the metropolitan centers exemplified by modern cities such as New York, Los Angeles, São Paulo, and Rio de Janeiro.[9]

As media texts, rap songs have no inherent meaning in their lyrics and sounds. Rather, rappers encode their music with certain meanings and messages, and their fans decode meanings and messages in similar, oppositional, or negotiated ways (Hall, 1980a). These encodings and decodings between producers and audiences have produced tensions in diasporic circuits of cultural exchange between Black people in the United States and Brazil. In his song "Desculpa me Jay-Z," Baco functions as both audience and producer, receiving Jay-Z's music and speaking back to him as a fan, a fellow rapper, and a nonromantic lover. He is also speaking to his audience, many of whom are also Jay-Z fans. He negotiates Jay-Z's rap ideologies, which are dominant and even aspirational among Black men in the African Diaspora, with his own local racial conditions, self-awareness, and desire to dismantle heteropatriarchy's hold on Black masculinity around the globe.

Over a somber beat, the Bahian raps in a low and serious tone, dividing the song into three parts that foreground alternative hip-hop masculinities. Baco begins the song by rapping that he is done, he is breaking up with Jay-Z. Addressing Jay-Z directly, he says that he doesn't love the Brooklyn rapper anymore. He doesn't want to see him. And he asks Jay-Z to never call him again. Baco raps that he isn't even mad at Jay-Z, expressing how much he loves the Roc Nation founder. This may sound absurd, a man breaking up with another man with whom he is not sexually involved. The real absurdity is that we lack a language to approach the idea that cisgender heterosexual Black men have relationships with one another, that we love one another, care for one another, and are nourished by one another. Baco's problem is that patriarchal masculinity does not view nonromantic bonds between men as relationships. Being in a relationship presumes social connection and bonding; it also makes men vulnerable. If Black men do not view friendships as relationships, then they do not need to nurture, care for, and evaluate friendships as they might in a romantic relationship.

The song expresses Black men's desires to transgress boundaries so that they can connect with one another outside of heteropatriarchal borders. Baco breaks up with Jay-Z yet still wishes to leave on good terms. His lyrics express his continuing affection and care for what Jay-Z has done for him. Rather than just "ghosting" (disappearing on) Jay-Z, Baco invests in a Black masculinity that privileges care and empathy for other Black men, especially in worlds that push them to disconnect from one another and their own selves. So Baco asks for forgiveness from Jay-Z in the song, demonstrating maturity through communication and mutual understanding. He is aware that his actions may hurt Jay-Z and thus wants to emotionally engage one last time to express his concerns and explain why he is moving on.

Even though this is a symbolic breakup, Baco is demonstrating a commitment to a politics of intimacy around reciprocal closeness, shared vulnerability, support, and protection, indicative of his commitment to such relationships in the future. The Bahian rapper realizes he must move on to a better place as he works through his own personal struggles. Baco is ready for growth, which necessitates leaving Jay-Z behind. The symbolic potential in this is that Baco knows he must interact with other Black men in his everyday life in this way. This is the only way to find deep modes of social connection, intimacy, and love that he could not with Jay-Z. That is the gift Jay-Z gives Baco, and Baco recognizes that as he moves on. Breaking up with Jay-Z, no matter how one-sided the whole thing may be, points to a love for Black men in ways we do not traditionally associate with Black masculinity. This is a form of care that is not assumed or expected from Black men, especially when so much value is placed on their physical capabilities.

At the end of the first verse, Baco throws his audience for a loop: the breakup is also with himself. The Bahian rapper has used Jay-Z as a mold to constitute his own identity and sense of self. He raps that he has attempted to emulate Jay-Z so much that when he looks in the mirror, he sees Jay-Z, not his own reflection. For Baco, Jay-Z is a symbolic cloak to hide from himself and his own imperfections. In the second part of the track, Baco raps why he must break up with Jay-Z. Baco realizes he is engaging in alienating behaviors only because he aspires to be like Jay-Z. He raps about his sexual fantasies with Beyoncé, Jay-Z's wife. He also raps about trying to be rich like Jay-Z, smoking cigars like him as pictured on his album covers (shout-out to *Reasonable Doubt* and *The Blueprint*). He wants to go out and drink like Jay-Z. Baco then reveals to Jay-Z, and by extension his audiences, that he has wanted to do all this to escape from his everyday life.

Baco knows he is being inauthentic to himself, a serious sin in the Bahian hip-hop movement. Brazilian rappers highly value authenticity, speaking to what is real in their own world (Camargos, 2015; J. C. Gomes da Silva, 1999). Yet Baco cannot do it. And trying to be someone he is not and suppressing his own desires, needs, and wants as a human being is ripping him apart. This inauthenticity must stop. The self-betrayal must cease. Baco raps that he fears getting to know who *he is*. With Jay-Z as a symbolic cloak to emulate, Baco did not need to see himself as a flawed and complicated individual. Instead, Baco preferred to pretend he is someone he is not.

In breaking up with Jay-Z, Baco also navigates the racial and gender identifications between Black men in the African Diaspora through similarity and difference. Baco and Jay-Z are Black men who are also rappers, but their experiences in those sociopolitical categories are different based on their local socioeconomic conditions *and* their diasporic positions. Identifications are not natural phenomena; they are the product of people determining which people are similar to them, the recognition of one's self in another (Hall, 1996). At the same time, people's group identifications negotiate internal differences that can fracture the group's cohesiveness. In the song, Baco discusses how he disavowed his own self in favor of a hegemonic icon of Black masculinity to secure comfort, empowerment, a way of being, and a cultural community. However, people cannot substitute representation for experience; the two shape one another in the Black cultural repertoire (Hall, 1992). Baco pursues Jay-Z as a ready-made Black masculine mold, which leads to his own alienation. This is similar to the process Fanon describes when the Black Antillean man attempts to become a white man, asserting his humanity by embracing a race-gender hegemonic norm (2008). In Baco's case, Black people are performing these scripts within the African Diaspora, trying to follow a path to a dominant norm that exerts influence over subordinate segments. Baco is not a Black man living under colonial rule, like Fanon; he is a Black man in the non-Anglophone Global South. Rather than trying to become the white colonizer, as Fanon describes, Baco is trying to become a rich Black celebrity from the United States. The song elucidates how Black men outside of the United States emulate US Black male rappers as they attempt to demonstrate their human value in local and diasporic communities. Jay-Z may be racially and culturally different from the hegemonic representation of the human, or Western white "Man" (Wynter, 2003), but he is close in terms of gender, class, language, and geography. Baco wants to act like Jay-Z to try to be more human. And just like Fanon, Baco learns that these dreams will never come true. These aspirations produce only self-alienation and reinforce a world that subjugates Black people and Black consciousness. Baco suffers a crisis: he cannot be who he wishes to be because he is sociopolitically positioned within his local environment. When Baco finally refuses to erase his particularities in his identification with a hegemonic Black masculinity in hip-hop cultures, he realizes that he cannot be in a homosocial relationship with Jay-Z because US rap music has become a form of self-alienation. Like Exú, Baco is at a crossroads, unsure where to go. Jay-Z is comforting, but increasingly less so the more Baco neglects his personal issues.

The track's last part reveals what is on the other side of Jay-Z. As he turns to his own authentic self, Baco raps about his depression, suicidal thoughts, self-esteem issues, retail therapy, if he should go to school, and should he pursue his dreams. It is easier to neglect his inner self than confront the significant amount of pain he has accumulated. Healing his personal wounds seems insurmountable. Still, healing is the only authentic way forward. There is no other way out from the world he lives in, no matter how much he consumes US hip-hop and mimics Jay-Z. Baco must take off the cloak, collect the fragments of his self, and piece himself back together. As the song winds down, he raps that he teeters between loving and hating himself, but comes to an ultimate understanding: he can no longer lie to himself, but must confront who he is on his own terms.

Rarely do we get Black men expressing their feelings, emotions, and desires with themselves and one another as in "Desculpa Me Jay-Z." Baco is yearning for a Black masculinity that supports his intense desire for intimacy, where he can show up as his full self, not hide his flaws, and freely express his emotions with others, especially Black men. He is leaving behind a heteropatriarchal model and fleeing to a "feminist masculinity" (hooks, 2004) where Black men express their feelings, needs, and desires and have healthy relationships with their community. Vandal may have become emotionally open, but that was only to himself. Baco became emotionally open to another Black man, creating a different relation between Black men than what is conventional. Even though their songs represent a desire for intimacy, people often do not find them legible because they counter hegemonic notions of Black masculinity in hip-hop, the African Diaspora, and Brazil.

Performing Care and Protection

Vandal's and Baco's songs critique the inadequacies of a Black patriarchal masculinity that keeps them from what they really desire in this world: intimacy. In the Bahian hip-hop movement of which they are a part, Black Bahians are putting this intimacy into praxis as part of their *aquilombamento* model, enabling Black men to support and care for one another in ways that trouble Western hegemonic gender norms. This happens in everyday life.

After a long day in 2014 of painting graffiti on a two-story building in Salvador's central area, the New Boys Crew graffiti collective and I lugged large blue tarp bags of spray paint, ladders, and other equipment back to their headquarters in the Ladeira de Preguiça favela. Even though no one in the crew lived there, it was a centrally located space for them to congregate in, as they came from other peripheries such as Castelo Branco and Ribeira. Being outside in the scorching heat, all of us understandably had ravenous appetites and were ready to devour some food and some cold drinks. Once we arrived back to the Ladeira de Preguiça, we went into the restaurant owned and operated by Dandara, the wife of graffiti collective member Flavio. She asked what we wanted to drink; most of us asked for lager, but some asked for a cold Pepsi. A few folks set up the grill, some getting the coals ready while others cleaned the metal grate. Jefferson and Cesar ran off to the butcher to grab some meat and to the corner store for some vegetables. The remaining folks sat back, relaxed, and sipped on a beverage as the sun made its way over the Bay of All Saints, sharing its last daily rays.

As it always does, time moved quickly, changing the sky's colors, now drenching us in its beautiful darkness. People began to retire to their homes, and fewer children ran carefree through the streets. The cobblestones streets were almost empty. The nighttime breeze off the water swooped in, dropping the temperature a few degrees, sending chills down our spines. Nature's clock was telling everyone that nighttime was quickly arriving and that folks must decide whether to stay or to go. The last few buses stopped running at 11 p.m. As Uber had yet to arrive in the country, it was imperative to either arrive at the bus stop with ample time to catch one of the last buses rambling through the pothole-filled streets or take an overpriced and shady taxi. While some folks were still lingering, I felt the pressure of time, unsure if I had enough cash to afford a taxi back home. I attempted to just leave, say my goodbyes, and head to the Comércio bus stop. I got to Ronaldo, a founder of the collective, who wouldn't let me go:

> **Ronaldo:** Where are you going? We're all leaving. Just hold up. We'll walk you to the bus stop!
> **BH:** Naw, naw, it's cool. I gotta get goin'.
> **Ronaldo:** Homie, we're all leaving in a bit. We'll all walk together. You can't be walking these streets by yourself at night.
> **BH:** I know how to get there. I've done it before. It'll be all good.
> **Ronaldo:** Bro. Chill. It's really okay. We want to make sure you get there safe.

When Ronaldo said, "We want to make sure you get there safe," the Portuguese words he used were "A gente quer que você chegar com segurança," a more literal translation being "We want you to arrive with security." I trusted that Ronaldo would make sure I arrived safely at Comércio and then to my home. His conception of security and safety meant that he was concerned for my own movements in the city, and he would not permit me to travel on my own, insisting that I remain with the collective. Ronaldo also had a broader commitment to ensure that Black men are not vulnerable to violence and even premature death, whether from police or someone who robs people on the street.

Since that night, I have not been able to let go of Ronaldo's phrase "chegar com segurança" and how it translates to both "arrive safely" and "arrive with security." What does it mean to ensure Black men's safety? For Ronaldo, it means protecting one another in praxis, asking someone like myself to trust him to get me home. This simple action reflects a politics of care, emotional bonding, and social connection for a Black masculinity not premised upon a patriarchal gender system. And it shows that Black men gain a great deal when we give up ideals like aloneness, isolation, physical prowess, and disconnection as our guiding traits.

I ended up waiting until Ronaldo and his crew were ready to leave. It might have only been another fifteen minutes, but that can feel like forever when you feel yourself racing against time. Eventually, we made our way down the badly lit slope. We were isolated, above those just below us down on Avenida Lafayette Coutinho, and certainly out of sight from those in the high city. If I am being honest, I felt much better walking with them. I did know that most of the neighborhood's residents were gregarious and hospitable; I have been welcomed in a few homes there and the local cultural center. But I also knew there were a considerable number of drug users, and many folks inside and outside of the hip-hop movement had warned me about making my way into the neighborhood. Whenever I entered or left Ladeira de Preguiça, I often saw and walked past them. I usually gave a quick head nod, the diasporic "hello" as a means of recognition and identification, but I tried to avoid any kind of conversation. Often, I feared that my accent would give me away as an outsider and they might mess with me in some way, either then or on another trip into the neighborhood. At the very least, traveling in the safety of the graffiti collective between the periphery neighborhood and the bus stop granted me relief from having to be hyperaware of my surroundings.

Ronaldo and his crew are by no means unique or exceptional. The *quilombo* practice of ensuring collective safety and security by walking together in public spaces is indeed common in the Bahian hip-hop movement, and really in Salvador more broadly. A sense of protecting the collectivity and relinquishing one's individuality reigned over numerous occasions of my ethnographic homework. That same 2014 winter, I ventured out to Plataforma twice a week. There, João and Carlos shared an apartment just below the Centro Cultural Plataforma. To arrive at João and Carlos's home, I took a bus to Comercio and then transferred to another bus on its way to Suburbana, approximately fifteen kilometers away. The bus ride can take anywhere from forty minutes to an hour and a half, sometimes two hours. Like many things in Salvador, mobility is never as easy as it should be. After riding the bus for however long, I got off at the Bom Preço grocery store on Avenida Afrânio Peixoto and made my way up no fewer than three hills into the Plataforma neighborhood. The walk easily added twenty to twenty-five minutes to get to João and Carlos's three-bedroom, barely furnished apartment (while I am talking about alternative Black masculinities, some things don't change) overlooking the glistening Baía de Todos os Santos (Bay of All Saints). Every time, I was reminded, usually as I descended on the final hillside slope to João and Carlos's apartment, that historians describe *quilombos* as being far away on hills in difficult-to-reach spaces (Price, 1996).

No matter the time of the year, the sunset in Salvador rarely goes past 6 p.m. This can be attributed to the fact that it is only

1,444 kilometers from the equator. Any type of evening activity with João and Carlos meant that my return trip to the bus stop on Avenida Afrânio Peixoto took place at night. Whatever time I left their apartment, João or Carlos walked me back to the bus stop. Whether it was 7 p.m. or 10 p.m., they dropped whatever they were doing and accompanied me back over the three hills. I have seen them stop conversations, arguments with their girlfriends, song recordings with their homies, and other activities to accompany me to the bus stop. No matter how long it took, they waited patiently with me at the bus stop until I got on my bus and headed back on my way. Once Carlos waited with me for two hours before I gave up on the bus and took a mototaxi instead. Each time, they reminded me to message them and let them know I had arrived safely at my home. Their generosity and kindness are significant because their home was a central gathering spot, but they never let me go to the bus stop by myself at night. They always made it a priority to accompany me there. Like Ronaldo, they were worried about my safety, and practiced an intimacy with me that is rarely remarked on between Black men.

One time in winter 2015, I spoke with Carlos about walking me to the bus stop. I told him that I loved these walks we took together and the quality time they gave us, but at some point, I could just walk myself to the bus stop. He looked at me like I was fuckin' silly. Looking back now, I can realize that I said that because I did not want to be a burden. For Carlos and João, I wasn't a burden; this was just something they do as part of their friendship. They also wanted to watch out for me. Carlos then proceeded to tell me a story:

Carlos: Naw, I don't feel alright letting you walk there by yourself. People don't know you. You notice that when we walk to the bus stop, I always introduce you to people? I want people to know who you are, so y'all are familiar. Also, I want people to know that you roll with me. Like bro, there are little things here that you can't pick up on. For example, this one time this young punk, maybe fifteen years old, rolled up on me. Had his hand like this [fingers pointed inside of his shirt like it was a gun]. This motherfucka tried to rob me! I said "Do you know who the fuck I am? You're gonna' try and ROB ME?!? Get the fuck outta here!" The kid tried to play it off "Aye bro, I'm just playing, you know?" The kid quickly ran away, scared at his fuck-up. Like I don't know that you would be able to tell if someone is tryna' rob you for real or not. If they're stupid enough to rob me, they'll definitely try to get you. And there's small little things that you still may not know about or can't read in the situation. And there might be little things that you do that tip off others that you ain't from here, like not even not from the US but not even from the neighborhood. I can't let you get hurt out here. But you know, you would do the same for me if we were in the United States.

Carlos's point is that despite my growing familiarity with social codes in Salvador, fully mastering them takes years, and I had yet to and maybe never will achieve this mastery. He refused to risk putting me in danger because I could be robbed, or the police might mess with me. At the very least, he would not want me to be alone; he wanted to be there with me, letting me know he had my back.

Many folks assume that marginal Black communities accept Black-on-Black violence. João and Carlos were both committed to a praxis that refutes that. They both felt an obligation to ensure my safety. For both, Black men are not disposable, even a US Black man they were still getting to know. For my safety, they asserted themselves in a dominant position over me. The goal is not simply to assert one's dominance among men, but to protect the collective. This is clear in Carlos's statement: "But you know, you would do the same for me if we were in the United States." This is a communitarian notion of protection, power, and security. It is reciprocal and can be flipped at any given time and place: Black men can exchange the position of protector, assuming it at certain times and deferring it at others. Carlos's assertion that the position of protector can be switched shows that it is not about obtaining a position of dominance, but rather preserving the well-being of the collective. This flipping of protection is about intimacy and closeness, the ability to trust that one will step up to protect the other whenever and wherever necessary. We were not competing to show who was the most masculine by asserting dominance over the other; we were in a relationship that valued protecting each other.

As the years went on, I learned to perform this collective strategy with more ease. It went from being an awkward intrusion on my, let's be honest, fragile Black masculinity and autonomy to becoming habitual, teaching me how to work under a *quilombo* model. We willingly subjected ourselves to this collective mentality. Later, in 2017, João created a rap-jazz live band group in the vein of Digable Planets, De La Soul, and A Tribe Called Quest to appeal to an older audience that prefers a live show in the evenings rather than after the midnight hour (if I'm being honest, me too!). Each Tuesday, the band would meet at 7 p.m. at a studio in the Dois de Julho neighborhood to practice, go over their sets, experiment, introduce new band members/instruments, and discuss band issues (new shows, venues, pricing, etc.). I would sit either in the producer's booth with Ivan, who works the sound board, or quietly in a corner in the performance room soaking in the sweet symphony of saxophones, drums, guitars, trumpets, spoken word, rapping, and singing. After the two hours, each band member would give the drummer their ten reals to pay for the studio rental fee.

Leaving the small recording studio just north of the Largo Dois de Julho, three or four folks would jump in Daniel's car. The singer/rapper would drive them home out to the periphery, leaving the remaining five to seven of us to walk over to Rua Carlos Gomes to wait for our various buses. We would banter on the way over. A band member might ask me how to say something in English. As many Black men do, we played the "dozens" on one another, teasing each other for various things. Even as we moved as a collective to the site of dispersal, the five-minute walk and subsequent time waiting for our buses were moments of coming closer and feeling more connected to one another. At times, I was the first person to get on the bus. There were other times that I was the last. But each time during those winter 2017 Tuesday nights, we all messaged the group on WhatsApp to let the others know that we had arrived safely in a city predicated upon anti-Black violence.

Black women also participate in alternative performances of Black masculinity that stress the collective over the individual, social connection over isolation, protection over domination, and care over violence. While Black men are usually the targets of state-sanctioned and extralegal violence, Black women form collectivities to protect themselves and, when necessary, Black men as well. Once, I ventured up to a periphery neighborhood to meet with Carla and Camila. That day, they were invited to be panelists for an event on the Bahian hip-hop movement, alongside other, more established hip-hop artists. The workshop was a significant acknowledgment of their work and recognition of their activism. Throughout the workshop, they spoke about the importance of a Black feminist militancy in the hip-hop movement to combat not only anti-Black racism, informal segregation, and socioeconomic inequality but also patriarchy, sexism, and misogyny. Their message was that Black men should be concerned with Black women's freedom; that issues of gender and sexuality are not separate from those of race and class. If the Bahian hip-hop movement is committed to Black collectivities, then they must take seriously Black women's issues. A liberatory future must deconstruct the structures of sexism and homophobia alongside racism, urban segregation, and class exploitation.

We had met up early to do a group interview. After the workshop, we walked to the exit gates on the university campus. Carla and Camila asked me how I was getting home. When I told them I was taking the bus back to Rio Vermelho, they said I should stay just inside the campus gates until my bus arrived. They stepped out onto the sidewalk themselves, glancing over to keep making sure I was okay. Honestly, I felt fine and safe at the bus stop by myself. Yet I felt it necessary and respectful to follow their protocol, as they had more experience in the area and wanted to look after me and my safety. It was not my place to challenge their authority. So I placed myself under their guidance and protection. Eventually a bus arrived, and they waved me forward to take it. Even though the bus signboard did not mention it was going to Rio Vermelho, the two women told me it would. I briskly walked over, gave them each hugs, bade them farewell, and then jumped on the bus. Like many Black men artists, they informed me to advise them when I got home. Their sense of duty did not end until they knew that I had arrived home safely, ensuring a diasporic sense of collectivity and survival.

Carla and Camila were also invested in a Black masculinity that can follow the lead of Black women to ensure the collective's safety. For them, protecting the collective is far more important than subscribing to colonial gender norms that attempt to naturalize masculinity's dominance over femininity. Again, the *quilombo* model holds space for alternative social behaviors for Black men in relation to other Black men and even Black women that exceed heteropatriarchal boundaries. In this case, we exchanged positions of authority and protection with one another. In this model, Black women can also be leaders who take care of the collective and protect those who are more vulnerable, even Black men, at any given moment. The goal is not to reproduce a patriarchal system but to preserve the *quilombo* by relying on the strengths of individuals and shielding those who are vulnerable from harm.

Alternative Modalities of Black Life

Quilombos were and are war encampments against the violence of coloniality, protecting their inhabitants against colonial and national forces bent on destroying them. Beatriz Nascimento (2018f) elucidates that *quilombos* are also about creating "a possibility in the days of destruction" (p. 190) where Black people can relate and assemble in ways not permitted in Brazil under either a colonial or national structure. This continues today. Central to the *quilombo* is the mission to collectivize as interdependent beings to protect the vulnerable, the weak, and the defenseless, regardless of age, gender, or other social categorizations. Food was central to the survival of the *quilombo*: *quilombolas* knew they had to nourish and care for one another literally and in other ways as well. Displays of physical violence were necessary only in defense of the collective. *Quilombos* represent the convergence of Black people seeking strength in unity and renewal, no matter how long the *quilombo* lasted or how big it grew. *Quilombos* were and are mobile and ephemeral, adapting to the exigencies of *quilombolas* at any given conjuncture.

It is imperative to stress that *quilombos* nourished Black people's ability to assume nonnormative social relations. A *quilombo* praxis absorbs outsiders, a philosophy and politics that date back to its Angolan roots in West Africa, where *kilombos* consisted of nomads who incorporated outsiders into their social, cultural, and cosmological worlds (B. Nascimento, 2021). In Brazil, Yoruba/Nagô, Gêge, Hausa, and Black creoles had differences among themselves, but they also formed their own *aquilombamentos* together as coalitions against slavery and white supremacy (J. Reis, 1995; C. Smith, 2016a). Queering Eurocentric notions of the heteronormative familial unit as an atomic model of the nation, *quilombos* do not fortify social reproduction through heteronormativity. They instead cultivate bringing more Black people outside the *quilombo* into the maroon community (Price, 1996). In Brazil, *quilombos* implemented this African institution in multiple ways: "households, kin groups, [and] offices have always been highly absorptive of outsiders. It is evident that all those African features were essential for Palmares, as a society constantly absorbing new members" (Funari and de Carvalho, 2016, p. 29). Despite differences and even tensions, *quilombos* depended upon absorbing outsiders to contest Brazilian white supremacy and racial violence as well as foster new possibilities of Black social life beyond the coloniality of gender.

5 | Artifice

On February 8, 2020, I hopped into an Uber and headed to meet my friend Marília in the Curuzu neighborhood of the Liberdade district. Along with Black people all over not just Brazil but also the African Diaspora, we were going to the annual event thrown by one of the most famous Afro-blocs, Ilê Aiyê: The Noite da Beleza Negra (Night of the Black beauty) event. The closest I could get was still at least six blocks away. I got dropped off at a local grocery store, its metal garage-style doors already pulled down for the night, met Marília, and walked twenty to thirty minutes with scores of Black people. On the closed-off cobblestone streets we trekked to the *senzala*, a highly noticeable three-story concrete performance hall, its vibrant red, yellow, black, and white exterior standing out in the neighborhood. Formally known as Senzala do Barro Preto–Associação Cultural Ilê Aiyê, it is the headquarters for Ilê Aiyê. Everyone wore their finest and most fashionable African-inspired threads: kente cloth jumpers, dresses printed with African-style patterns, headwraps, and the traditional *baiana* dress. Knowing I had to come correct, I wore my favorite shirt from the Katuka Africanidades boutique, a black button-up with red and white circles, which always reminds me of Exú.

In February everything feels like a Carnival event. It was 9:30 and the night was young, so full of energy and anticipation. Marília and I bought our R$55 tickets for the contest but stayed in the streets drinking *caipirinhas* and *caipiroskas* and eating some snacks. We ran into people who had come into town for the event, both friends we had not seen for a while and friends we had seen just that very week. Around 11 p.m. we entered the venue, wading through hundreds of Black bodies joyfully squeezed together, smiles wide and eyes sparkling; together we cheered on the Black women contestants as they made their way to the stage, accompanied with judges on one side and the hosts on the other. Vying for the crown of Ebony Goddess (*deusa do ébono*), each contestant gracefully and elegantly danced to the front of the stage and then back, demonstrating her mastery of African movements and cultures.

Dance is only one of the contest's criteria. Ilê Aiyê's website has the complete list: "The aesthetics of the contest is judged by the hair braiding, the fabric prints, the grace of her dance, but, above all else, the candidate's consciousness that speaks to her Blackness (*negritude*), how she demonstrates her self being active in the community in this way" (Ilê Aiyê, n.d.). Each contestant wore a "natural" hairstyle and some type of African-inspired clothing, using color schemes from gold-brown-yellow hues to red-yellow-white. Other contests judge women predominantly on their physical appearance, so the cultural focus was refreshing. But it was not lost on me that Black men were the judges, as in so many other beauty contests around the world. I also noted that an unusual number of local government agencies and national brands, including Skol beer, SALTUR (Salvador Tourism), Avon, Bahia Gas, and the Bahian state government, sponsored this event out on the periphery. I wondered why. Clearly, they wanted the advertising space, but why did they choose this event over others?

To be honest, I already felt ill that night, and the street food made it worse. The intense heat and humidity from the crowded audience became too much to bear.[1] The combined odors of sweat, perfume, cologne, and beer did not help either. Even though I hated to leave early, I called an Uber and headed home to watch the rest of the contest on TV. There, I saw local resident Gleiciele Teixeira Olivera crowned Ebony Goddess as thousands applauded. Weeks later, on the final night of Carnival, I saw her dancing atop Ilê Aiyê's *trio elétrico* (street float) in the Campo Grande circuit wearing similar attire. As she rolled by, folks in the street yelled and cheered for the new Ebony Goddess.

The Night of the Black Beauty dates back to 1980, so this was the forty-first time the event had been held. Each year, the theme refers to an African nation or another Black-majority country in the Americas, such as Jamaica. According to Ilê Aiyê's website, the Night of the Black Beauty communicates a Black *conscientização*: a racial affirmation and ancestrality that Black people can externalize through aesthetics on their bodies. Ilê Aiyê, Olodum, and other such groups have fought valiantly for "positive representations" of Black people that do not conflate

Black Brazilian history with only slavery or Black Brazilian people with socially subordinate positions such as domestic workers and doormen, or worse, with criminals, vagabonds, and savages. Ilê Aiyê is a significant cultural institution in Salvador's reafricanization, connecting Black Bahians with an African civilization, geography, and history in part through an aesthetic rubric that encompasses hair, clothes, dance, and style. There is great importance in reclaiming the past and renarrating their own history in strong opposition to how the dominant white masculinist gaze has defined Black Brazilian history and social subjectivities. But even events like Noite da Beleza Negra have their own limitations: they are still patriarchal, state- and corporate-sponsored, and essentialist. Black men still judge Black women on their appearance and expect them to perform domestic duties and obligations for the Black family and nation. Sponsors embrace these events because they fit into national narratives that celebrate African-derived cultures. And the events rely on an idea that Black people have an inherent nature that they can recover only through their African roots. Together, they fail to tie aesthetics to race as a sociopolitical category or racism as a structure. They also leave little if any room for gender fluidity, an aesthetic outside of an idea of the "natural," or exploring Blackness outside of a mythic past.

Refusing Natural Aesthetics

Institutions, agencies, and actors who participate in Salvador's reafricanization, like Ilê Aiyê, emphasize the "natural," an ideology that Black people must return to their original state of being in premodern Africa. Their desire for the natural is both internal and external. Internally, one must recuperate one's inner self as a timeless African, which will boost one's self-esteem and dismantle the social stigma that society attaches to Black people. Externally, Black people should manipulate their bodies to conform to a natural aesthetic, a rubric that specifies how African people supposedly appeared, styled themselves, and behaved on the continent before colonialism and enslavement. No doubt powerful, it also assumes that Black people must save themselves from their abject state of being that is anchored in slavery, poverty, and misery. Black people can redeem themselves from their current situations by returning to a timeless, static, and homogeneous community past. Many believe that events like Ilê Aiyê are important in erasing ignorant people's cultural prejudices against Black people and their African roots. The idea is that if Black people took more pride in their heritage, they would develop stronger self-esteem and could finally overcome! But that conception of the past in fact never existed, and the "natural" reduces race to biology, culture, and/or heritage, giving race an essentialist quality. This emphasis on the natural also puts the burden of overcoming racism on Black people, asking them to aesthetically change who they are and their political positions to self-redeem and be deemed valuable.

In historical and modern *quilombos*, Black people have labored, through their own aesthetic practices, to assign meaning to their own and other Black people's bodies as beautiful, normal, desirable, and worthy. Many have done so by resisting, not conforming to, Eurocentric aesthetics that assigned meanings of immorality, ahistoricity, and placelessness to Black people, by interrupting how the white dominant classes signified Black people's bodies, especially from the lower classes, as only abject, the opposite of Eurocentric aesthetics and beauty standards. In historical *quilombos*, Black fugitives used Candomblé and other African-derived cultural practices to rewrite the visual scripts of Black people as just denigrated nonbeings and chattel property whose purpose was to labor and biologically reproduce the next generation of property. Black people used their *ancestralidade* to see these supposed racial deviants as aesthetically pleasing, desirable, and tasteful.

Aesthetics are culturally constructed (Edu, 2019). However, they are not neutral; people use aesthetics to mark certain groups as more desirable than others. They then use the desirable group as a marker to judge less-than-desirable and undesirable groups based on their proximity or distance from the desirable group. Raymond Williams wrote that aesthetics articulate a "phenomenal beauty" (1985, p. 30) that conveys taste, sensation, value, joy, and other pleasurable affects in relation to external appearance. But aesthetics are not apolitical; they are immensely *political* (Adorno et al., 2007; Bourdieu, 1984; Marcuse, 1979), embedded in the order and ordering of things, connoting relational points of domination, resistance, and rupture within systems of power differentials. Throughout the world, media, people, and other social forces designate whiteness as a rubric of aesthetics to determine what is beautiful, shaping our ideologies and (sub)consciousness (Tate, 2009); the rubric uses whiteness to subjugate Blackness (Mercer, 1994). In response, Black people across the African Diaspora mobilize aesthetics as a site of symbolic intervention into the meanings attached to their bodies. Ilê Aiyê is representative of this trend in Salvador da Bahia and part of the "reafricanization" described in the second chapter. Black aesthetics symbolically protect Black people against the degradation of a Brazilian white consciousness that operationalizes a Eurocentric, white supremacist, heteropatriarchal, and capitalist matrix to deprecate Blackness, signifying it as entirely undesirable (S. Carneiro, 2019b; hooks, 2018; B. Nascimento, 2018c). In short, Brazilian society has long stigmatized, derided, and repressed African aesthetics, which it associated with an abject Blackness (Gonzalez, 2018c), so Black people have sought to assign to African aesthetics, especially on their bodies through hairstyles and fashion, meanings of beauty, community, and pride.

In Salvador da Bahia, Black Bahian hip-hop artists and their communities are producing, performing, and representing their own aesthetics that mark an ideological shift from the natural to the artificial, establishing an alternative phenomenal beauty that does not fit within Eurocentric or Afrocentric standards. Certainly, the "natural" holds significant power for Black aesthetics in the diaspora (Tate, 2009). Merriam-Webster's online dictionary defines "natural" as "being in accordance with or determined by nature"; "having an essential relation with someone or something"; "growing without human care," "existing in or produced by nature: not artificial"; and "closely resembling an original: true to nature." In Black aesthetics, people view certain hairstyles and appearances as "natural," just innately happening without human interference. But we know this to be false (Mercer, 1994). Natural aesthetics still require care, manipulation, and processing. The "natural" discourse readily feeds into the ideology that Black people have certain appearances, tendencies, and essences that are innate, whether biological or cultural (P. Pinho, 2010), reifying racist discourses that Black people are closer to nature and unfit for Western civilization. As the Ilê Aiyê vignette illustrates, the state and corporations are willing to embrace the natural because it folds nicely into folkloric Blackness, locating racial difference as a matter of culture and antiracism as a matter of cultural tolerance. If the state, corporations, and Brazilian society can accept and even support folkloric Blackness, then there cannot possibly be any racism in Brazil, especially when they subsume folkloric Blackness under a mixed Blackness necessary to produce Brazilian nationalism.

When Black people *aquilombar-se* in the Bahian hip-hop movement, they are culturally constructing an aesthetics of the artifice that beautifies the Black masses, which is to say, those who do not express themselves as timeless Africans. In general, some people frown upon the "artifice," associating it with "artificial," conjuring meanings of fake, unnatural, inauthentic, and cheap. But I mobilize "artifice" according to Merriam-Webster's online definition of it: first, as ingenuity, "a clever or artful skill," as well as "an ingenious device or expedient"; second, as a trick or "an artful stratagem"; and third, "false or insincere behavior." How might we think of Black aesthetics through art, strategy, and trickery that demand skill, thoughtfulness, and labor; as a critical interpretive vehicle of cleverness; and as unruly behavior that intervenes in the racial and gender social order? I want to think of the artifice as a set of Black aesthetic practices in the Bahian hip-hop movement's *aquilombamento*. First, the artifice is a process by which Black people create their aesthetics. Next, the artifice appears artificial, having kitsch attributes that define it against the norms of highbrow tastes. Lastly, the artifice expresses Black bodily sensation, value, and pleasure among the Black masses. This artifice can be like the abject, not an entity to avoid but rather an empowering concept that produces alternative tastes within Black social, cultural, and political systems.

As an emergent *quilombo*, the Bahian hip-hop movement refuses more than just Eurocentric aesthetics; it also refuses African aesthetics that visually redeem Black people by restoring them to an African civilization filled with gender norms, patriarchy, and purity: a civilization that runs parallel to the West.[2] Black Bahian hip-hop artists' politics of refusal do not abandon how a dominant Eurocentric consciousness in Brazil signifies the Black person's body as abject. The Bahian hip-hop movement takes abject Blackness and renders it beautiful, upsetting how mixed and folkloric Blacknesses distance themselves from the abject. They participate in a queer politics that intervenes with gender and sexual norms in the racial order. I am less interested in Black people's aesthetic attempts to redeem themselves by bridging a mythical past with Western bourgeois norms to elevate themselves above the Black masses. I am more interested in Black aesthetics that *draw* on the past but move on, interrupting Western mores embedded in both Eurocentric and Afrocentric aesthetics. I want to conceive of Black bodily aesthetics as always evolving, refusing, and taking flight as acts that challenge Brazil's gendered anti-Blackness. This requires turning to the Black aesthetics based on the artifice that valorizes and beautifies that which is abjected, excluded, and repressed.

Blackening Hair

Hair is a critical component to Black aesthetics around the globe. Hair is one of the most important markers of one's racialization, especially for Black people (Hall, 2017). Like many places around the world, Brazilian society has stigmatized Black people's hair textures as being ugly and a marker of their racial deviance (Caldwell, 2004). In turn, Black people turn to hair as a political site of struggle in the cultural arena to valorize themselves (Mercer, 1994). Black Bahian hip-hop artists are keenly aware of this dynamic, using hair as a marker of political struggle for marginalized Black youths and one entry point to forming emergent *quilombos* in Salvador da Bahia. They do so by Blackening ("enegrecendo") their bodies, especially their hair (Barreto, 2005).

In 2019, Darlene, a prominent Black feminist graffiti artist in Bahia, posted on Instagram a photo of herself with straightened hair and blonde highlights. In the caption, she wrote that these were the things she used to do to her hair, especially when she was living in São Paulo. After she became racially self-conscious as a Black woman, she stopped straightening her hair and let it grow into more "natural" hairstyles. When I saw her Instagram story, I immediately DMed her with a surprised emoji face and a comment about how I couldn't believe the old photo of her. She replied that she understood the sentiment herself, that it is surprising to look back on that part of her life and realize how far she has come.

Even though Brazil has a large African-descended population, many Black Brazilians internalize and adopt Eurocentric white beauty standards, especially regarding hair, because they are aware of their social rejection (S. Carneiro, 2011). To be accepted by society, they care for, style, and keep their hair in very modest and unassuming ways that do not stand out in Brazilian society. Their attempts to whiten their appearance are met with encouragement and approval (S. Carneiro, 2011). For men, this usually means short hair that is combed to the side, without a crisp hairline from a razor edge or a sharp electric clipper outliner. Both men and women straighten and color their hair to obtain a more Eurocentric aesthetic. As a teenager playing for the

Santos Futebol Clube, international football sensation Neymar was visibly darker in skin tone and had short coarse black hair. With international success and a European career, his skin tone has become noticeably lighter, and people postulate that he must be avoiding the sun and/or using high SPF sunscreen. He also started straightening his hair and frequently coloring it blond. Neymar distanced himself from Blackness in other ways: when a reporter asked the star football player about racism, he said he wouldn't know anything about it because he is not Black.[3] Recently, he came out in support of Jair Bolsonaro in the 2022 elections, despite Bolsonaro's far-right conservatism and racist attacks on Black Brazilians. Many Brazilians would be viewed as Black or Afro-mestiço if they did not straighten or color their hair; instead they pass or try to pass as white or white-*mestiço*.

Today, Darlene wears her hair in natural hairstyles like an Afro or box braids and is an important Black feminist graffiti artist icon for many in the wider community, not just in the Bahian hip-hop movement. Darlene's story illustrates how Black Brazilians can come to embrace Black aesthetics, especially with their hair, as part of their Black *conscientização*. In her critically acclaimed book *Quando me descobri negra* (When I discovered I am a Black woman), Bianca Santana (2015) describes how Black Brazilians come to identify as Black in their consciousness and express it on their bodies in Brazil. Santana writes that this process is not a given, and that racial identifications often change over a person's lifetime.[4] The São Paulo author notes that while she is thirty (at the time of her publication), she had been "Black" for only the past ten years. Growing up, she did not see herself as Black but as a Brazilian woman who did not experience race or racism. She would straighten her hair and stay out of the sun to be lighter. She adopted a Eurocentric consciousness in her mind-set and bodily aesthetics. Over time, she realized how society saw and treated her, even as a lighter-skinned Black woman. She also started paying attention to the racist things people would say to her. As she became more aware of this, she discovered her Blackness at twenty years old and started to develop her *conscientização* while also changing her hairstyle. Darlene and Bianca Santana both became Black not just internally but also externally by making their Black social and political identification culturally visible on their bodies.

Identity conveys one's being, who you are and who you come from, as well as one's "becoming," claiming a strategic political position about where you are going (Hall, 1990, 1996). In Brazil, Black people do this internally through a Black *conscientização*, and externally by becoming part of more Black social circles and "Blackening" their physical appearance, especially hair. Raquel de Andrade Barreto (2005) first used *enegrecendo*, or Blackening, to describe how Black feminists "Blacken" Eurocentric feminisms in the Americas. Today *enegrecer*, to Blacken, is used for a variety of Black identification processes. Here I extend Blackening to the hairstyle politics that valorize Black people in an array of visual markers that evolve and expand upon the natural, showing this process as a work of art by and for the Black masses.

In January 2017, friends and I gathered outside the Amsterdam Nightclub to see Fall Clássico perform. We arrived early at 11 p.m., joining hundreds of other Black youths congregating outside the hillside venue that overlooks the majestic Bay of All Saints. The water was sparkling even at night. Many folks were smoking, drinking, and socializing. I remembered vividly how the concert attendees had played with "natural" aesthetics using artificial colors, textures, and styles. I thought to myself their hairstyles were extraordinary works of art. This insight fundamentally altered how I understood Black bodily aesthetics in the Bahian hip-hop movement and their purpose within *aquilombamento*. Many people that night Blackened their hair by adding bold and extravagant colors, textures, and other styles. Many had Afro hairstyles of various sizes. Others had dreadlocks, some that were just starting and others down past their shoulders. Numerous folks had braids (or plaits). Many of these braids used synthetic hair to give them longer braids than they could normally grow on their own. Others had "twists," the separation of the scalp's hair into small sections which are then twisted together. I saw Black women with pink box braids, green box braids, and other nonblack colors. Black men had synthetic dreadlocks that were shiny metallic silver in color. Black men put jewelry and "frosted" tips on their dreads, that is, coloring at the end of each dreadlock. Young Black men bleached their hair not for an Eurocentric blond look but rather as a platinum-blond look that is artificial both in its coloring and its placement on darker Black Bahians. Each one of these examples illustrates how Black people Blacken themselves through artifice as works of art and often with camp aesthetics, an exaggerated style that calls attention to itself. They decorated their Black bodies, associated with an abject Blackness, with low-class and nonnormative styles, and dared to signify them as beautiful, tasteful, and pleasing.

If you look hard enough, you can see that Black people get box braids with a discernibly different hair texture than their own. Numerous Black people with wavy and curly hair, like 2c, 3a, 3b, and 3c hair types, have box braids that mirror someone with coarser and more tightly coiled hair, like 4a, 4b, and 4c hair.[5] Box braids can give someone a "Blacker" appearance and by extension affect their social subjectivity. For Black Brazilians who are lighter in skin color with wavy or curly hair, their identification as Black can be met with resistance from Black and non-Black people. People will tell them they are not Black because they are not dark or because they do not experience the worst consequences of racism. These intraracial tensions have inhibited larger Black social movements (Hanchard, 1994). Many lighter Black Brazilians acknowledge their color privilege, that they don't experience racism to the same extent as darker Black Brazilians, and they also convey how they experience their Blackness and structural racism, albeit on different scales. Their identifications work through difference rather than assuming an innate sameness.

Blackness is complex in Brazil because people perceive it as a matter of color, and thus discrimination is a matter of colorism, not race and racism. The two are not equivalent, but they are certainly linked. Color is central to racial classifications and structural racism. As a hierarchical system of knowledge, coloniality produced and maintains colorism within a white supremacist matrix that valorizes whiteness, Eurocentrism, and Christianity over Blackness, Africanity, and African-derived religions (Bispo dos Santos, 2015). Across various socioeconomic indices, color correlates *strongly* with race and racism (Telles, 2004). Lighter Black Brazilians fare slightly better than darker Black Brazilians within structures of racial domination. When Black people have a hairstyle perceived as "mixed," that is, wavy or curly, they may opt to Blacken their hair to culturally express Black pride, solidarity, and/or stylistic preference. In the Bahian hip-hop movement, we can read lighter Black Brazilians' hair aesthetics as a matter of Black identification that disrupts "chromatic classifications that institute differences within Blackness" (S. Carneiro, 2011, p. 73). White Brazilians have been able to fracture Black social movements and political activism by dividing Black Brazilians along color lines, classifying some as Black and others as "mixed," neither Black nor white. In turn, many Black Brazilians have internalized this, preventing large-scale political mobilization (Hanchard, 1994). Rather than identify with whiteness and/or miscegenation, lighter Black people identify with Blackness with increasing frequency.

Many people believe that a "natural" hairstyle means the opposite of straight(ened) hair. But numerous Black people are born with straight hair. Also, some Black women *and men* need synthetic materials and/or human labor to achieve the appearance of a natural hairstyle. My friend Marília is a dreadlock hair stylist, and she tells me that even those who already have dreads come back to her every few months for maintenance. Box braids may have a natural aesthetic, but they are styled through artificial materials and means. Many Black people combine synthetic and natural hair to create the appearance of long and thick braids. Obtaining a "natural" aesthetic is sometimes available only by drawing on the artificial. Yet these are still acts of the artifice.

Even those who have a natural hairstyle sometimes change their minds and opt for a different style, showing that Black people view their hair as an artistic endeavor that they are free to change at will. They are not locked into one hairstyle; they are free to manipulate their hair to get a different look. When I met João and Carlos in 2013, they each had dreadlocks, with João's going well down his back and Carlos's just starting to reach his shoulders. Their hairstyles were part of their political commitments, as Black male rappers in the Bahian hip-hop movement dedicated to both ancestrality and negritude. In 2019, João cut his dreads off, surprising many in the hip-hop movement. When I asked him why he decided to do it after growing his hair in a dreadlock style for more than a decade, he said: "I just wanted the curls." João did not shave his head completely, leaving a couple of inches of his 3a/b curls. But he let his hair grow back. Now he frequently styles his hair in cornrows, another natural hairstyle, like a younger Snoop Dogg and Kendrick Lamar. Though João went from one "natural" hairstyle (dreadlocks) to another (cornrows), he still had to manipulate his hair to go between styles. Natural is not an essentialist quality but an aesthetic that one artistically curates and makes, even with one's hair.

Black people manipulate natural hairstyles in other ways as well. Carlos grew his dreadlocks for almost a decade. Unlike João, he did not cut off his dreadlocks completely, shaving the sides but leaving the dreadlocks on top. When I asked him why, he said he wanted to be more "suave," meaning to have a smoother and more stylish haircut. In practice, this means he wants to play around with his dreads as a style among other styles and aesthetics. Carlos regularly goes to a barber to cut the hair on the side of his head. Sometimes, he gets a high bald fade, like the classic Nas haircut, but with his dreadlocks up on top still. Other times, the sides are cut down to a "one" or "two" guard on barber clippers. He regularly gets designs in his hair, like zigzags, straight lines, patterns, and other shapes that combine fading and sharp edges with barber clippers, trimmers, and razor blades. Black hair can have both a natural style, like Carlos's dreadlocks on top of his head, and an artificial style, like the artistic designs on the side of his head at the same time, to express one's Blackness in creative ways.

While many Black women and men share similar hairstyles, this does not mean that gender is not at play. Black women must also confront people who attempt to police them if their hair is perceived to be too masculine. They have to be aware of whether they appear too "masculine" and not properly "feminine." This "ungendering" dates back to the Middle Passage (Spillers, 1987), where Black women could not embody womanhood and femininity like white women. People have used hair to judge Black women and determine that they deviate from Western gender norms.

Nonetheless, many Black women in the Bahian hip-hop movement use their hair to embrace a femme androgyny. They disrupt both Western and Afrocentric patriarchal beauty standards and do not conform to Western gender modalities that aesthetically exclude them. Instead, they decide to style their selves and their bodies in ways that speak to their own racialized gender expression. A notable example is DJ Nai Kiese, one of the few Black woman DJs in the Bahian hip-hop movement. For many years, she sported a dreadlock style. Shortly after Carnival 2019, DJ Nai Kiese posted on her Instagram account a picture of herself with her new haircut: short hair and a barber-designed part curving alongside the right side of her head. With more than six thousand followers, she has almost two hundred comments on her post. All the responses are positive, exclaiming about her beauty both with her former dreadlocks and also now with short hair: "marvelous," "inspirational," "beautiful," and other Bahian slang words that convey praise, such as "barril" and "foda."

In the same Instagram post, DJ Nai Kiese is also wearing a white top that exposes her shoulders, a Candomblé necklace, a metal chain, and large, round white earrings. The Candomblé clothing in this context speaks to her new hair and overall style as a gender-neutral rebirth, using her *orí* to start anew, and even changing her stage name. In this case, her haircut also symbolizes a rebirth for her.[6] When someone begins their Candomblé initiation, the initiate must shave their head to symbolize their reentry into the world as a new subject; when Black women cut their dreadlocks, they must cut their hair quite close to their scalp. In the United States, we call this "the big chop," a common and necessary technique for Black women to adopt new hairstyles, also signifying a new moment in their life. The "problem," if you will, is that cutting their hair down so close to their scalp results in a "man's" hairstyle.[7] Many prefer that only Black men have their hair cut so close to their head. When a Black woman does it, she is perceived as too masculine, not properly feminine, and a threat to Western gender norms internalized in the African Diaspora. DJ Nai Kiese's new hairstyle is natural, neither processed nor manipulated to look white. However, people do not always perceive a short hairstyle as natural for Black women. There remains a prevailing assumption that Black women should have hair, whether natural or synthetic, of the same length as white women. At the very least, it should not be *so* short like a man's hair. In contrast, when Black women and men praise DJ Nai Kiese for having short hair, they intervene with this coloniality of gender. Her supporters are valorizing how she disrupts these socially accepted norms concerning hair, race, and gender.

When DJ Nai Kiese cut her hair, she was not donning a masculine persona. She was resignifying beauty standards on Black women's terms. This is in opposition to Western and colonial aesthetics as well as Afrocentric standards that maintain gender hierarchies, obligations, and limitations for Black women. She continues to mark Black femininity as a site of strength, challenging the dominant associations of femininity with piety, purity, and dependence on patriarchal protection. She detaches femininity from the norm of whiteness. At the same time, she incorporates feminine elements as she wears dresses, uses makeup, and utilizes other feminine beauty practices. In combination with her hairstyle, she creates a Black femme androgynous aesthetic. Black androgyny does not have to be one part feminine and one part masculine; it can be a fluid construction that permits more expansive notions of beauty that extend beyond what the natural engenders. It is more art than science.

The politics of Black hairstyles mobilizes pleasure, taste, and creativity. Brazilian barbershops, especially Black barbers in the periphery, are world famous for their clean fades, crispy edges, designs in the hair, speed, and innovative techniques. Salvador has no shortage of barbershops. A Friday night on a weekend of festivities can have a barber cutting hair late into the night, sometimes as late as 11 p.m. A fresh haircut, meaning both stylish and very recent, is extremely important. This is especially true for any hip-hop event, where artists and fans alike make sure they get a fresh cut before going out and being seen in public. Barbers also provide eyebrow shaping, using a razor to create eyebrows that are perfectly contoured and curved back to the crispest point at the end. To be clear, men get these services too. I often joke with friends that men (rather than women) have the prettiest eyebrows in Brazil. Many clients ask their barbers to put lines in their eyebrows. Some are vertical and others are slanted. Some people want only one line, while others want multiple lines.

Black hairstyles signify different things for different people, which can have serious and even deadly consequences. According to Julio, a local rapper, graffiti artist, graphic designer, and video game maker, there are nuances to these designs, cuts, and lines that encompass both hair and eyebrows. As we talked outside his place of work, a local university where he was a bus attendant, he told me some designs and cuts are associated with gang factions in Salvador's peripheries. Those who are not part of the gangs would not dare get these designs themselves: there could be problems if they were spotted by members of a gang faction, or other people might associate them with a gang and distance themselves, or cops might recognize the markings and stop to aggressively interrogate them.

As many are from the periphery, Bahian hip-hop community members are familiar with what haircut styles signify. Most people who are not from the periphery do not fully understand, or they see no difference, associating all these styles with criminality. They view bold Black youths with fade haircuts, brightly colored hair, pretty eyebrows, skinny sideburns, and crisp mustaches as violent outlaws. People in society get nervous or scared of young Black men with colorful and playful hairstyles, which they see as immodest. In public spaces of consumption, like a grocery store or a mall, store employees and security guards profile, harass, and even violently attack Black people. Police officers confront Black youths with these hairstyles and conduct *abordagens* (forceful and violating bodily searches). The police do not care to understand or decode the nuances of which hairstyle or eyebrow line belongs to which gang faction.

In February 2020, just before the Noite da Beleza Negra, military police in Salvador stopped a group of Black male youths in Paripe, a neighborhood in the Suburbana region. One officer harassed Diego, a sixteen-year-old Black boy with a strawberry-blond tapered Afro hairstyle. The police targeted him because of his hair (Freelon, 2020). Neighbors recorded the police's verbal and physical assault on Diego. One officer yelled at him: "To me, you're a thief. You're a vagabond. Look at this disgrace of this hair here. Get rid of your hat. Do it! Your hair is a disgrace. What are you? Are you a worker, [homophobic slur]? Huh?"[8] These symbolic aggressions were accompanied by ripping the youth's hat off and kicking and punching him (Globo, 2020). The police used Diego's highly expressive hairstyle to tie him to a threatening Black masculinity and criminalize him.

Poor and working-class Black youths in the hip-hop movement take these signs of abjectness and valorize them as beautiful, stylish, and markers of Black taste to be desired and praised by other marginalized Black folks. When Black men embrace their curls, coils, kinks, and Afros with creative manipulations, they embrace their Blackness. People view these Black men as out of place in the Brazilian imaginary that will accept only "good hair," which is to say straight hair or a modest "natural" hairstyle. Diego violated the racial moral order that permits some forms of Blackness if they conform to certain codes of respectability, redemption, and valor. In Diego's case, the police saw his hair as symbolic of Black men's criminality, which is why he was called a thief and a vagabond. Diego had an exaggerated Black beauty that exceeded a folkloric Blackness based on gender normativity, cultural recuperation, and racial modesty.

The state resorted to its phallic tool of domination, its police force, to discipline and emasculate Diego for veering away from permissible bodily aesthetics. For them, Diego could distance himself from an abject Blackness if he changed his hairstyle to Eurocentric and Afrocentric norms that Brazil can tolerate. Because Diego did not do this, the state believed it must correct him for not being properly masculine, especially because his hair was seen as too effeminate. The state reinforced its racial and gender hierarchies by using homophobia to emasculate and feminize Black men, pushing them out of the dominant modality of masculinity as a state of their abjection. Deviant Black men and boys are violently coerced to self-correct and conform to dominant norms to be read as worthy, tasteful, and part of society. As Black men and boys are already assumed to be suspicious and criminal, the police, even Black officers, are often supported by an anti-Black civil society that also takes these hairstyles as evidence of Black criminality.

Fashioning *Aquilombamento*

The Bahian hip-hop movement also incorporates clothes and fashion to refuse the aesthetics in folkloric and mixed Blackness, and also to resist degradation in abject Blackness. Its aesthetics of artifice extend beyond what Black people do with their bodies to what they put on their bodies, using what cultural capital they have to make themselves a canvas of representation that disrupts human hierarchies (Hall, 1992). The Bahian hip-hop movement's fashion is intensely diasporic, linking their location in Bahia to Africa *and* the United States with crisscrossing diasporic aesthetics.

In 2014 and 2015, I undertook a considerable amount of research at the Kilombo Bar in the Rio Vermelho neighborhood. The two-story club had an upstairs dance room, an upstairs lounge area with a bar, and a back patio with scattered chairs and tables where people would take smoke breaks or have group conversations away from the blaring music upstairs. From the street one would see an inconspicuous building, yellow in front with the paint chipping on the bottom and the sidewall adorned with local graffiti, an açai-juice bar on the lower level, and then just the fence on the top level. The Kilombo was immensely popular with local rappers, who frequently threw parties there, sometimes two to four times a week. Some parties were more dancehall focused. Others played only hip-hop. But the lines between the two genres often blurred.

I would usually arrive before midnight. This gave me time to check out the scene and make some notes in my phone before the night got too busy and I got carried away. As I walked in the front door, I would stop to chat with the local vendors selling clothes, accessories, and CDs by rappers from Salvador and other cities, checking in about what singles and albums were new and who was rising in the national and local hip-hop scene. Then I would go up the wooden stairs, grab a drink from the upstairs bar, and hang out on the upper-deck couches by the inside dance floor.

Usually, I was one of the first folks there, along with people setting up: organizers, bartenders, DJs, and a few of their friends. I would exchange pleasantries with them, asking the performers if they were releasing any new music or were performing soon. They would ask after my research and often suggested new interviewees for me. The venue typically did not fill up until around one or two in the morning, but then the parties lasted long into the night, as late as four or five in the morning. Sometimes they lasted even longer, as carless youths waited for the city buses to begin their earliest routes. Arriving early let me observe the crowd on the back patio, sitting in plastic chairs against the graffitied concrete wall or on the rooftop looking over the beach before heading inside to the dance floor.

Their fashions caught my attention early on. The following are my field notes from June 9, 2014:

> Many of the other patrons wore typical Bahian clothes, that are tighter or more beach influenced. Others wore baggier clothes, basketball jerseys (I keep seeing the same Miami Heat Shaquille O'Neal #32 jersey that I saw for the first time in 2008), and snapback hats. The hats featured cities such as Los Angeles or Chicago. Some even had New Era logos but I doubt that they were licensed hats due to the poor graphics. Most had hats with the latest graphics and fashion designs, such as the name of the city stitched underneath the bill or "elephant" print. These were hats that one would find in US shopping malls, targeted for urban Black youth.[9]

An urban ballcap, called a *boné* in Brazil, holds an esteemed place within hip-hop aesthetics, conveying style, beauty, and fashion for the Black masses. This is different from, say, a fedora hat, which is called a *chapeu*. Black Bahian hip-hop youths were especially keen on New Era baseball[10] hats because they connected them to other hip-hop communities and urban Black populations. Artists, activists, fans, men, and women *all* adored the New Era baseball hat; you could garner considerable praise from one's peers and romantic interests by wearing one. In fact, a New Era hat can make a whole outfit. A woman might look fly in high-top shoes, such as Adidas or Chuck Taylors; black tights or a miniskirt; and a baggy tank top or a baggy T-shirt. But if she is wearing a New Era hat too ... game over. Her style just increased exponentially. The same can be said for men. Baggy jeans, a pair of sneakers, and a graphic-design T-shirt or tank top are super-stylish. But top it off with a fresh New Era baseball hat and he just scored extra points in the eyes of many.

There are rules to the fashion game when it comes to hats. There are two options. The first is that the New Era baseball hat must bear the logo of a sports team, usually from the NBA or MLB but sometimes the NFL in cities with highly visible Black populations that are known around the diaspora. We're talking New York, Chicago, Miami, Atlanta, Detroit, Los Angeles, and the Bay Area. Even my own Seattle Supersonics New Era baseball hat received high praise. Numerous folks gave love to Gary Payton and Shawn Kemp. But you're not going to see many hats bearing teams from Salt Lake City, Portland, Green Bay, or Oklahoma City. Black Bahian hip-hoppers want a particular team because they are familiar with US rappers, Black athletes, or Black culture from those cities. They also want the hats in the latest styles that they see in media and popular culture, like US hip-hop videos. Many hip-hop youths also sought New Era hats by urban boutiques, mostly from the United States. More recently, they are favoring nonbaseball hats, like "dad hats" (a hat with less rigid material construction and a curved bill) and "five panel hats" (a floppy hat made of flexible material with five rather than six panels like a baseball hat) by large sportswear companies such as adidas, Nike, Champion, and Fila. The *boné* ties Black Bahian youths to other global Black urban youths who participate in Black popular cultures and fashions that are at odds with the racial moral order. In Salvador da Bahia, the hat is a diasporic material object of artificial styling that connects Black people in Salvador's peripheries with urban Black people in the United States.

While I noticed the New Era hat, I was not necessarily sure how Black Bahian hip-hop artists and fans saw it. I thought to myself that perhaps they did not find it as meaningful as I did there. One of my exchanges with local rapper Maceo confirmed my suspicions. We met at the Kilombo Bar. As always, he arrived around two in the morning. When we sat down on the flimsy plastic chairs on the back patio, he was immediately fascinated with my purple Blackscale New Era fitted baseball hat. He wanted to know how much it cost, where I got it from, and if I could bring others like it the next time I traveled to Brazil. That year, I brought a handful of New Era baseball hats with me, some of which I had recently bought just for this trip. I did not want to wait a whole year for Maceo to get his hands on something he prized so much. The next time I saw Maceo, about a week later, I gifted him the blue Kidrobot fitted hat that I had brought with me. He was hyped when I gave it to him, telling me that no one else would have a hat like this, meaning one from a New York City boutique, and he would wear it the next time he performed. This New Era baseball hat had a greater significance than most *bonés* because no one in Brazil would have it; it was truly rare.

The next year, I brought Carlos a Detroit Tigers New Era snapback hat from the local Lids store in my city. I also gave João a T-shirt of J Dilla, the famous Detroit-born producer, drummer, and rapper who died of cardiac arrest in 2006 at the age of thirty-two. The previous year, I had asked them if they could go to any US city, which one would it be? I expected them to name a city like New York, Chicago, Los Angeles, or Atlanta. I was surprised when they shouted "Detroit" almost simultaneously. They said they loved Detroit because they loved J Dilla. I told them that Detroit temperatures can drop to −29 degrees Celsius (−20 degrees Fahrenheit) in the winter. Their jaws dropped. It did not matter. Detroit was their answer. A J Dilla shirt and a Detroit Tigers hat aesthetically connects them with other urban Black youths—including other J Dilla fans—in other peripheries. They saw a commonality with Black people's racial conditions in Detroit, cultural resistance, and marginalized community. These clothing items externalized that diasporic love for themselves and for others to see. While they are both committed to ancestrality and negritude, they are also invested in links with other marginalized Black communities. The New Era hat became an aesthetic point of self-styling that expressed a Black identification with the African Diaspora instead of with the Brazilian nation.

Today, there are New Era kiosks in malls around Salvador and other large Brazilian cities that sell baseball hats of teams with high marketability like the New York Yankees, Brooklyn Nets, and Los Angeles Lakers. This is very recent. For many years, these hats were extremely difficult to obtain because they were not typically sold in malls or ordinary stores, especially if they were by a boutique brand or of a US sports team. In 2014, I learned about Afreeka, a boutique streetwear store that had just opened that year in Salvador. Located in the Barris neighborhood, the store sold New Era baseball hats plus local Brazilian hip-hop apparel such as T-shirts, sweatshirts, CDs, and chains. It was a remodeled artist's loft with graffitied walls, a few barrels used as tables, a tiny makeshift fitting room, modest sound speakers, and an upstairs office. At best, it would comfortably fit ten people. Afreeka was not just the name of the store but also its in-house brand, adorning T-shirts, hats, necklaces, and other paraphernalia. The name takes the word "Africa" and replaces the "fri" with "free," evoking the English word, and the "c" with a "k," an African spelling. Many Black Bahians saw the store as a symbol and space of diasporic resistance that combines the images of Africa, freedom struggles in the United States, and styles of urban wear as points of Black resistance and markers of a reimagined community. A local rapper owned the store. It was very common to see him hanging out upstairs in the office with Bahian hip-hop artists. People threw frequent events there, called a *sarau*, or soiree, with themes that ranged from slam poetry to erotic storytelling. Artists would share poetry, do rap, and paint graffiti while attendees attentively listened and watched. In some ways, these replaced the soirees that took place at Sankofa Bar, providing a different refuge space for Black people in the city's central district. Even if just for a few hours, the store fostered and nurtured *aquilombamento* for various Black artists, activists, and community members.

At that time, I was curious how stores and vendors were able to obtain hip-hop clothing items to sell to their clients who placed a high value on certain items like the New Era baseball hat. In 2014, New Era hats cost around R$220 at Afreeka, which was $90–$100 USD, but in the United States the same hat cost only $25–$35 USD. When I interviewed the manager, he said that local youths basically demanded New Era hats even though he could get national brands at much cheaper prices. When he said this, he gently shrugged his shoulders and his face informed me that it did not make sense to him, but that he knew he was supplying a demand and a particular taste that his clients wanted.

One reason the New Era baseball hats cost so much at that time is that people were moving them through informal global markets and distribution chains. Globalization has facilitated the movement of items in markets across the globe. At the same time, globalization flows through locally specific political economies. In 2014, one Brazilian national clothing store sold New Era baseball hats, but the options were few, usually New York Yankees or Los Angeles Dodgers hats in bright colors that most Black Bahian hip-hop youths did not want. Someone in Brazil could not even order a baseball hat from the New Era website or US companies such as Lids or Foot Locker that sell New Era baseball hats, because none of these companies shipped their merchandise to Brazil. The Afreeka manager described the complex supply chain. "Runners" make numerous trips from Brazil to the United States every year to purchase hip-hop-style apparel from retail stores and outlet malls and bring it back to Brazil. They usually leave from São Paulo because its Guarulhos Airport has the most international flights, including more direct flights to the United States, and cheaper options. Once the runners return from a trip, they sell their goods to boutique stores around Brazil. Some runners also have their own boutique stores and use these trips to stock their own inventory. I once met a runner who operates his own hip-hop fashion store in Southern Brazil. He said he would travel to various cities in the United States frequently to purchase clothing, hats, and shoes to bring back to sell in his shop and to other vendors. On his return trips, he did not claim these items in

Brazilian customs, and sometimes the customs officers would confiscate his merchandise. Considering the formidable challenges and expenses of flights, accommodations, and potential lost merchandise, the price of a New Era hat in Brazil quickly escalates from its US retail price.

One way that Black Bahian hip-hop youths signify abject Blackness as beautiful is by blurring gender in their fashion aesthetics. Their Black queerings are what make the Bahian hip-hop movement more threatening than, say, Ilê Aiyê, an organization that invests in draping Western gender roles in Afrocentric garb. This gender fluidity in the Bahian hip-hop movement caught my attention early on, all the way back in my preliminary research in 2013. That June, local artists and organizers put on a hip-hop festival at the Parque Solar Boa Vista. After I interviewed João that day, I walked around, eating *acarajé*, listening to performers, admiring the graffiti murals being painted, and generally people-watching. I saw a young Black woman who reminded me of home, particularly of the singer Aaliyah, the wildly popular US R&B singer from Detroit whom I loved in the 1990s (she tragically passed away in a 2001 plane crash in the Caribbean).[11] Her baggy khaki pants were like the kind US West Coast gangsta (also São Paulo) rappers were wearing and sat just below the waistband of the men's boxers she wore. Her tank top bared her midriff; she wore dark sunglasses and a fitted New Era hat. Her hair was long and dark black, but she had shaved the right side of her head close to her scalp. While she performed femininity with her long hair and women's tank top, she also donned masculine aesthetics with her baggy pants, her boxers, shaved side, and New Era hat. Whereas Brazilian society denigrates Black women for being too masculine, this Black woman used masculine aesthetics to signify her beauty.

Men also disturb the supposed natural distinction between masculinity and femininity in their fashion aesthetics. Masculinity might dominate hip-hop cultures and styles, even among women and girls, but some Black men choose femininity to queer gender norms. In June 2017, I accompanied João to a photo shoot in Pelourinho with two younger hip-hop artists—they would use the photos to advertise their upcoming hip-hop freestyle battle on social media. Lázaro, a young Black queer man, wore a red tank top and a flowy red dress (no pockets from what I could see); the others were in typical masculine hip-hop baggy clothes, skater shoes, *bonés*, and baggy T-shirts. Throughout the photo shoot, Lázaro stood alongside them or in the middle of them, but never behind them, a position where one might expect a woman to stand in relation to men. Instead, he brought his feminine clothes and bodily aesthetics to a position equal with his friends in their masculine clothes and aesthetics.

Lázaro also uses his queer Blackness and gender fluidity to challenge Brazil's racial *and* gender order of things. For example, his Instagram page reads, "A threat is detected," referring to himself as a threat to Brazilian civilization. While Brazilian society stigmatizes Black men as a threat, Lázaro resignifies them as empowered and able to rail against dominant structures. Lázaro refuses to conform his Blackness to Eurocentric bourgeois norms around gender and sexuality. Instead, he takes flight from them, reestablishing links between Blackness, gender, and bodily aesthetics. Lázaro also styles this threat as sensuously beautiful and alluring. In another Instagram post of his, he dons leopard-print underwear with a lower cut that provocatively rides up high on the hip and a matching robe, three necklaces that tug at his neck, like a choker collar, and a diamond-shaped earring flashing on his left ear; he is holding a gun and grinning to show off his gold teeth up top. On the one hand, Lázaro is wearing a feminine-clothing print and jewelry, and his underwear style is associated with effeminate gay men. On the other hand, he has gold teeth and a gun, both suggesting more masculine expressions. In his Instagram and quotidian performances, Lázaro uses a queer-embodied aesthetic that blends masculine and feminine stylings to artistically style a Blackness that Brazilian society denigrates.

Both the Black woman at the hip-hop festival and Lázaro queer-gendered norms to signify their Blackness as tasteful, exquisite, and beautiful. Black people's gendered performances do not have to conform to Eurocentric norms to be sensually pleasing; their gender fluidity is deviant, artistically paving a way for Black people to value one another in contrast to how Brazilian society deems Black people beautiful if they adhere to Afrocentric modesty, gender norms, or even an exploitative hypersexuality. Lázaro takes the popular belief that Black men are threats and pushes it further: he is also a threat to gender and sexual norms. He invites his viewers to find him attractive even though some might feel scared of a gun-wielding Black man wearing women's clothing and jewelry. The red dress he wore in 2017 draws on the power of Exú, the ability to cross over between various worlds; Lázaro himself shifts, not necessarily between the metaphysical and the material but between the masculine and the feminine, with ease. In that regard, we can see him as a trickster figure, one who is "signifyin'" (Smitherman, 1977), or playing on the gaps in meaning-making processes and the aesthetic symbols of masculinity and femininity among Black people.

The Beauty of Abject Blackness

Throughout Brazil's history, Black people have assembled *quilombos* as safe havens for marginalized Black people. In these maroon communities, Black people could take refuge, rest, freely express a Black consciousness, and reorder social relations that defy Western logics of race, gender, sexuality, and class. Assembling a *quilombo* is an opportunity to produce a different symbolic order as well. Black people's search for the *quilombo* is also a search for a Black aesthetic that remakes the relationship between Black people's bodies, tastes, values, and beauty. Black people did not discover a Black visual aesthetic; they had to fashion it themselves through their genius, their labor, their skills, and their innovation. They fabricated it through artifice.

In a *quilombo*, the relationship between Blackness, aesthetics, and politics provides a symbolic alternative to the dominant Brazilian conceptual map. In both the colony and the nation, Brazilian elites, institutions, agencies, media, and ordinary citizens have drawn upon a Eurocentric framework to assign Blackness the meanings of ugly, undesirable, filthy, and abominable. The meanings attached to abject Blackness justify Black people's marginalization in various social and political relations, including romantic relationships. The Brazilian conceptual map makes two aesthetic exceptions for Blackness as abject. The first is mixed Blackness, in which Brazilians desire Blackness because they have diluted it with whiteness through interracial mixture, so that Blackness is more beautiful the closer it gets to Eurocentric bodily aesthetics. The *mulata* figure, which I described in the introduction, is exemplary of this: with curly rather than tightly coiled hair, bronze rather than dark skin, slim body with large buttocks and hips, and thinner rather than wider nose and lips.

In Brazilian society, the other exception to abject Blackness is folkloric Blackness. Ilê Aiyê's Noite da Beleza Negra exemplifies how folkloric Blackness renders some Black people beautiful. Afro-blocs, like Ilê Aiyê, seek to aesthetically intervene in the association of Black with dark, evil, and immorality (Gonzalez, 2018c). As part of the reafricanization movement, these Afro-centered actors, institutions, and agencies took what was seen as abject, Africa as a symbol, and transformed it into a source of pride, self-esteem, history, tradition, and beauty. The Brazilian conceptual map can accept folkloric Blackness because it is a Blackness that has reformed itself and become civilized within a Western matrix of value. Africa the symbol is no longer abject: it is beautiful once a Black person has recuperated themselves, restoring their self to its previous being before colonialism and slavery. The shift from abject to folkloric Blackness is to make Africa and its people around the world seem as if they are parallel to Western civilization, a reflection of growth, development, and progress. Black people continue this process by constructing African (diasporic) history based on a Western template that adheres to bourgeois logics of gender, class, and sexuality (Hanchard, 1994). The Western template is evident in the pageant's gendered relations, in which Black men judge Black women on their appearance and how the event performs gendered duties and obligations for the Black community. The problem is that African-based aesthetics like Ilê Aiyê's are now tied to a folkloric Blackness rather than an abject Blackness. This leaves abject Blackness, now without Africanity as an aesthetic referent, still in place. Africanizing Black aesthetics was important because it sought to intervene with the degradation of the Black masses. Now it tends to hold the place of "high culture" in the diaspora in contrast to the "low cultures" of the Black masses, still stuck in abjection.

In contrast, the Bahian hip-hop movement invests in Black aesthetics, namely the artifice, to cause disarray in the symbolic and social order of things. Black people can be beautiful outside of a false choice between mixed and folkloric Blackness. Rather, the Bahian hip-hop movement takes abject Blackness and renders it beautiful, upsetting how mixed and folkloric Blacknesses distance themselves from the abject. Black Bahian hip-hop artists do not believe that marginalized black people must adopt a new position; rather, they connect marginalized Black Bahians to a new set of aesthetic relations and arrangements (Madison, 2003). When various actors and groups created mixed Blackness and folkloric Blackness aesthetics, they left abject Blackness in place as the baseline value for Blackness. They merely provided alternatives for Black people who sought cultural inclusion into the Brazilian community. As African-centered symbols, discourses, and cultures became incorporated into the multiethnic nation-state, many Brazilians made a cultural and aesthetic distinction between folkloric Blackness, a permissible Blackness tied to a premodern civilized Africa, and an abject Blackness, the stigmatized cultural practices of the Black masses on the periphery.[12]

When Black people make abject Blackness beautiful, they are engaging in a *quilombo* practice that recognizes a dignified human existence in marginalized Black people. They transform the abject into beauty without a discourse that they must redeem themselves or seek inclusion into the nation. One reason that Black people fled the colonial planation and took flight into the hillsides was to secure liberation on their own terms, to assert bodily sovereignty in ways that were fundamentally unavailable in Brazilian colonial society and remain unavailable to this day in the modern world. Black fugitives fled slavery as a condition *and* Brazil as a social system and aesthetic order (Moura, 1981). Even after abolition, Black Brazilians did not and still do not have full freedom within Brazil. Emancipation is not the same as freedom. Emancipation relies upon the juridical system and thus normalizes the Western state apparatus that is invested in determining who has what freedoms and on what scales: "Black freedom is often offered only in opposition to the history of enslavement" (Walcott, 2021, p. 2). Black people fled the plantation and Brazil because they still could not assert bodily sovereignty.

The relationship between Black people's bodies and freedom is a contentious one, especially in the context of emergent *quilombos*. The state and society often criminalize Black people as they *aquilombar-se*. This struggle for freedom revolves around who can control Black people's bodies. When Black people fled the plantation, they stole back their bodies *and* the right to alter the cultural messages and codes attached to their bodies that were dictated by Brazil's Eurocentric and white supremacist conceptual map. Across the diaspora, Stuart Hall notes, Black cultural creators have used the body "as if it was, and it often was, the only cultural capital we had. We have worked on ourselves as the canvases of representation" (1992, p. 27). I want to take Hall's point even further: Black Bahian hip-hop artists claim their bodies and use their cultural stylings, artistic labor, and aesthetic practices to assert their bodily sovereignty, marking the abject body as beautiful.

It is important to remember that in colonial and imperial Brazil *quilombos* were not embraced; the crown, colonial forces, and white society stigmatized *quilombolas* as enemies of the colonial structures of racial, gendered, and classed hierarchies. They associated Black people in *quilombos* with an abjectness that justified their demonization and dehumanization. *Quilombos* were far from normative and stood as threats to the racial somatic order. Yet *quilombos* sought to situate the stigmatized Black masses as beautiful and Africanity as a sign of desirability in creating a symbolic economy with different notions of taste outside the colonial regime. Today, rather than following the aesthetics of Africa, now under a folkloric Blackness that reifies the Brazilian nation, the Bahian hip-hop movement maintains *quilombismo* ideals in making beautiful those whom Brazilian society subjugates as abject, which is still the Black masses. In this case, Black hip-hop artists privilege the styles, creativity, and taste of marginalized Black people who do not conform to a premodern Africanity or a Brazilian ethnoracial hybridity. However, the Bahian hip-hop movement is invested in more than just the aesthetics of abject Blackness. Their styles, taste, and artistic endeavors also extend to other forms of representation that move beyond the body as a site of representation.

6 | Mediating *Quilombo* Politics

On February 6, 2015, right before Carnival and during the peak of Salvador holidays, the night gave the folks in the Cabula neighborhood a nice reprieve from the sun that had overheated them all day. It was already the weekend, and favela residents were drinking some ice-cold lagers, playing music, dancing, and socializing with one another in the streets. But the peaceful evening quickly changed into something else. Midsized blue trucks drove in and parked, and military police in bulletproof vests with heavy artillery poured out of them. They quickly rounded up Black male youths ages fifteen to twenty-seven throughout the area. Why? Days later, the state said the police officers claimed the youths were involved with robbing banks. But more importantly, they accused them because they were poor, Black, and from the periphery. Society often views racial profiling as a preventive measure to protect white tourists from São Paulo, who buttress Bahia's tourism-based economy (C. da Silva, 2019, p. 137).

After rounding up the Black youths, the police conducted an *abordagem*, a stop-and-frisk procedure that functions as both a public performance and an exercise in state power. The youths were lined up side-by-side on a street, facing a wall, with their backs to the police officers. The police moved among them, patting down each "suspect." Each Black youth knew the drill: spread your legs and lace your fingers together behind your head. Of course, this is never enough for the police, as they kick the youths' feet farther apart while pushing and prodding them to the side or in front. One can only imagine the hateful, racist, and derogatory things the police officers were saying to them. The police "searched" the suspects for weapons and contraband, but really they were grabbing, poking, and squeezing everywhere on their bodies, from the meatiest to the most tender parts. The young Black men no doubt flinched, tightened up, and released numerous half breaths of pain, but all of them knew that reacting too much would only invite more attention, ridicule, and inspection.[1] Police perform these violent searches to punish and emasculate the Black male youths *and* to terrorize Cabula residents who are watching. The message is clear: they can easily perform this scenario over and over, treating other Cabula residents as criminals with impunity.

The night's events were not over. The police loaded up twelve of the Black male youths, four teenagers and eight adults, in their squad vehicles and drove them to a nearby hill on the backside of the favela. Neighbors heard gunshots and feared that the police were ruthlessly shooting down their friends and family members. But they learned for sure that the police had murdered the Black youths only when they saw photos from the morgue posted on social media. Many went down to the morgue only to see their loved ones' lifeless bodies, filled with bullets, eyes smashed in and bones broken (C. da Silva, 2019). The police had beaten and tortured many of their victims before killing them. Autopsies revealed that these young Black men died with their knees on the ground, defenseless and probably shot in the back (Ciconello, 2015; Hafiz, 2016).

Many outraged Brazilians refer to this as the Cabula massacre, a mass murder at the hands of the state. As resident Marina Lima said, "My taxes paid for the bullet that killed my grandson." Even if her grandson, Natanel, and the eleven others did rob a bank, an unlikely scenario, then why did the police kill them? Why did they not just bring them to jail to be arrested, processed, and put on trial? Through the media, the police said they acted in self-defense, that the suspects did something that endangered their lives. The police represented their victims as violent antagonists, a threat to police officers and Brazilian society at large. They claimed self-defense in their formal reports, too. But the autopsies show the police shot the victims in a defenseless position from behind, undermining claims that they were under violent duress. While local residents and Black activists and organizers such as React or Be Killed rallied against this state-sanctioned terrorism, the larger public barely batted an eye. This representation of self-defense depends upon societal beliefs that poor Black youths are prone to violence, and thus that the police should proactively kill them before they can kill others.

Even worse, the state glamorizes how the police perform racial violence against Black people as spectacular, patriotic, and exhilarating.

Bahia state governor Rui Costa of the Workers' Party (PT) called the police heroic and delivered this atrocious public statement: "[The police officer is] like a striker in front of the goal trying to decide, in seconds, how he is going to put the ball into the goal. When he scores, all the fans in the stands will clap and the scene will be repeated several times on television. If the goal is lost, the top scorer will be condemned for his failure." Costa glorifies these murders, portraying Black people as opponents to the home team and framing Black death as cause for celebration, like a Brazilian national team football victory. As a part of Brazil, the police know their mission, to kill Black male youths—like Ronaldo and Neymar know their mission, to score against the other team. Both are heroic acts of patriotism, garnering Brazil's love and affection. Failure to execute this mission could result in humiliation, punishment, and ridicule. Just as the media will always show and glorify a Brazilian footballer's spectacular goal, they will do the same with police officers who murder poor Black youths from the periphery. While these murders may have different actors each time, the Brazilian media maintain an ongoing loop of premature Black death in Brazilian televisual cultures (Henson, 2020).

This chapter explores how Black Bahian hip-hop artists represent their political alternatives in contrast to the Brazilian state's criminalization of their existence and spaces. They re-create the *quilombo* model to assert sovereignty, the right to rule over themselves, their community, and their spaces, to protect themselves against Brazil's never-ending war on poor Black communities. *Quilombos* were not just spaces of refuge and cultural autonomy: they were political communities with their own structures of statehood, government, and sovereignty (E. Carneiro, 1958; Farfán-Santos, 2016; Kent, 1965). Black hip-hop artists conjure this political history in their music videos, representing themselves as legitimate authorities who exercise sovereignty over their communities. Their *quilombo* practices are more than ideological, spatial, social, and cultural matters; they are also political matters.

Refusing Brazilian Necropolitics

This opening vignette depicts how the Brazilian state represents itself as the supreme authority, the only institution whose force is legitimate and can be used to kill people who fall under their jurisdiction. The Brazilian state is largely unconcerned that it disproportionately targets poor and working-class Black people. In Brazilian political representations, such as media or police reports, they show that Black people might have cultural citizenship but do not have the same social and political citizenship as non-Black Brazilians (Caldwell, 2006). Thus, Black people experience a paradoxical relationship to citizenship and membership in the polis (C. Smith, 2016a). The state expects them to vote, pay taxes, and follow the law. Yet Black people have no expectation that the state will protect them. This is how the state and extralegal forces can kill Black people with impunity at catastrophic levels without moral outcry (Ferreira da Silva, 2001) outside Black or activist communities.

In fact, the Brazilian state, like the Bahian governor and police officers, is actively invested in killing Black people and then celebrating these murders as a national pastime. The state portrays these murders as necessary to preserve Brazil as a multiethnic and congenial nation. It uses its sovereignty, the supreme power to exercise legitimate force and violence, against the Black masses, creating a racialized "necropolitics" (Mbembe, 2019) that determines each population's human worth by subjugating "life to the power of death" (Mbembe, 2003, p. 39). The Black people the state ties to mixed Blackness and folkloric Blackness may live longer than those it ties to abject Blackness. When the state ties Black people to abject Blackness, it must stop, interrogate, harass, harm, and even kill them. In response to the Cabula massacre, Cidinha da Silva (2019) describes Black activist efforts to identify, critique, and dismantle Brazilian necropolitics. She writes: "It is necessary to problematize the structural racism of Brazilian society that generates violence and endorses the extermination of Black youth" (p. 141). I read this problematization in two ways. The first is obvious: publicly protesting the state's violent performances against Black people. The second is critiquing the ideologies, discourses, and representations that justify, normalize, and even celebrate such violence.

The Bahian hip-hop movement uses rap artists' music videos to problematize Brazilian necropolitical ideologies and everyday performances. These artists also represent alternative political systems in which Black people band together, nourish one another, and protect their communities against violence and harm. Here, the periphery is a Black space distinct from Brazil, with its own political logics, meanings, and practices. Throughout numerous music videos, including the four I will analyze, Black hip-hop artists portray the periphery as a sovereign space, one that the Brazilian nation is constantly at war with; here Black people are fighting to protect socially excluded Black people from a political institution that excludes them and is intent on killing them. Black Bahian hip-hop artists participate in an "antiracist visual politics" (Gillam, 2022) that disrupt the Brazilian state's anti-Black structures, ideologies, and practices. Rather than seeking inclusion within this apparatus or pursuing freedom within the nation, Black hip-hop artists propose other political systems that protect fellow *quilombolas*, establish political boundaries, create their own economies to nourish the Black masses, and develop a justice system that focuses on repair rather than retribution. Black hip-hop artists use media to imagine, perform, and practice *aquilombamento* as another set of political possibilities, construing the periphery as itself a site of freedom.

Stop Killing Us!

As the Brazilian state attempts to naturalize its violent assaults on Black Brazilians, Black hip-hop artists deconstruct the state's lethal tactics and media discourses that generate and normalize Black death. They challenge how other Brazilians devalue Black people's lives and make their premature deaths seem natural. The artists valorize the lives of those within the Black masses whom the state and even society criminalizes and kills. In addition, they band with one another to decry these activities and form a different political entity.

On December 20, 2018, the music video "Moço Lindo do Badauê" (Beautiful boy from Badauê) was released on YouTube by AquaHertz Beats. Bringing together Opanijé, Nelson Maca, Wall Cardozo, Aspri RBF, and Xarope MC, the collaboration between these Black male rappers and poets provides a televisual homage to the murder of Mestre Môa da Katende (born Romualdo Rosário da Costa), an artist-intellectual revered for almost forty years in the Black Bahian community. The music video takes place in Mestre Môa's neighborhood, Brotas, a periphery neighborhood that is approximately 70 percent Black and sits just east of the Arena Fonte Nova football stadium. It is both a televisual funeral procession for Mestre Môa and a declaration for Black life against Brazilian necropolitics.

On October 8, 2018, the well-known artist, educator, composer, poet, and capoeira master Mestre Môa da Katende and his cousin Germino Pereira died. Paulo Sérgio Ferreira de Santana, a local barber, stabbed and killed them both in a bar by Diqué Tororó, not far from Brotas, during the first round of the 2018 presidential election. Môa da

Katende and Santana had argued over presidential candidates. Môa da Katende voted for Fernando Haddad of the Workers' Party and Ferreira de Santana voted for the far-right candidate Jair Bolsonaro of the Social Liberal Party. The heated discussion quickly escalated. The two began to fight, and at some point, Ferreira de Santana pulled out a knife and stabbed Môa da Katende twelve times in the back, eventually killing him, and also attacked his cousin Germino. Later, Ferreira da Santana confessed to his crime and was sentenced to twenty-two years in prison for the murders (A Tarde Online, 2019).

After Mestre Môa's death, my social media page was flooded with pictures and eulogies of him by not only hip-hop artists but just about anyone in Salvador: artists, activists, intellectuals, and friends. Mestre Môa had created alternative social and cultural spaces, like his capoeira school, where he had many students over the years. Capoeira is an Afro-Brazilian martial art that incorporates music, singing, and dancing. Black people developed it during slavery but had to conceal their martial-arts training from slave owners and other potential enemies, so they added musical elements to make the fighting appear to be entertainment (Lewis, 1992). Today, many Black people still practice capoeira in Brazil (Kurtz, 2020). At Mestre Môa's school, Black people could train in this musically infused martial art, learn about Black Brazilian political resistance, and develop their racial self-esteem. And even though Mestre Môa was not a hip-hop artist, he was a huge influence on the movement. People saw him as a paragon of both ancestrality and negritude, guiding poor and working-class Black people away from abject Blackness without conforming to permissible Blackness. His teaching engaged African-derived cultural practices, philosophies, and ways of being that connect Black people to their own ancestral knowledges and ontologies, from capoeira to Candomblé to his own *afoxé*, a Carnival group he created that uses African ancestral knowledges and religious cultures from Candomblé and expresses them in a nonreligious fashion in public settings. Mestre Môa was deeply invested in negritude in his community work, teaching the youths and others in his communities about African-derived cultures and knowledges to boost their self-esteem. Mestre Môa's emphasis on ancestrality, negritude, informal education, and community outreach resonated deeply within the Bahian hip-hop movement. So his murder was a grave loss for the Black Bahian community.

Like that of other community members, Mestre Môa's informal social work was not institutionalized. Thus the death of its leader was also the death of his work: the networks he forged across different groups. While *quilombos* are mobile, ephemeral, and malleable, the sudden disappearance of an emergent *quilombo* like Mestre Môa's results in devastating effects on when, how, and where Black people can foster *aquilombamento*. The premature death of this widely respected figure and elder is a reminder to other Black people of their own precarity under both state-sanctioned and extralegal modes of race-based violence. Santana's murder of Mestre Môa shows how easy it seems to be to end a Black person's life without regard for them, their family, their community, and their social importance.

Roughly two months after Mestre Môa's death, the one poet and four rappers released their music video as an homage to the beloved arts educator, delivering a message of memory, critique, resistance, and spiritual strength to poor and working-class Black people. Shot in the Ladeira de Nanã e Praça dos Artistas, the music video begins with spliced clips of Mestre Môa from the film *Raiz Afro Mãe* (Afro mother roots). It also features images of ancestral cultures: Nelson Maca wears a Badauê *afoxé*, Mestre Môa's *afoxé*, shirt. Community members are playing the *atabaque*, a large wooden hand drum. The famed dancer Negrizu dances in wearing Pan African–inspired pants. Capoeira players play their berimbaus, a single-string percussion instrument.

Each Black man on the track details his memory of Mestre Môa's death and adds a political message. Nelson Maca delivers its heavyweight poetic punches, asserting that Mestre Môa will not be forgotten. Referring to Afro-Brazilian cosmologies, he says the arts educator will come back to the community through rebirth, taking on a new form. Mestre Môa may have left his body, but his presence is not gone. Maca refers to conceptions of life and death in Black communities in which even though a person is killed, it does not mean they are dead. The differing values and social purposes here are to extend the life of Mestre Môa beyond his physical passing, keeping his memory alive and politicizing the ease with which Black people are killed in Brazil. The video then turns to rapper Wall Cardoso and from the streets of the favela to a cliff overlooking the city. These cliffs are places where Black people can perform Candomblé rituals away from a periphery's densely populated areas. Cliffs are also where police murder Black male youths before clandestinely disposing of their bodies by throwing them over the edge. Wall raps that even though Mestre Môa has been killed, the struggle does not end, confronting a genocidal Brazilian nation-state thirsty for committing Black violence. Cardoso makes explicit Brazil's violence toward Black communities, rapping that the "green and yellow flag" is stained with red. People refer to Brazil's flag as the "green and yellow," indicative of its predominant color scheme (with some blue and white). The red stains Cardoso refers to are from the blood of Black people ruthlessly killed by the state, society, and paramilitary groups every year. Brazil regularly registers homicides above fifty thousand and sometimes even more than sixty thousand a year. Black people are the overwhelming majority of the victims, ranging between two-thirds and three-fourths of those killed (Waiselfisz, 2014). While red, green, and yellow are Pan African colors, Cardoso notes that those colors also symbolize how anti-Black violence stains the Brazilian nation.

Standing where so many Black men meet their fate at the hands of the state, Cardoso ends his verse by chanting with the others, "Stop killing us!" This has become a mantra for numerous Black activist and political organizations such as React or Be Killed. Black activists, educators, and artists resist how the state, media, and society so easily accept Black people as recipients of extreme violence. They issue the "stop" command against the multilayered forces that contribute to Black death, both immediately and chronically: the state, non-Black Brazilians, and other Black Brazilians. The video then ends with Xarope of RBF and Lázaro Erê of Opanije. Xarope raps that Black people are armed: not with firearms or weapons to kill others, but with the *orixá* spirits who will protect them, bring justice, and deliver retribution in some way to those who harm Black people. He draws on alternative cosmological networks, in this case Candomblé deities, to protect Black life and arm Black people against danger. Finally, Lázaro Erê raps that victory, honor, and glory are what Black people deserve and will achieve.

Not everyone will see Santana's murder of Mestre Môa as a racist incident or even part of a broader structure of anti-Black violence. Some will point out that Mestre Môa's killer is Black and argue it was just an argument that got out of hand and resulted in violence. But this reinforces the "non-synchrony" (McCarthy, 1998) of Blackness, that Black people can turn on one another for their own aims and desires. Frantz Fanon (2008) examined these non-synchrony dynamics where Black people do not act together and share similar interests in the Francophone world: Black Antilleans, like Fanon's fellow people on the Caribbean island of Martinique, see themselves as closer to Frenchness and thus whiteness. For this reason, Black Antilleans then feel it is their right to administer anti-Black racism to Black Senegalese, doing the work of white supremacy. In this context, a French Caribbean has a higher standing than a French African, using that to elevate their position and diminish the latter's. In our Brazilian case, Santana was Black but aligned himself with white supremacy. Bolsonaro's followers, even Black Brazilians, have conservative views in general and racist beliefs against Black people, especially in the lower classes. Many believe in vigilante justice, leading to calls for the public to have access to firearms. Santana saw himself as better than someone like Mestre Môa, who was also Black, deeply involved in African ancestral cultures and a Black community, and voted for the Workers' Party candidate. Like police officers, Santana believed Black people are disposable and thus can be killed. This is not uncommon: many Black "citizens" show their allegiance to Brazilian society through their disavowal of and antagonism toward abject Blackness. They wish to stand in for and perform whiteness, especially in their ability to punish Blackness. On the flip side, Santana also learned that his Blackness comes back to him; he too is a racial threat and someone the state can dispose of.

Because the collective shot the music video in Brotas, they show a different geographical aspect of Bahia, which is usually represented by Pelourinho or the ocean beachfront. The music video contrasts the two social *and* political worlds in Salvador da Bahia, one of middle-class and upper-class neighborhoods and another in poor and working-class Black neighborhoods that society sees as outside of Brazil and thus beyond legal protection. Rather than showing Brazilian civil society, like in Pelourinho, the music video shows where society displaces abject Blackness. This strategy sets up an opportunity to transform abject Blackness into diasporic Blackness, a radical mode of *aquilombamento* in opposition to Brazil. Beatriz Nascimento deftly argues that Black people's freedom arrives in the periphery, not on the "asphalt," or middle-class neighborhoods. Black people's freedom outside of Brazil has a cost: "You lose the possibility of being in contact with the *zona sul* (a posh and very affluent Rio de Janeiro district), with the freer, more independent lifestyle in the favela" (2018f, p. 193). Nascimento's insight suggests that Black people can form and are forming alternative political organizations that attend to their freedom, their rights, and their ability to determine life and death.

Militancy on the Periphery

The Brazilian nation-state wages war on Black communities on the periphery (Ferreira da Silva, 2001; K.-K. Perry, 2012), and Black Bahian hip-hop artists frequently call attention to this fact. War is a constitutive feature of modern societies, producing a conquering self who must defeat a racial enemy, on local or foreign soil (Maldonado-Torres, 2008). The conquering self is a white masculinist ideology that maintains coloniality as a strategy of power in sociopolitical structures, cultural representations, and ideological practices (Maldonado-Torres, 2007; McClintock, 1995). Hip-hop artists resignify their stigmatized subjectivities from being threats to being political warriors who fight against Brazil and protect their marginalized communities.

In 2017, Udi Santos and Brena Élem formed Visi00nárias and used hip-hop as a vehicle for social change.[2] They brought and continue to bring Black feminism into their music and videos to recognize Black women's roles, politics, and knowledges in social movements. Their name signifies them as visionary women with two 0's to mirror eyes, seeing that the Bahian hip-hop movement must account for race, class, *and* gender in creating alternative social and cultural systems. Guided by their slogan, "To all the (dark) Black women, it has to change," the two young Black female producers and rappers embed themselves in militant circles, social activism, and community organizing, from putting on education workshops to using social media as a platform for educating their followers, being part of International Black Women's Day in the Caribbean and Latin America, and using their music and videos to represent Black women differently. Hip-hop is, then, about sociocultural systems *and* political activism.

Their debut music video, "Visionárias," is set on the train tracks by an old, dilapidated factory on the coast of the Bay of All Saints in the Plataforma periphery neighborhood, suggesting a desire to bring Salvador out of a romanticized past and into contemporary struggles against anti-Black racism, sexism, and classism. In the video, Salvador has a reality outside the Bahian imaginary, entangled with the same social, economic, political, and historical forces as more "modern" cities like São Paulo and New York City. Visi00nárias shows Salvador's deindustrialization: many factory shops have been closed, taking away job opportunities for the Black masses. Even though African culturalisms proliferate in Pelourinho, Black people confront conditions similar to those in other Black diasporic populations where hip-hop emerged.

The contrast between how people imagine Salvador and its material conditions has a historical context. For centuries, Brazil's economy depended on Northeast plantations, agrarian economies, and enslaved labor. Western empires began to look down on slavery and the slave trade. They were also fearful of Black people's desire to run away, rebel, and even riot, destabilizing the social order in the Americas. These same empires pushed the rest of the world to invest in industrialization, urbanization, and a modern workforce, the bedrock of capitalism at that time. Brazil was the last nation in the Americas to abolish slavery, ending it in 1888. At the time, national elites sought to shift the economy from the agrarian-based Northeast to the quickly urbanizing and modernizing Southeast, in cities like São Paulo and Rio de Janeiro, where factories were springing up (Bacelar, 1997). The federal government invested in Southeastern cities' infrastructure: roads, public transportation, electric grids, and so forth, largely ignoring the Northeast and its agrarian society (Costa, 2000). These collective actions isolated the Northeast, which found its political influence gone and its economy faltering. Since the late nineteenth century, Salvador's industry has had some success with seafaring, domestic crops, manufacturing, and the oil industries. Yet these industries did not propel Salvador's economy to the heights reached by other Brazilian cities such as São Paulo, Rio de Janeiro, and Brasília. Tourism is a key industry, but it also generates gentrification and confines poor and working-class Black people to the periphery (C. da Silva, 2019). Salvador has the highest unemployment rate of all the state capital cities, contributing to Black people's socioeconomic precarity and overall racial conditions, as described in chapter 1.

In their music video, Visi00nárias visually situates Black communities and cultures in the periphery to call out racialized class inequalities *and* to disrupt how people speak for Black women, effectively silencing them. The two Black female rappers want to speak for themselves. The Brazilian state and cultural agencies romanticize the *baiana* as the quintessential Black Bahian woman. She is warm, welcoming, and smiling. She cooks food such as *acarajé* (a shrimp-stuffed fried fritter) and *moqueca* (a palm oil–based white fish stew) for her family and clients. Her job is to pass along African folkloric cultures. She is a "Mama Africa" (P. Pinho, 2010) figure for the Brazilian national family. Instead of the *baiana*, Visi00nárias focuses on the *preta suburbana*, a dark Black woman from a periphery in the city's surrounding suburbs. In Brazil, a suburb does not usually have positive connotations; for many Brazilians, it means periphery communities that exist on the outskirts of the city. While society marginalizes the *preta suburbana*, the two MCs portray her as a Black radical figure who fights against oppression.

As Udi Santos and Brena Élem make their way up the train tracks, rapping and dancing toward the camera, Santos raps about her takeover of the hip-hop game and her own environment as a visionary Black woman from the periphery. She raps that she wanted an exit from the unfair social conditions she was born into. Rather than leave the periphery, the space of her material existence, she rhymes that she instead changed herself and the rules. Her lyrics are about going to metaphorical war, killing the so-called rulers in her world, and becoming the leader herself. She raps that she made her father proud and that she would certainly take over the top spot again and again. Santos's rapping points out that Black people do not have to leave the periphery to change their life for the better; they can change themselves right where they are and use their communities for social change. Santos asserts that Black people will not find liberation getting away from the periphery; in Brazilian spaces, they will still confront racism, classism, and sexism from the state and society. When she kills the mediocre "kings," her lyrics suggest that she is referring to those who believe they are in charge of the periphery, which can mean patriarchal men in the hip-hop movement or even the Brazilian state. Killing the kings means she can step in as a Black woman and institute a different system and norms, what she calls "rules," for Black people in the periphery. If Black people will play by a different set of rules, then the vision for another world can manifest. Santos showcases a *quilombo* sensibility because she valorizes the Black masses, proposes alternative social and political systems, and resignifies the periphery as the starting point of Black people's liberation, not their oppression.

When Santos flips the script on the rules of which Blacknesses are valued and which are not, she develops and enters into a different set of political arrangements. For her, the Black masses are not at the mercy of Brazil's sovereign power. Black people can create their own sovereign power to press back against Brazilian necropolitics. Metaphorically, Santos ridicules and kills kings, supreme rulers, through suffocation. She does not want to be on the other side of this war; she wants to remain on the side of the oppressed and fight back. Instead of being docile, Santos becomes militant, heading into war, fighting to take down the system rather than be included in it. Her desire to become the sovereign head is not so that she can preside over the status quo but so that she can change the world. Having killed the kings, a metaphor for the Brazilian state, she takes the place of the sovereign ruler and has legitimate authority.

Banding with other marginalized Black people, Visi00nárias draws on a legacy of Black radical militancy to upset the current social, political, and cultural system that excludes them. In the song's hook, Santos and Élem rap together that they are creating a disruption against a conspiracy. They are working with and for marginalized people, installing a new scheme and information system for them to realize their vision of a better world. We can understand the song's hook as a metaphorical revolt. They play with the meaning of inflammation, alluding both to setting fire and causing discomfort. Setting fire invokes various Black radical acts, such as enslaved Black people's revolts and rebellions in which they set fire to Salvador (J. Reis, 1995; Schwartz, 1995). These histories also generate discomfort for the Brazilian national imaginary because they challenge the belief that Brazilian slavery was benign and harmonious. Visi00nárias agitates against the conspiracies, or dominant ways of thinking, that naturalize national history and a political order, calling for an insurrection against this structure of racialized suffering. But this first requires an alternative system, what they call a scheme, that gives Black people a political order in which they can relate to one another differently. Visi00narias conveys new information so that Brazil's most vulnerable populations can understand and participate in this new system.

After the first chorus, it is Élem's turn to spit her rhymes, articulating her vision for tearing down systems of oppression. Like Santos, she refuses to accept that Black Brazilians can secure the good life only outside the periphery. She raps that even though she comes from a harsh reality, she is a strong Black woman who makes her own fortune. She adds that she will confront oppression and even die doing it, a good death in her book. She is unbothered by privileged individuals and their crying; they are all just clowns to her. Then she raps that she is interested in saving other socially excluded people: the bandits, the womanists, the graffiti artists, those from the ghetto, crazy-ass women (*maloqueiras*), and the poets. In her lyrics, Brena Elim charts out an escape from Brazil and into her own *quilombo* space on the periphery. Rather than trying to join the privileged life and become part of an anti-Black Brazilian society, she wants to stay in the periphery, join up with other marginalized peoples, and confront injustice rather than avoid it. She understands that the cost may be her own life, but she knows it will be a noble death because she is fighting against oppression and for Black people's liberation.

The Brazilian nation-state depicts poor Black people from the periphery as national outsiders. The two women of Visi00nárias use this alterity as a point of militancy in their identification, belonging, and resistance. This militancy is also visual, part of their fashion. Wearing camouflage clothing, they depart from the usual depictions of Black women in Brazil, refusing the hypersexualized *mulata* as well as the traditional *baiana*. Instead, they are soldiers in a war against a society that incessantly labors to discipline and punish Black people who fail to perform acceptable forms of Blackness.

Usually, militancy, the ability to showcase one's political acumen and strategies in combat, is expressed in a heteropatriarchal masculine framework that relies on physical power and mastery. Visi00nárias disrupts militancy's association with masculinity, signifying that it can include both political strength and femininity. In Brazil, many Black social movements are led by misogynist men, relegating Black women to the margins (Hanchard, 1994) as "foot soldiers" (K.-K. Perry, 2013).[3] Visi00nárias conjures Black women's political leadership: they are generals, commanders, lieutenants, and sergeants in the hip-hop movement. These Black women are feminine warriors, combining the clothing styles of Black women on the periphery, such as short dresses, with camouflage print. Black women do not need to take a back seat. Santos and Élem also assert *themselves* as leaders in the Bahian hip-hop movement, showing they are ready to lead Black people into battle. They too have knowledges, insights, and strategies that are useful for *aquilombamento*. Black women are not simply passive objects that need protection. They are actively engaging in ideological, material, and symbolic warfare against the systems that oppress them. They are also investing in protecting the collective, especially those who are weak, elderly, or vulnerable, regardless of gender. The Bahian hip-hop movement thus invests in *aquilombamento* beyond education and consciousness-raising; it puts together a political configuration that opposes Brazil in part by upending both raced and gendered norms.

Visi00nárias's music video politically reconfigures Black women who refuse Black and white patriarchies in Brazil as revolutionary agents in the Bahian hip-hop movement. In Brazil, many people see a *preta suburbana* as a *piriguete*, a sexually liberated and dangerous figure who sits at the "interconnection between racism, class, gender, and sexuality" (Gomes do Nascimento, 2010, p. 5). The word *piriguete* is a contraction that combines the words "dangerous" and "girl." She is a racialized and classed figure that Brazilians associate with a promiscuous lower-class Black woman from the periphery. She cares little for social norms. But Brazilian cultural critics argue that what makes the *piriguete truly* dangerous is that she is in control of her body, her desires, and her behaviors (Gomes do Nascimento, 2009; Machado Larangeira, 2016); owning her body and sexuality, the *piriguete* exemplifies how marginalized Black women practice and assert bodily sovereignty. The *piriguete* is dangerous because she is a sexually aggressive woman who crosses racial boundaries of permissible femininity. This stigmatized figure does not embody or conform to white womanhood—still Brazil's ideal of femininity, modeled on purity and piety; nor does she perform a *mulata* womanhood whose hypersexuality fulfills white men's patriarchal desires. Instead, the *piriguete* is a Black woman whose sexuality society deems excessive because she actively desires men rather than passively serving as the object of men's desires. Her excess appears elsewhere: in her makeup, hair, revealing clothing, and accessories. These desires and behaviors disturb the moral order of Brazilian civil society.

In the Bahian hip-hop movement, Black women on the periphery reappropriate the *piriguete* as a means of empowerment.[4] Even though Brazilian society and many Black Brazilians demonize the *piriguete*, Visi00nárias empowers this marginalized subject as a radical leader. When Élem raps that cockroaches believe they are butterflies, she is creating a metaphor for how marginalized Black women, like the *piriguete*, refuse the judgment of a white masculinist gaze and replace it with their own view of themselves. She is also signaling that Black women should refuse how society devalues Black women and construct their own systems of beauty and valorization that do not rely upon colonial, sexist, and anti-Black logics.

As Santos and Élem lyrically and visually represent Black women as revolutionary agents of social change, they are engaging in their own critical cultural politics. Part of this is a "performance of possibilities" (Madison, 2003) for Black women. These performances are critical because they do not ask Black women to change or adopt a new position. Instead, they situate marginalized Black women, such as the *preta suburbana* and the *piriguete*, in a new set of relations and arrangements (p. 471). They see their task as, in the words of Henry A. Giroux and Peter McLaren, "to win an already invested, already positioned individual or group" (cited in Madison, 2003, p. 471) to an alternative system that is grounded in a politics which resists the forces that oppress them rather than acquiesces to them.

De Facto Sovereignty

Historical *quilombos* stood in political opposition to the Brazilian colony. Black people joined these maroon communities because they were searching for alternative political systems to the Brazilian colony. Together, Black fugitives accepted the *quilombo* leader as a sovereign figure, granting leaders like Zumbí the power to rule over them. Today, the Bahian hip-hop movement replays this relation, configuring a different sovereignty and authoritative figure for Black people that stands in opposition to the Brazilian nation.

Sovereignty is the supreme authority that creates laws, assigns citizenship, distributes violence, and governs a jurisdiction in the name of the public good (Krasner, 2001; Schmitt, 2007; Wallerstein, 2004). In the Western Hemisphere, colonial and national sovereign powers have labored to strip Black people of geographic belonging in order to justify their violent and harmful practices against them (McKittrick, 2006; Wynter, 2003). In their white conceptual maps, Black people belong neither to an African homeland nor to an American host land; they languish in geographic and political uncertainty. As a result, a sovereign power, such as a monarch or governor or president, can deny Black people political rights, citizenship, and basic humanity in their jurisdiction. Brazilian sovereign powers reduce Black people to "bare life" (Agamben, 1998), a human life with no political rights but still under the domain of law. Without belonging to a sovereign nation-state that will protect them, Black people experience a state of exception in the Americas (Weheliye, 2008) where the rule of law is always suspended, citizenship is negated, and violence is gratuitously distributed.

Black people's political relationship to American nation-states raises political dilemmas around belonging and sovereignty. Black people have created their own political practices to contest de jure sovereignty, that is, legally recognized supreme authority. When Black people escaped the plantation, they participated in Black radical political action: they stole back their bodies from a jurisdiction that provided no rights, only subjugation, dishonor, and violence (Patterson, 1982). It was an act of asserting bodily sovereignty, stating that Black people have the right to rule, control, and govern themselves, and protect themselves against violence. Bodily sovereignty can also lead to territorial sovereignty. Beatriz Nascimento's *quilombo* theories describe Black people's relationship to their bodies and territory as such: "African people are an extension of the earth and vice versa. *We are the land, the land is us.* The body literally becomes the territorial continuity between Africa and Brazil. This grounding is symbolic and material" (C. Smith, 2016c, p. 80). When Black people fled the plantation and created *quilombos*, they established a geographical belonging between themselves as African people and the land they settled upon to re-create a Black-oriented political system on Brazilian soil but not under Brazilian jurisdiction. They created their own sovereign powers that ruled over their communities and spaces, exercising political rights that they do not have access to under Brazilian rule.

Black Bahian hip-hop artists convey a de facto sovereignty, practical control and jurisdiction, over their Black spaces. Black hip-hop artists present the periphery as an emerging *quilombo* with sovereign power to protect, nourish, and provide for marginalized Black people who are treated as noncitizens by the Brazilian nation-state. Their sovereignty is paradoxical, recognized by its members as legitimate yet unrecognized by the Brazilian nation-state that claims a monopoly on sovereign rule.

The Bahian rapper Coscarque represents an alternative political community in his music video "Scarface." The video refuses Brazil's racialized necropolitics, instead nourishing Black people on the periphery and providing the necessary goods for them to live well. The three-and-a-half-minute music video features Coscarque in a recording studio with members of Ugangue Familia, a local rap collective. The thirty-eight-year-old rapper spits into the mic with his crew bouncing to his potent lyrics over DJ KL Jay's beat.[5] The other eight video participants are also Black men, many wearing baggy shirts and *bonés*. At times, the video cuts to three Black men in hats, baggy sweatshirts, and sunglasses. The middle person wears a bandana over his face while holding up the Ugangue flag against the backdrop of the Salvador cityscape, signaling to the knowing viewer that the video takes place on the periphery.

In the song, Coscarque undertakes a "signifyin'" (Smitherman, 1977), or Black wordplay, that exploits gaps in meaning and creates misdirection. While misdirection is often a tool for confusion, Coscarque uses it to disrupt how Brazilian society labels poor Black people as criminals and outsiders, resignifying them as part of a radical collective. In the music video, he portrays himself as the Scarface of Salvador, referring to symbols in the 1983 US film starring Al Pacino, made popular in US Black hip-hop culture. Coscarque takes this symbolic icon from the United States and uses it to intervene with local meanings of Blackness, belonging, and criminality in Salvador da Bahia. Instead of avoiding the stereotype of Black people as drug-trafficking criminals, Coscarque leans into it. He reinvents himself as Tony Montana, the Cuban kingpin of a drug-trafficking organization, and uses trafficking vocabulary like "illicit," "traffic," "risk," and "organized crime." Like Montana, Al Pacino's character in the movie, Coscarque is a social and political outsider to society, someone who does not properly belong in the polis. But Coscarque is trafficking information, not illegal drugs. In the Bahian hip-hop movement, information and knowledge are hip-hop's fifth element after rapping, DJ'ing, breakdancing, and graffiti (Messias, 2015). Black hip-hop artists mobilize it to foment a Black *conscientização*. In the music video, Coscarque compares his lyrics to "organized crime," signaling that his information trafficking is actually more dangerous than drugs because of his ability to speak to the Black masses and mobilize them into a *political* organization.

In the video, the periphery, like the original *quilombo*, is a political territory. In front of the mic, Coscarque depicts himself as the leader of this crew of marginals. He asserts himself as a sovereign leader of the periphery just as Zumbí was the sovereign leader of Palmares. His Zumbí *boné* and AFREEKA sweatshirt express negritude and ancestrality as cultural and political symbols. Coscarque welcomes Brazilian racial outsiders such as the Ugangue Familia into his periphery. Coscarque uses the Ugangue flag to represent an alternative political affiliation. *Ugangue* is actually an acronym, the letters standing for the Ghetto Union and Hip-Hop Culture Family. At the same time, the word is the Brazilianization of the US word "gang." While Brazilian society sees hip-hop, ghettos, and gangs as negative, Coscarque makes them meaningful as a set of organizing concepts and symbolic resources Black people can use to construct their nonblood kinship structure. Coscarque performs this political practice by inviting poor Black people from the periphery to join him in his own *quilombo*. Just as the historical *quilombo* welcomed outsiders (B. Nascimento, 2021), Coscarque's own *quilombo* welcomes Brazilian outcasts such as punks, skateboarders, and Black women into his alternative political community. With him, they will be VIPs, valuable family members who protect each other against Brazilian violence. Ugangue uses family as a trope for a type of nonstate-based nationalism. Around the diaspora, Black nationalism has certainly reproduced a heteronormative kinship unit and nationalism (Gilroy, 2004). As a *quilombo*, Ugangue is substantially

Figure 6.1. Coscarque's cover art for his single "Scarface"; used with permission of the artist (2013)

different in that it does not rely on biologically reproducing itself, instead absorbing outsiders as the basis for its bond-making and community expansion. It queers heterosexual norms (Cohen, 1997). The Ugangue flag comes to represent a different nation for socially excluded Black people. Ugangue is a means by which Black people in Brazil can imagine themselves belonging to a different community than Brazil.

In Coscarque's lyrics, Black sovereignty is a key theme that stretches across the song. As a *quilombo* leader, Coscarque asserts his power to rule over his Ugangue family and his periphery territory. For him, this power is not insignificant, just as Zumbí's sovereign power was not insignificant, as the latter negotiated peace treaties with Brazilian colonial forces. The Black Bahian rapper establishes the degree of his power, suggesting its largesse.

> Quem se opõe ver suas ações caindo?
> Igual o governo da Dilma junto com seus ministros
> Monitorado vivo o risco, sei dos riscos corro riscos
> Atuação inconfundível tipo Denzel Al Pacino
> Trafico informação e meus negócios flui
> Antes de dizer fui diz que é noiz na porra do bagui
>
> Who opposes seeing their shares fall?
> Equal to Dilma's government and her ministers
> Monitoring the risk, I know the risk. I run the risk
> Unmistakable performances like Denzel, Al Pacino

> I traffic information and my businesses flow
> Before speaking, I was there, said it's ours, fuck this shit

Coscarque's power is equivalent to that of the Brazilian government, the president, and department heads. He is concerned with governing his jurisdiction, creating alternatives like public security ("monitoring the risk"), infrastructure ("I traffic information"), a political economy ("my businesses flow"), and authority ("said it's ours"). He is the supreme authority over his own territorial jurisdiction that has its own rules, infrastructure, and economy that differ from Brazil. As a political entity, Coscarque's emergent *quilombo* on the periphery is parallel to, not separate from, Brazil. It is a similar model to many historical *quilombos* that had their own political rule, economy, and infrastructure, but still interfered with the Brazilian colony, rescuing the enslaved, stealing supplies, and undermining its structures of gendered anti-Blackness (J. J. Reis, 2016).

As he drops the song's hook, Coscarque refuses Brazilian necropolitics that relegate Black people to bare life. Rather than a depraved existence, Coscarque sees his sovereign power as having a duty to provide and care for the citizens in his polis:

> ¿Quer saber quem é que fornece?
> ¿Quem é que abastece e tem a da boa?
> Liga pro Cosca
> Essa é daquelas que enlouquece
> Vicia as pretas e muleques
> Também vem lá da maloca
>
> You want to know who is providing?
> Who has the supplies? And who has the good stuff?
> Connect with Cosca
> This is one of those that goes insane
> Addicted to Black people and punks
> Now here comes the craziness too

The Brazilian nation-state often excludes the periphery from ordinary public services, like waste collection and running water, and commercial services. For periphery residents, it can be difficult to get goods delivered and services rendered in their neighborhoods (Henson, 2016a). Many periphery communities create informal networks to do these things for each other. Coscarque assumes this mantle in his music video to provide for and nourish his citizens. Signifyin' on the trafficking vocabulary, his "good stuff" is not drugs; instead, it is goods, services, and infrastructure like food, clothing, and other necessities. Black people no longer need to exist in a depraved world and suffer premature death; they too can lead a good life with dignity in the periphery as an emergent *quilombo*. They are no longer excluded from the public good; they are central to the public good.

As a sovereign power, the modern state can be an abstract entity consisting of multiple layers of elected politicians, appointees, government chairs, and juridical officials. Many people see the state as decentralized, messy, and inaccessible. Coscarque provides another alternative. Every time he raps for people to call him, he pulls out his cell phone to demonstrate that he is material and accessible. This sovereign power is not distant, buried in bureaucracy. As the authority over his periphery, Coscarque is accessible in the community, addressing the needs of his constituents and providing for them.

Black Feminist Systems of Justice

Black Bahian hip-hop community members commonly critique the Brazilian justice system for its failure to deliver justice for them. They refer to the violent nature of the police force, a judicial system that endorses it, and a penal system that does everything but rehabilitate people. Worse, the state's multilayered system does not treat the white middle classes in the same way. A white middle-class citizen's life is seen as valuable, and thus the state sees it as worthy of protection, justice, and rehabilitation: a political redemption if you will. For Black Bahian hip-hop community members, the Brazilian justice system is a façade, working to punish, confine, and even kill poor and working-class Black people. Even though Black Bahian hip-hop artists critique the Brazilian state's repressive justice system, they do not believe that there should be no justice system; they just want one that delivers justice for them without inflicting further harm on Black communities.

Black Brazilians have historically constructed their own political organizations, movements, systems, and institutions to challenge Brazilian anti-Black racism, provide refuge for Black people, and imagine another world that is freer and more just. In practice, these political efforts have been mixed, contradictory, and even at times severely inadequate. Historical *quilombos* were not entirely "free"; newly arrived members were sometimes indentured until they could replace themselves with a newly escaped fugitive who would join the maroon community (Beatriz dos Santos, Nascimento-Mandingo, and Chazkel, 2020; B. Nascimento, 2018g). More recent examples of *aquilombamento* demonstrate how sexism and patriarchy are persistent problems. The Black Movement has often ignored women, gender issues, and sexism in general (Hanchard, 1994). Afro-Carnival groups like Ilê Aiyê reproduce a heteropatriarchal structure that demands Black women perform domestic duties and obligations to the Black family and community (P. Pinho, 2010). The Bahian hip-hop movement also has its own problems: men reduce women to objects, rarely recognizing them as agents who are sociopolitically active (Sobral Freire, 2018). Even in Coscarque's "Scarface," we see the repeated trope of an authoritative Black male leader banding with other Black men and leaving women by the wayside.

Ideally, *quilombo* politics involve more than just valorizing Black people's lives, becoming militant actors, and establishing de facto sovereignty. They seek collective liberation, justice for Black people against racism, sexism, classism, homophobia, religious intolerance, and transphobia. The problem is that many emergent *quilombos* over the past century have focused on racial justice without attending to how racism is interwoven with other structures of oppression. These blind spots concerning intersectionality have had devastating effects on Black women, harming them outside and inside radical movements. As the Combahee River Collective (2015) argues, liberating Black women would necessarily result in everyone's liberation because it would require the eradication of racist, sexist, homophobic, and classist structures.[6]

Black Bahian feminists advance *quilombo* politics by imagining a different justice system that addresses harm which does not involve the repressive Brazilian state and its judicial system. This is evident in Visi00nárias's "⅓ da tropa," which considers how Brazilian society and even the periphery still rely on sexism, misogyny, and patriarchy toward Black women, or what Moya Bailey deftly describes as "misogynoir" (2021): the specific type of anti-Black racism that Black women face. Moreover, it shows how Black men's sexist, misogynist, and patriarchal attitudes toward Black women are also racist. Just because they are Black men does not mean that race and racism are not factors in their sexism toward Black women. Visi00nárias tackles misogynoir violence and asks how to create a justice system that does not rely upon colonial logics of Black disposability. Santos and Élem refuse the Brazilian repressive and juridical apparatuses, namely the police and the courts, and instead imagine a world where Black women are free and Black communities can hold Black men accountable without exposing them to Brazilian machinations that produce Black premature death.

Black people often represent the periphery, like the *quilombo*, as a space of refuge and freedom that they cannot find in middle-class and upper-class spaces. Different Black people experience refuge and freedom differently. For Santos and Élem, Black people must continue to raze the gendered colonial edifices that establish and maintain unequal social relationships and power dynamics between men and women. On their YouTube music video page, their description reads: "[We will] Haunt your MACHISMO, your MISOGYNIST AIR, haunt your PREJUDICE, haunt those who KILL US! UNITED WE ARE, ⅓ OF THE SQUAD!" They call attention to how gendered violence intersects with racial politics as well as how Black women collectively respond. In Brazil, men establish their social status by asserting their masculinity through a patriarchal lens that normalizes patriarchal power and consequently physical dominance over women, especially Black women (Hautzinger, 2007). Black men also participate, as they feel the need to overcompensate in their displays of heteropatriarchal masculinity. Visi00nárias is committed to holding Black men on the periphery accountable for their violence, harm, and abuse of Black women without furthering violence against other Black people.

Interlocking systems of oppression and nonlinear journeys toward freedom have long placed Black women in a particular bind. Black men suffer from Brazilian racism, but they can also use their gendered power to get closer to their own freedom and push Black women further away from theirs. So, what do Black women do? Do they accept racialized and gender-based violence against them, by their own people in their own communities, in the name of racial solidarity? This approach perpetuates misogynoir against Black women. Or do they call on the state for help—the state that assumes Black women deserve violence, and that arrests, incarcerates, and kills Black men as an act of civic duty? This approach also relies on an apparatus that views Black people as expendable and unworthy of protection. Santos and Élem turn to Candomblé spiritualities to obtain justice in emergent *quilombos* and evade the genocidal Brazilian state. In their political philosophy, ancestrality maps out a template for *quilombo* justice that governs Black people's actions, including consequences for those who transgress the rules, laws, and norms in Black communities.

The music video begins outside with a small fire, some leaves and shrubs, and candles burning. We next see a Black man inside in his living room, where he turns on his television and the Visi00nárias logo appears on his screen. Confused, he tries to change the channel, to no avail. Far away, Santos and Élem are in a computer laboratory creating interference with the antagonist's life. The duo's music video description says that they will haunt those who kill Black women, going after their machismo, misogyny, and prejudice. Based on that, we can assume that the antagonist has done something egregious toward a Black woman, something that Visi00nárias believes needs punishment. The antagonist is representing the countless men who harm Black women.

Though unaware of Santos and Élem's electronic interference, the antagonist becomes frightened and leaves his house.[7] He hastily gets into his car, only to be met with more spiritual trouble: his car won't start. Freaking out, the man is even more scared and just runs away from his home, into the streets of his periphery neighborhood. Slowing down, he looks at his cellphone, now taken over just like his TV and his car. The video splices in short clips of Santos and Élem, sometimes in everyday attire and sometimes in Candomblé clothing in front of the small fire. The antagonist finds himself haunted by the Visi00nárias logo in other locales, such as the TV at his neighborhood bar. Eventually, he returns home, exhausted, and falls asleep in his living room chair. When he wakes up in the morning, he steps outside, and Santos and Élem pass by, glaring at him before looking at each other and eventually laughing.

The music video is a Black feminist political mediation that circumvents the nation-state, affirms Black people's right to territorial sovereignty, and protects Black women's right to bodily sovereignty. The duo does not turn to the Brazilian state, well known for its violent approaches to Black communities, for justice. Instead, they utilize Candomblé to obtain justice. They hold the antagonist accountable for his unnamed misogynoir yet keep him from the Brazilian nation-state that would see his life as expendable and create further harm without addressing the harm already caused. They follow a Black feminist commitment that "struggles together with Black men against racism but also struggles with Black men about sexism" (Combahee River Collective, 2015, p. 213).

How will Visi00nárias haunt those who harm Black women? This is a multi-step process that relies on creating a Black feminist *quilombo*, what they simply refer to as a squad. Santos raps that she is one-third of their squad, and Elém raps this too. That leaves one more third to constitute their *aquilombamento*. Based on their Black feminist political ethos, viewers could read the last one-third as themselves, another Black woman, or a Candomblé *orixá*. If a Black woman, it could be someone who was harmed or another Black woman joining the two Black female MCs to address the harm to a Black woman. If an *orixá*, it would be an Afro-Brazilian deity who is joining both Santos and Elém or even just guiding the two Black female MCs, who have already formed their trio with another Black woman. Regardless of their intended formation, Visi00nárias posits that a Black feminist *aquilombamento* formed by Black women and ancestrality is critical to pursuing justice in their emergent *quilombos*.

In the eyes of Visi00nárias, finding justice is like traversing a delicate tightrope: one must walk intentionally, carefully, and with laser focus. Justice cannot result in punitive measures that push Black people closer to premature death, feeding Brazilian necropolitics. At the same time, it cannot permit Black men's harm, violence, and abuse against Black women to go unpunished, which would also sustain Brazilian necropolitics by doing the work of the anti-Black nation-state. So they provide a model of what a world would look like without police (e.g., Kaba, 2021). Instead of the state's repressive apparatus, Visi00nárias turns to Candomblé cosmologies and conjure deities to distribute justice. They summon Iansã, the undefeatable goddess who reigns over wind, lightning, and violent storms (personal communication, 2019). Along with other river goddesses, Iansã uses her mystical arts for retribution, protection against evil, militating against heteropatriarchal dominance, and erasing socioeconomic inequalities (Thompson, 1984). In the music video, Visi00nárias incorporates ancestrality into their Black feminist politics to hold men accountable for the machismo, misogyny, discrimination, and violence highlighted in the music video description.

Why would Visi00nárias need to exact justice against someone? Because the Black man caused harm to a Black woman. What harm the antagonist did is unclear in the music video. I want to read this absence as also having meaning, tied to why Santos and Elém are pursuing justice through Candomblé rather than the state. I want to take this reading further, emphasizing the importance of not depicting the harm. One, the music video moves away from what Hortense Spillers (1987) describes as "pornotroping," the pleasure a viewer gets by watching someone commit violent acts against Black women. Second, a person is not required to witness an act of transgression to know that someone has caused harm to a Black woman. I read it as a symbolic charge for viewers to believe survivors when they report gender violence. While white women can more easily secure legal or patriarchal protection, many Brazilians blame Black women for the violence against them, literally blaming the victim by attempting to show that they somehow deserved harm.

Because Visi00nárias does not involve the state, with the two women pursuing justice on their own, one might view them as partaking in vigilantism: they go after the antagonist themselves, punishing him as the Black woman squad sees fit. That type of reading reinforces stereotypes that Black people are miscreants who operate outside of law and order. I want to head in another direction: the duo challenges Brazilian justice norms that commit to redeeming white people and condemning Black people, who remain forever in a state of damnation. White redemption began with Man1, a Christian theological framework, where God saved (white) Christians from sin and granted them freedom on earth and eventually heaven. It later shifted to Man2, a political philosophy, where Western white Man has transcended his natural state and can be a member of political society (Mills, 1997; Wynter, 2003). If Man2 commits a crime, he can redeem himself in the judicial system, because society deems his life as redeemable and invests resources in saving him. In both religious and political redemption, Black people are not just undesirable: they are unredeemable, nonhuman, and antithetical to a political existence. Visi00nárias proposes a different political world where Black people are desirable, redeemable, and constitutive of modern political systems, just not in the nation-state. To do that, they put forward a Candomblé cosmology, in this case Iansã's reign over death and rebirth, as the guiding political philosophy for justice within an emergent *quilombo*'s sovereign practices. Iansã represents Black women's *legitimate* rage, like the goddess's ability to control storms, winds, and lightning, at the harm Black men cause. At the same time, the music video suggests that Black women can insert themselves into a different political system of sovereignty and life chances. Whereas the Brazilian nation-state exposes Black women to premature death (e.g., C. Smith, 2021) through its structural racism, sexism, and classism, the music video is a media text that represents an alternative, in which

Black women protect other Black women and create a different political standard against violators. Furthermore, the video also positions Black men in a different life and death from state necropolitics: in this justice system and this video, the antagonist makes it to the end alive, even if scared.

For Visi00nárias, Black people must conceptualize and practice justice differently in any emergent *quilombo*. Like many Black Bahian hip-hop artists, they do not believe that the Brazilian nation-state can be the political apparatus that delivers them justice. In the nation-state, justice is served in the name of whiteness while reproducing racism and sexism against Black people on different scales. Visi00nárias provides an answer to the complex questions around Black sovereignty in the Americas: if Black people assume control over their geographies and construct and enforce policies over life and death, then how do they avoid re-creating the same outcomes of Black premature death as the modern nation-state? The *quilombo* protects its inhabitants from necropolitics, but the Black female MCs show the *quilombo* must have its own codes to judge people *and* to have its own radical remedies. Casting Candomblé deities onto Black male perpetrators is a way to address harm without pushing Black men to premature death, focusing instead on the collective well-being.

Quilombo Sovereignties: Then and Now

Quilombos provide a different take on the political, challenging Western thought, the modern nation-state, and contemporary sovereignty. *Quilombos*, then and now, are alternative political systems in which Black people assert control over their bodies, spaces, social norms, and justice systems. Too often, Brazilian society reduces *quilombos* to simply cultural geographies, ignoring Black people's political desires to control their own land (Bowen, 2021) and to refuse Brazilian political systems that deny them citizenship and treat them as enemies (C. Smith, Davies, and Gomes, 2021). *Quilombos* have their origins as war encampments in Angola (B. Nascimento, 2021, p. 299), back when *kilombos* were politically struggling against other, rival camps in Africa. As Black people have retooled the *quilombo* throughout Brazil's history in response to white supremacy's various manifestations, their political uses of it have also evolved, offering alternative political goals, priorities, and systems. Beatriz Nascimento writes: "The quilombo is progress, it produces or reproduces itself in a moment of peace. A quilombo is at war when it *needs* to be at war. And it is also the retreat if the fight is not necessary. It is a wisdom, knowledge. The continuity of life, the act of creating a happy moment, even when the enemy is dangerous, and even when he wants to kill you" (2018f, p. 190; emphasis added). The *quilombo* is more than a war institution. Black people extend the *quilombo*'s political mission to create and maintain peace by fostering political thought for its inhabitants. Even if a *quilombo* is at war, its members are committed to resisting Brazil's insatiable desire for Black death by extending Black people's lives and providing a happy existence for them. For Black people, war for war's sake is unnecessary. They form *quilombos* because they are concerned with building a public good that revolves around Black people's survival and well-being.

Quilombo politics are not a matter of policy preference, voting rights, or juridical structure. They are not even about cultural or political representation. *Quilombo* politics unsettle the nation-state as a legitimate sovereign power that controls and governs Black people's social, cultural, and political worlds. The sovereign decides the exception: those actions, including violence, that can take place outside the legal norms, codes, and community (Schmitt, 2006). The sovereign also decides who it includes/excludes and who it can persecute outside the normative juridical structure and norms. State sovereignty must culturally produce a political enemy that threatens the national community. This enemy can be real or imagined, as long as its meaning is strong enough that the national community believes it could commit violence (Schmitt, 2007). For many minoritized peoples, the state of exception is not a temporary suspension of political norms; it is the norm (Benjamin, 2003; Weheliye, 2008). The state calls upon its ideological apparatuses to produce enemies, often in racialized terms (Althusser, 1998; Hall et al., 2013; Rana, 2011). The state's production of a political enemy is also the production of a national community. With the support of society, Brazilian colonial and national sovereign powers have constructed Black people as racial outsiders and political enemies (Campos, 2005; E. Carneiro, 1958), banding together disparate peoples in opposition to this enemy to forge a unified national identity and consciousness (M. A. Soares, 2012).

The music videos presented in this chapter show how Black Bahian hip-hop artists see poor and working-class Black people on the periphery as their fellow political citizens in a *quilombo* polity, not as noncitizens, nonbeings, and nonhumans. That is, *quilombo* theory sketches out a political theory that differs from its counterparts in the Western tradition. For Black people, the *quilombo* is how they politically responded to Brazil labeling them an "enemy within our doors" (E. Carneiro, 1958, p. 33) and the condition of captivity, an existence without political rights. Black people have endowed the *quilombo*, whether historical or emergent, with its own sovereign power, controlling and ruling their spaces with an agreed-upon set of laws, rules, norms, and penalties to organize Black life outside the polis.

Many Black Brazilians have long viewed *quilombo* sovereignty as equal to Western sovereign powers, and often those powers have treated *quilombos* as sovereign powers. Each time a new governor took over, the leader of Palmares would sue him for peace and pursue a treaty between the colony and the *quilombo* as a sovereign polity (Kent, 1965). When Portuguese and Dutch colonial forces sought to extinguish Palmares and other *quilombos*, they went to war against them as they would any sovereign polity. In 1671, a Brazilian governor described Palmares as just as much of a threat to "this State" as the Dutch colonial forces (E. Carneiro, 1958, p. 33). The Portuguese saw Palmares as a sovereign polity parallel to its own and other competing colonial administrations. In the latter half of the twentieth century, Black Brazilian activists argued for a *quilombo* state that would be "a free, just, egalitarian and sovereign state" (A. Nascimento, 1980, p. 168). Today, Black Bahian hip-hop artists still push for a *quilombo* state that politically protects Black people from the modern nation-state, nourishes its citizens, and delivers justice for them.

When necessary, the *kilombo* (the *quilombo*'s predecessor), the historical *quilombo*, and the emergent *quilombo* have violence at their disposal. However, this violence is used against those who threaten them, not internally. Throughout Brazil's history, *quilombo* communities have not pursued war; they protected themselves against those who have already waged war against them (E. Carneiro, 1958). Their violent actions have been made in pursuit of freedom, such as rebellions in early nineteenth-century Bahia (J. Reis, 1995). The fundamental relationship between Brazil, as both colony and nation, and Black people, especially fugitives, is that where the former depicts the latter as an enemy and uses violence against Black people in the name of sovereign power and authority, Black people have responded by removing themselves from this relationship, attempting to establish their own communities, like *quilombos*. However, Brazil amplified its derision and violence against these maroon communities, attacking its self-declared enemy in a foreign territory. This dynamic extends from the colonial era against historical *quilombos* (Kent, 1965) and now spills over into the contemporary situation as police forces attack the periphery in the name of Brazilian security and peace (Franco, 2014). These historical attacks on *quilombos* demonstrate how Western modernity continues a never-ending war between the white conqueror and the racialized conquered (Maldonado-Torres, 2007).

In this case, Black fugitives constructed a Black political sphere unlike its Western counterpart; radically, Black people forged bonds with one another, producing their own community to rely upon in the state of exception, whether the plantation or the periphery. While Black people create *quilombos* as a mechanism for legitimate war and violence, they do not follow the same friend/enemy dichotomy Carl Schmitt theorizes as central to Western political sovereignty. This is part of its evolution from the *kilombo* as a nomadic war encampment. Black fugitives form *quilombos* as a political institution, not as a war-waging institution. They are focused on producing Black life, not subjugating it to the power of death. Beatriz Nascimento has seen that *quilombo* political concerns revolve around protecting the Black collectivity, not conquering another group. The main political concern is not violence; it has always been to create peace, happiness, refuge, and care to prolong Black life and stave off Brazilian necropolitics.

Quilombos construct a different political model of freedom that is more expansive and leads to collective liberation. For Black people, freedom is not exclusionary or a zero-sum game. It is a never-ending reservoir, always able to expand. Around the African Diaspora, white people's freedom is exercised against Black people's unfreedom (Wilderson, 2010). *Quilombos* are an alternative: people do not see one person's freedom as tied to another person's unfreedom. As a political praxis, one views one's freedom as fulfilled through another person's obtaining freedom. Rather than biological reproduction and filiation, Black people build the *quilombo* by absorbing outsiders and envisioning them as potential community members, *not* as an internal enemy. In *kilombos* in Africa, Black people practiced this by conquering another African group, expanding their own community, and bringing the conquered into their own social and cultural systems. In historical *quilombos* in Brazil, leaders sent their warriors to raid plantations, free more enslaved Black people, and bring them back. Sometimes, a *quilombo* community indentured some newly arrived Black people for a period of time. However, an indentured Black person in a *quilombo* could secure freedom by freeing another Black person from slavery and bringing them back to the *quilombo*. The historical *quilombos* were not racially exclusionary; they also included Indigenous people and poor white people. The goal was always to continue expanding freedom for others.

Today, the Bahian hip-hop movement continues this legacy, creating emergent urban *quilombos* where Black people can band together politically against violent attacks, pull more people in, create alternative economies that emphasize care and nourishment, protect one another against premature death, and ensure that Black freedom is not plagued by misogynoir. They hail Brazil's racial outsiders as part of their community, inviting them to participate in their *quilombo* spaces and contributing to alternative social, cultural, and political systems. Each time a Black person joins an emergent *quilombo* in contemporary Brazil, Black people as a whole are inching closer and closer to the collapse of the nation-state and their eventual freedom. While hip-hop artists do not ignore the importance of Brazilian sovereignty, they call for their own modes of rule and power over their spaces, communities, and people to determine life and death, social norms, and the political punishment that can be doled out. None of us are free until all of us are free.

7 | Real Women

On February 2, 2020, I woke up early in the morning to trek down to the *festa de Iemanjá* (Festival of Iemanjá), a religious celebration that has taken place every February 2 since 1924 on the ocean in front of Rio Vermelho (Couto, 2010). More than one million other people were also making their way to Rio Vermelho to pay their respects to Iemanjá, the Candomblé deity of water, motherhood, beauty, and death. The blacktop of the Rua Oswaldo Cruz arterial street was almost invisible in the sea of white and blue clothing, Iemanjá's colors. After passing the military police checkpoint, we all arrived in the thick of the festival. Music flowed across the street and through us. Riding the wave of people to the ocean, I saw the countercurrent of people coming back, with water still dripping on them, cold lager beers in hand to kick-start the rest of the day's festivities. The flow of people did not miss a beat once it hit the ocean, where people were already knee-deep in the ocean. The crowd stretched along the beach for miles. Flowers stretched even farther, offerings from those who had already been there. Boats filled with flowers, mirrors, and perfumes floated out into the water to show Iemanjá how much she is loved, going to her rather than asking her to come near the shoreline. Like so many others, I got my knees wet, tossed my flower in the water, and spoke Iemanjá's salutation: "Odoyá."

I had one last stop to make: Iemanjá's house. I walked back up the beach, through waves splashing at my feet and the waves of people in the crowds, to get in line to enter the small structure (approximately one hundred square feet) with white and blue mosaic stones plastered across its exterior. After twenty minutes, I entered the small room, already crammed with other people spraying her dolls with perfume and laying their flowers on the floor. Both Catholic and Candomblé

Figure 7.1. The House of Iemanjá in the Rio Vermelho neighborhood; photo by the author (2022)

religious practitioners were here, reciting sacred passages for her. Before I passed out from the lack of oxygen, I escaped through the side door.

Built in 2008, this altar, like so many other Afro-Bahian processions and spaces, is sponsored by the state government. While Iemanjá is an Afro-Brazilian deity, the house represents her as a white woman in *her own house*. Outside, a white porcelain sculpture of Iemanjá stands on top of an approximately nine-foot-tall flowerpot. Inside were dozens of Iemanjá dolls, nearly all of them white with flowing straight brown hair and often with blue eyes. The audacity, you might say. I know I did. I counted quickly, estimating that there could have been no more than a half-dozen Black or even "brown" Iemanjá dolls inside the altar. The white-to-Black Iemanjá doll ratio was easily 10:1, a white sea with a few Black dolls peppered throughout. Yet the city is 80 percent Black and renowned for African cultural pride. In my mind, things were *not* adding up.

Candomblé is a highly flexible and malleable religio-cultural formation that draws on various African traditions, such as the Jejé, Nagó, and Bantu, and incorporates Indigenous traditions such as *caboclo* and

European influences. Like other religious holidays in Salvador, and in Brazil more broadly, the *festa de Iemanjá* celebrates and reveres Candomblé religious deities while publicly acknowledging their African-derived juxtaposition with Catholicism.[1] Such juxtaposition is the belief that one can find an *orixá* in another revered figure, based on their features and characteristics; under slavery, many Black people linked their deities with Catholic saints to clandestinely practice their religions and cultures.[2] Iemanjá is juxtaposed with the Virgin Mary. In African cosmologies, Iemanjá is not just the deity of beauty but also the supreme mother who protects all her children (Amado, 1984). Thus, pairing her with the mother of Jesus seems logical, as her significance in Candomblé mirrors the Virgin Mary's in Catholicism. Like Iansã, Iemanjá possesses biopolitical powers as a "militant witch" (Thompson, 1984, p. 74) over life and death, using her mystical powers to protect against evil and deliver retribution. She uses her mystical powers to protect her children, much in the same way that Catholics pray to the Virgin Mary for protection. In celebration, the *festa de Iemanjá* devotes an entire summer day to Bahia's most cherished Candomblé goddess.

There is a sociohistorical context for Candomblé's juxtaposition with Catholicism, often called Afro-Catholicism. Many people believe that once Black people were savagely ripped from Africa and inserted into the transatlantic economies of the Middle Passage, they forgot their African historical and cultural roots (e.g., Frazier, 1939). The colonial environment exacerbated this belief in the Americas, where the planter class savagely forced enslaved Black peoples to convert to their religions, such as Catholicism. They sought to totally detach Black people from Africa, but paradoxically would not welcome them in the Americas as human people either. They saw the conversion of enslaved Black people to another religion as a means of redeeming abject heathens morally while continuing to naturalize their subpersonhood. Black Brazilians turned to an Afro-Catholic juxtaposition between African-derived religions they brought with them through the Middle Passage with the colonizers' Catholic religion (Bastide, 1978).[3] For Candomblé practitioners, Catholicism is a mask that hides African deities and their meanings (Roca, 2005). They were less concerned with what the Catholic saints looked like than with what they did (Ogunnaike, 2020). When Black Brazilians prayed to the Virgin Mary, it would appear to the slave owners, priests, and colonialists that Black people had succumbed to Catholicism, its religious meanings, and its social ordering of the colonial slave society, but many Black Brazilians were actually praying to Iemanjá. Mary was a convenient signifier to hold Iemanjá's meanings and knowledges in Brazilian slave society.

Many African-derived religious practitioners are unbothered when white Catholic saints represent their gods. However, a society cannot separate religion from race and racism, especially since Europeans long used their religion to produce race and justify racism. For centuries, Black Brazilians have found ways to *aquilombar-se* in practicing their religions so that they could find, establish, and safeguard their humanity with dignity when Brazilian society has negated it (A. Nascimento, 1980). Historian Andrew Apter (1991) writes that Afro-Catholic juxtaposition is not always mapped onto discourses of racial and cultural resistance, such as oppressor/oppressed, elite/popular, white/Black.

For years, Black Brazilians have been resisting the racial whitening of Iemanjá by continuing to assign her mystical and powerful qualities to Black women, not white women, in their cultural representations. On July 3, 2020, Opanijé posted on Instagram an image of the House of Iemanjá with the caption: "Black skin, white clothes glowing in the day. My victory is imminent. It is not a utopia" (2020). São Paulo's Emicida raps in "Baiana" that for Black people, Iemanjá is Black, not white. Artists like Zeze Olukemí and Larissa Luz regularly post pictures on social media with the caption, "Iemanjá is a dark Black woman (preta)." Luz even made a song titled "Yemanjá é preta" (Iemanjá is Black) and released a music video for the song on February 2, 2021, in which she accompanies other Black women in Candomblé attire on a boat in the water, paying their respect to the *orixá*. Within a cultural studies framework of representation (e.g., Hall, 1997), these Black hip-hop artists' critique is nuanced. In Candomblé, Iemanjá's meanings, messages, and codes may be carried over to the Virgin Mary without tension. However, this is a transmission of cultural meanings in religion. For Black hip-hop artists and many others, the medium of Iemanjá is important; the form of Iemanjá fundamentally changes the content and subsequently the signifying chain of discourse. In Brazilian society the representation of Iemanjá as a white Virgin Mary is *also* a transmission of cultural meanings of gender and racial hierarchies in Brazilian society. When Black hip-hop artists argue that Iemanjá is a Black woman, they are disturbing how Afro-Catholic juxtaposition can fall under white feminine ideals of motherhood, beauty, and kinship that displace and dehumanize Black women in Brazilian society.

In this chapter, I shift the focus on the juxtaposition of Iemanjá away from Catholicism and white womanhood to the Bahian hip-hop movement and Black women. This is a trend among Bahian graffiti artists who represent Iemanjá as what local graffiti artist Sista Katia calls "real women," that is, ordinary Black women seen among Black Bahians every day. This shift incorporates the Candomblé belief that a deity can be juxtaposed with another revered figure with similar features and characteristics in a way that also intervenes with Brazilian society's existing gender and racial hierarchies regarding who is human and who is not. For them, ordinary Black women are revered figures. This repudiates the idea that Black people must conform their Blackness and their selves to white norms to be valuable and thus be recognized as human. Instead, Black people can assert their humanity with one another on their own terms. As I argue later in the chapter, representing Iemanjá as a Black woman is a way to assert a human subjectivity outside of Western, white "Man" (Wynter, 2003) and secure human dignity for Black women and by extension for all Black people. Their representations assert a subject who is often the antithesis of Man, while also providing a different human orientation for Black people at large.

I have organized this chapter in such a way that it gradually moves us from heteronormativity, patriarchy, bourgeois class status, and nationalism as pathways toward Black people's humanity. It refuses the logic of Eurocentric Judeo-Christian redemption (Black people are valuable and worthy only as they leave abject Blackness and venture toward a folkloric or mixed Blackness) and focuses on *aquilombamento* away from permissible Blacknesses. It shifts from an idea of the human in which we mold ourselves to the template of Man, participating instead in a broader human constellation with proliferating ideas of who can be human that gravitates around Black people's relationship to Black motherhood, what Michelle Wright (2004) calls a "point of orientation." This chapter does so by turning away and running, running fast, toward those who are dehumanized in the Western episteme because they do not conform to Man: the street vendor who must labor rather than enjoy Bahian culture; the large Black woman society sees as diseased, unhealthy, and undesirable; the Black mother that Brazilians stigmatize for her excessive number of children. Instead of replacing Man with Black mothers, this chapter argues for a variety of human subjects who are positioned in relation to Black motherhood as a dialogical method for negotiating difference.

Refusing the Whitening of Black People's Humanity

Candomblé iconography is susceptible to the logics of whitening as the religion comes out more publicly, shedding the Catholic cover and becoming more popular in Brazilian society and representations. Historians note that the whitening of Candomblé is related to colonialism, where colonizers defined who the human was in racial and religious terms. Helena Theodore argues that "there was a demonization of Black and Indigenous religions from what Europe saw as being civilized, human. In this context, the human is European, white, and has blue eyes" (Schreiber, 2020). This legacy lives on. The struggle over the racialization of Iemanjá is tied to the struggle between permissible (mixed and folkloric) and impermissible (abject and diasporic) Blacknesses. The anthropologist J. Lorand Matory (2005) notes that early twentieth-century white-*mestiço* Regionalist intellectuals such as Gilberto Freyre and Jorge Amado praised African-derived religions, making cultural syncretism and racial hybridity into pillars of a new Brazilian racial democracy mythos. For them, Northeastern Afro-Brazilian cultures were central to Brazilian culture. Many Brazilians view white Iemanjá as emblematic of a folkloric Blackness that is now available for all Brazilians without disrupting how they also dehumanize Black people according to the logics of abject Blackness.

In Brazil, one's ability to claim their humanity is inextricably connected to race, culture, and religion. Over the years, many Black people have attempted to assert their humanity on Eurocentric terms: Western civility, white cultural norms, and Christianity. There is a saying in Brazil, supposedly a compliment: "You're Black with a white soul," suggesting that despite Black people's racial appearance, they have the internal attributes of a white person and thus a closer proximity to humanity than most Black people. Many Brazilians contribute to a racial orientation that upholds whiteness as an ideal of humanism and Blackness as its negation, something from which to distance oneself. With the help of white and white-*mestiça/o* Brazilians, Black Brazilians participate in this white human ideal through "whitening," adopting Eurocentric cultural norms, distancing themselves from the Black masses, inserting themselves into white social circles, dating and marrying someone lighter than themselves, and (they hope) producing children lighter than themselves (Pierson, 1944; Skidmore, 1993). Many Brazilian elites hoped that if Black people valorized whiteness enough, they would keep diluting African ancestry and culture in the national population, eventually eradicating Black people altogether.

If Man is the "overrepresentation" of the human (Wynter, 2003), then ordinary Black Bahian women are seemingly the antithesis to the human, cutting across geography, race, gender, class, sexuality, and religion. For me, the whitening of Iemanjá at her own festival brings up the following questions: Why is an Afro-Brazilian deity still represented as a white woman? How does this whitening also tie into hegemonic constructions of who constitutes (and does not constitute) the human? And what are other racial, gender, and religious grounds for representing the human that affirm rather than negate Black women's humanity?

Candomblé has been central to marginalized Black Bahians' ability to create alternative spaces of Blackness. Rachel E. Harding (2000) argues that Candomblé cultivates "an alternative meaning of Africanness, an alternative identity of blackness" (p. xvi). The religion challenges the stigma of Blackness as abject and moves to a diasporic Blackness where Black people can *aquilombar-se* and assert their own humanity. Beatriz Nascimento identifies the Candomblé *terreiro* as a *quilombo* reterroritialization (C. Smith, 2016c). In the colonial era, many Black people created *quilombos* precisely to practice their African-derived religious rituals (J. Reis, 1995; C. Smith, 2016a), even if just for a few short days, otherwise known as *petit marronage* (Price, 1996). In these *quilombos*, Black people also asserted their humanity in multiple ways that extend outside of religion and socially deviate from Man as the defining mold of the human.

Throughout the Americas, Black cultural traditions blur the line between the sacred and the secular. Religious epistemologies overflow into our everyday lives and interpretive frameworks. The shift from juxtaposing Iemanjá with the Virgin Mary to juxtaposing her with ordinary Black women is also important because it disrupts Brazil's affinity for *exceptional* Black people, those who are exceptions to abject Blackness. Focusing on real women means an emphasis on the quotidian and the everyday rather than the exceptional and unique that Brazil appropriates into its image as a racial democracy. This shift aligns with Abdias Nascimento's visual philosophies in his own paintings of Candomblé: "My *orixás* are living and vivifying beings that inhabit Africa, Brazil and all the Americas, right now. They are part of our daily secular life, a legacy of history and the ancestors. That is why I have named them after living people: they defend our heroes and martyrs and are committed to our people's search for identity, freedom, and dignity" (A. Nascimento, 2014, p. 20). Nascimento's philosophy of visual cultures is that *orixás* do not need to be affixed to Catholic saints. They can be represented through other figures, and not even exceptional ones, just "ordinary" living people.

Graffiti is one of hip-hop's defining elements, a visual realm that complements rapping's lyrical, DJing's sonic, and breakdancing's kinesthetic realms. In the Americas, hip-hop communities value graffiti as a medium that through which they can express their antiracist and feminist perspectives. Like others, I situate graffiti within the larger field of visual cultural studies, interrogating how the visual is central to culture, representation, and meaning-making processes. I draw on "critical visual methodology" (D. G. Rose, 2012), which tackles not only what an image is but also how to look at an image and the context in which it appears. The visual often takes a back seat to the sonic, the lyrical, and the performative within hip-hop cultures. I am not looking to find the true meaning of these representations, but rather to "trace the play of power" (Fiske, 2010, p. 36) in how graffiti artists represent Iemanjá with "real women," ordinary Black women in Salvador, as a weapon against controlling images that depict Black women as bad mothers, hypersexual *mulatas*, African queens, or domestic servants. In each case, Brazilians use these controlling images against Black women to deny them their humanity as well as the ability to self-narrate their own histories (hooks, 1989). When graffiti artists represent the deity with ordinary Black women, I argue that they assert Black women's humanity through motherhood (Wright, 2004), a dialogical orientation that puts in place an alternative human model that circulates through an emergent *quilombo*'s social, cultural, and political systems. Whereas Brazilian society must define one's citizenship and humanity against Black women, the emergent *quilombo*, I argue, shows how one's humanity starts and revolves around the relationship to Black motherhood as the orientation for Black life.

Black Mothers versus Bahian Racial Capitalism

Many in Salvador bemoan the fact that that the city officials, cultural groups, and agencies represent the city through the lens of Jorge Amado (1912–2001), a prolific white Bahian author. They refer to this as the "Amadofication" of Salvador. Amado published his first book, *O país do*

Carnaval (The country of Carnival), in 1931, and his thirty-sixth and final book, *A hora da guerra* (The hour of war), was released posthumously in 2008. Four themes recur throughout the devout Communist's novels: Black women's hypersexuality, a romanticized proletariat, interracial mixture, and religious syncretism. In his books about Bahia, Amado depicted Black residents as happy and hopeful against the backdrop of Salvador's deteriorating economy and their dismal socioeconomic conditions. He was writing at a time when Brazil was trying to articulate its national identity as distinct from the Portuguese, its former colonizer, and the United States, a country with a similar history of colonialism and slavery (Skidmore, 1993). Bahia had lost its political and economic influence to Southern states such as Rio de Janeiro and São Paulo in the nineteenth century; Amado was one of several Regionalist intellectuals who asserted that Bahia was the Brazilian cultural center and that its contribution was the most important in the Brazilian nation. A throughline in his work is that Black people might be poor, but they are happy because they routinely practice their African cultures, are sexually liberated, and always party with alcohol. Though he was not a social scientist, his literary representations implied that Salvador had no ethnic or class conflicts; here opposites joined together for the greater Brazilian public good. From 1961 until his death in 2001, Amado was the twenty-third chair of the Brazilian Academy of Letters, a very prestigious literary society; he was therefore able to exert influence on Brazilian national identity and culture beyond his popular novels. One reason why Amado's work is so popular is that it fits under the larger myth of the Brazilian racial democracy: first, that Bahia is a national model of harmonious race relations, and second, that Black Brazilians contribute (sexual) passion, culture, and a desire to party to a festive and optimistic *mestiço* nation that can overcome racialized structural inequalities.

Local graffiti artist Calongos disrupts the "Amadofication" of Salvador in his portrayal of Iemanjá in the Dois de Julho neighborhood. I first saw the mural in 2014 and was drawn to its vibrant colors and alternative view of Salvador's celebrated cultures. My friends told me that he was a very prolific graffiti artist who does work all over the city. Calongos represents Iemanjá against the backdrop of racial exploitation and capitalist accumulation. Unlike in Amado's Bahia, the Black Bahians portrayed by Calongos are not part of a happy-go-lucky proletariat, but rather are exasperated laborers who suffer under what Cedric Robinson aptly calls "racial capitalism" (2021), the theory that both

Figure 7.2. Calongos's mural of Iemanjá; photo by the author (2013)

capitalism and racism emerge from the old order and are integral to a modern world system that is reliant on slavery, violence, imperialism, and genocide (R. D. G. Kelley, 2017). Until its eventual fading (personally, I cannot remember it lasting past 2018), the mural was highly visible to thousands of Black Bahians as they went about their everyday lives: on their way to work, while taking the bus, and during other routines in their working-class/lower middle-class neighborhood. Sitting just below the Pelourinho area, the mural was close to Salvador's iconic space of celebration, but it also felt worlds apart.

Often, hegemonic representations portray Salvador as brimming with African cultural festivities, practices, and rituals, as if no one is ever working or these festivals are not in fact work sites. The Black male youths in the mural are a representation of Black men's position within racial capitalism today, rather than in folkloric geographies of African culturalism. One can read this thematic in Calongos's mural itself: it centers on Iemanjá sitting with a Black male youth in front of his beverage cart while a Carnivalesque party takes place in the background. Structurally, many Black men must work in the informal economy as dockworkers, fishermen in the surrounding bay waters, and selling snacks and goods on the city buses and on the street. Street vendors sell not just coffee but also soda, coconut water, beer, liquor, street meats, souvenirs, peanuts, gum, candy, and other inexpensive items; their incomes fluctuate depending on which days they work, how long they work, which festivals they can work, and what location they can secure. Regardless, margins are consistently low. Many Black street vendors use festivals such as Carnival or *festa de Iemanjá* to boost their wages, as they are able to charge higher prices than normal and also profit from the higher traffic of people who are surely drinking more than usual. Consider the following prices at the 2019 Carnival. Beer vendors sell little nine-ounce beer cans for three reals, or two for five reals.[4] They can buy them wholesale from distributors with a bulk discount of fifteen beers for R$24.90, or R$1.66 each. Then the vendors have to pay for transportation, storage, the cart, meals, ice, and cups, all of which cut into the margins. Society devalues these young Black men so much that their labor, as strenuous as it is, generates very little income.

The street vendor is just as important in supporting "the Bahian culture industry" as the cultural performers on stage (Henson, 2020), yet people who venture to Salvador to consume and experience folkloric Blackness ignore the economic characteristics of such an industry and have poor Black people serve them on the streets.[5] As they focus on the cultures on stage, participants can feel safe in the belief that Salvador is a city of African culturalisms and ignore capitalism's role in perpetuating racial inequalities, even as they pay absurdly low prices for their food and drink from mostly Black street vendors. Focused on their own pleasure, they do not see that some people are there to work, exchanging their labor for an informal and unsteady wage under undesirable conditions. They are operating on bourgeois beliefs that everyone has time off from their jobs to participate in festivals. But Calongos shifts the visual focus from the audience for such festivities to the informal workers, namely Black male youths. The street vendor might be on the margins of the event and of society, but he is at the center of this art.

Behind the worker we see scores of folks dancing joyously. The sun scorches the earth with its red, yellow, and orange rays, engulfing them. The laborer is in stark contrast to them, and to the happy and convivial Black people the state and literary elites like Amado use in their representations of Salvador. The laborer is visibly exhausted, evident by the sweat and exasperation on his face. He is far from the happy proletarian worker in an Amado novel. The mural invites the viewer to re-see Black Bahian people in contrast to dominant representations of Bahia; ethnic and class conflicts arise between those who can gleefully play in Bahian cultures and those who must work in a highly stratified society.

The mural also foregrounds issues of gender and sexuality as they cut across race and class. In the background, people are dancing in heterosexual pairings, as couples, socializing with their romantic interests, either just for a night or for years to come. This leaves the Black street vendor out of the local libidinal economy. Some Brazilians desire certain types of Black men, like the *negão*, but they exclude poor and working-class Black men from participating in this heteronormative sphere. Even though the street vendor may be heterosexual, he cannot take the opportunity to capitalize on this moment and go as a participant, mingling with potential love interests. He has to engage as an informal laborer, displaced from care and love. He is not cared for because he is not entitled to social benefits like holidays from his employer or concern for his own well-being. He is not loved because there is an economic threshold that Black men must cross to be desirable: they must be patriarchs who protect and provide for their family and community.

In Calongos's mural, the placement of Iemanjá next to the street vendor is a symbolic gesture to reconnect her to the Black masses, anchoring her with the socioeconomic and political realities of their racial conditions. In contrast, the Bahian culture industry revolves around folkloric Blackness so much that it socioeconomically excludes the very community that brought Iemanjá meaning and prominence in Brazil. She has no cultural specificity to the Black masses and their classed, gendered, and spatial specificities. A white Eurocentric consciousness has displaced her from Black people. Instead, the state and society represent her in such a way that she is a ubiquitous icon, available for the whims and desires of people with enough discretionary income to participate in the Bahian culture industry as a festival-goer rather than a laborer.

In the *festa de Iemanjá*, most people venture to the water to visit Iemanjá; they go to her. In the mural, it is the opposite; she ventures from her watery realm and onto the earth to find and protect Black male youths. Iemanjá is attending to the Black male youth, who is clearly suffering in this tropical environment: she gives him relief from the hot and humid air with a watery breeze flowing from her aqua blue body, cooling and hydrating him. She protects him from his harsh working environment. Her fan is both a symbol of beauty *and* "an emblem embodying the coolness and command of these spirits of the water" (Thompson, 1984, p. 72). But instead of her fan, she uses her own body to command the winds for the Black male street vendor, bringing him peace and calm as she does for all her devotees (Thompson, 1984).

I want to read Iemanjá's placement as a visual representation to illuminate how Black people build systems to protect and care for one another. Iemanjá is giving the street vendor life, pushing back on the clock of premature death that disproportionately afflicts Black male youths in Salvador. She refuses to let the street vendor die prematurely, putting aside her own desires for the greater good. Calongos's representation disturbs the biopolitical logics that incessantly push Black people toward premature death, slowly and/or abruptly. Premature death is not confined to immediate and violent styles of death. It also encompasses the various socioeconomic inequalities that strain Black people, stealing extra time from them every single day so that they die before they should. In this mural, Iemanjá pushes back on the clock of death, hoping to keep the street vendor alive as long as she can.

The mural also disturbs the heteropatriarchal social bonds between Black men and women. In Brazil, men usually determine Black women's worth, and they severely devalue Black women to maintain their authoritative and dominant masculinity. The mural represents an alternative: Black women are the ones who determine value, focusing their energy on those who are vulnerable and pushed to the brink. Iemanjá is not concerned with the folks dancing in the background. They are clearly okay. They are in fact more than okay. However, the Black street vendor is struggling, appearing to the viewer as weak from the sun, vulnerable to exhaustion and heat stroke. As she comes to save him, Iemanjá assumes a protective role over him, wielding a queer sensibility. Drawing from local mythologies of Iemanjá, we can read her relationship to the street vendor as both romantic and maternal, evoking alternative social and cultural systems of relating and connecting. In his book *Sea of Death*, Jorge Amado describes many Black Bahians' queer relationship to Iemanjá that interrupts heteronormativity and gestures toward a different system of human relations. The book follows Guma, a young Black Bahian who was born out of wedlock, grew up with his uncle, and eventually became a sailor. He falls in love with and marries Livia, a well-to-do Bahian woman, but his true love is Iemanjá, who lets him roam free on the sea. Amado describes Guma's queer relationship to Iemanjá:

> [Guma] never had a mother. And when he found her it was to lose her immediately, desiring her without loving her, almost hating her. There is only one woman who can be wife and mother at the same time: That

is Iemanjá, and that's why she is loved so much by the men of the waterfront. In order to love Iemanjá, who is mother and wife, you have to die. Many times Guma thought of jumping off his sloop on a stormy day. Then he could travel with [Iemanjá], he could love mother and wife. (1984, p. 32)

Iemanjá is not a human being; she is an Afro-Brazilian deity. The "mother and wife" combination does not advocate for incest. I argue that it opens other possibilities of being with and through Black womanhood. This mother-love combination thus merits further exploration, especially regarding the cultural messages about Black women that we can decode from Calongos's mural.

Reading Iemanjá as a Black woman who functions politically as a lover and mother illuminates the mural as a visual representation of an emergent *quilombo* that refuses acceptable Blacknesses in Bahian society, like those dancing under the sun, and takes flight to commune with the Black underclass in safeguarding one another's lives. What if we were to see Iemanjá as both mother and lover to the street vendor in Calongos's mural as Amado sees her in relation to Guma, the dockworker in the 1930s? This does not mean that they are mirror images of each other. Instead, we can take the mother-lover trope and put it within a different discourse regarding Black women. As a lover, Iemanjá summons men to join her in the depths of the sea; they literally jump to their deaths to be with her. Unbothered by monogamy, she has dozens of lovers in the sea without judgment from society. Each Black man who joins her knows that he is not the sole recipient of her love but is one of a vast number of recipients, forming a collective of love. Not only is she capable of these queer transgressions, but her profound love and affection challenges how life and death are constituted in Brazilian modernity, particularly for the poor Black man whose life is always already in precarity.

In Bahian popular culture, Iemanjá is the eminent mother, having an unlimited number of children. Again, she dismantles a hallmark of heteronormativity: children biologically produced by a married heterosexual couple, forming the standard kinship unit. Most importantly, a Black woman, Iemanjá, is directing these queer modes of Black love and kinship, an alternative social world according to her vision. She represents a Black matriarchy that demands individuals, even Black men, submit themselves to the collective in the name of the greater good. In this queer collective, Black people find cascading forces of love, kinship, and affinity that trouble the heteropatriarchal power structure. How does one assert patriarchy over lover and children when one is the child of your lover and the lover of your mother? How does one assert patriarchy when you are not the only one but rather one of many? One cannot; they insert themselves into a matriarchal tradition that opens possibilities, rather than foreclosing them.

We can also explore the way Calongos's mural undermines how Brazilian society ruthlessly stigmatizes Black women. Depicting Black women as hypersexual *mulatas* or *piriguetes*, the Brazilian state and its white-*mestiço* citizens objectify and/or punish their sexuality for what they perceive to be a deviation from Eurocentric norms. In this mural, Black women's hypersexuality is not attached to deviance but is a part of their divinity, as Iemanjá cares for multiple men in her community as a lover. They are free from the shackles of heteropatriarchal power, which would make women property that men should own and rule over through patriarchal law. Unshackled, Black women can love and care for Black men as a collective effort, not as property to be owned.

This extends to Black motherhood. In Brazil, Black women are social activists as mothers and advocate for social justice as mothers (e.g., C. Smith, 2016b). For them, motherhood is a political identity. For example, São Paulo rapper Emicida's music video "Chapa" features the Mães de Maio (Mothers of May), a political organization of mothers who called for justice after the police killed 493 Black, Afroindigenous, and poor men, their sons included. Just as Iemanjá is a political lover in the mural, she, like Black women, is also a political mother, working to save her sons from premature death. Brazilian society looks at Black mothers as bad mothers unequipped for motherhood. In the Americas, societies expect Black women to do "motherING," like being an *amanante*, a nanny who breastfeeds white women's children, but rarely grants them "motherHOOD," the social rights and privileges granted to mothers as well as the time and other resources necessary for mothering their own children (Gumbs, 2016a). Brazilian society politicizes Black motherhood. Under slavery, Brazil did not see Black women as potential or actual mothers, just biological producers of more chattel property that white slave owners could own, sell, and buy. These logics continued from slave society to the present (Spillers, 1987). Black women can perform motherly tasks for their children and others, like giving birth, breastfeeding, and supervising children, but society does not view or treat them with the respect shown to white middle-class women or grant them the time and other resources necessary for motherhood (M. A. Soares, 2012). We can read the relationship between Iemanjá and the street vendor in the mural as an extension of Black political motherhood, as a point of divinity, not derision.

At the same time, Calongos's rendition of Iemanjá as a visual signifier that can potentially recode Black feminine scripts is limited: Black women's value still comes from their relationship to men, namely their partners and sons. One cannot ignore Iemanjá as the pinnacle of motherhood and desirability, but there must be more to reading Black women and realizing their human value by focusing on them and not just what they do for Black men.

"Gordivas": The Real Women of Bahia

During one of the last nights of my summer 2015 research trip to Salvador, I returned to the Kilombo Bar. There, I noticed a new mural of Iemanjá by Sista Katia in the downstairs patio area, greeting patrons as they entered. The new mural was on the back concrete wall directly across from the new side entrance, where the patrons would notice it as they entered and paid the nightly cover of R$10. (The club owners moved the entrance from in front of the building, which faced the ocean, to around the corner on a side street. The side entrance seemed to promote more socialization on the back patio, while the front entrance seemed to move patrons immediately upstairs.) Many patrons paused before the mural in awe, taking in its beauty before they went upstairs to the bar and dance floor. Throughout the night, many folks would come back down to relax and to look at the mural again.

In his mural, Calongos depicts Iemanjá as a Black woman who is both mother and lover to the men of the Black underclass. In contrast, Sista Katia depicts Iemanjá as an ordinary Black woman among the real divas in Brazilian society, not the hypersexual *mulata*. Sista Katia is in her mid-thirties and from São Paulo; she moved to Salvador almost twenty years ago. Even though she is *paulistana* by birth, she firmly considers herself Bahian. While Sista Katia is also white, she is a reminder that some white people historically participated in *quilombos* and supported Black alternative social and cultural systems (B. Nascimento, 2018f). Some white graffiti artists, activists, and community organizers labor, like Sista Katia, alongside Black people to undermine systems of white supremacy, anti-Blackness, heteronormativity, patriarchy, fatphobia, and racial capitalism. Sista Katia is invested in visual representations of

Figure 7.3. Sista Katia's mural of Iemanjá; photo used with permission of the artist (2017)

"real women," the Black women Bahians see every day, especially representations that valorize Black women of all body sizes. She herself depicts these real women as Iemanjá, representing them as what she calls a "gordiva," meaning "fat diva." In popular culture, a diva is a famous celebrity, usually a singer, who is extravagant in appearance and gesture, and who can be perhaps arrogant and difficult to satisfy. Etymologically, the word derives from the Latin word for a goddess. In her visual work, Sista Katia elevates ordinary Black women to the level of celebrity and divinity to interrupt prevalent controlling images that extol the *mulata* as popular and divine while stigmatizing and demonizing other Black women. Sista Katia represents Iemanjá as darker in her skin tone *and* as voluptuous. The selection of dark skin is not unusual considering that Salvador is a predominantly Black city and has more African-descended Brazilians than elsewhere in the nation. However, it is a stark contrast to how Iemanjá is usually portrayed by the state and even in souvenir trinkets such as postcards. Iemanjá is not white as she usually is in visual representations sanctioned or created by the state and Bahian society. This ties Iemanjá's qualities of beauty, motherhood, and militancy to Black women.

Sista Katia's representation of Iemanjá refuses pervasive idealized representations of womanhood and embodied beauty standards: she is shown overflowing in beautiful fleshy excess, uncontained by

Eurocentric beauty standards. Her curvaceous arm folds and creases at the elbow, and her forearm is at least the same size as the upper arm, if not more rotund. At the end of her arm, her hand is ever so slightly signaling a body that is glowing in its abundance of beauty. Her flesh does not *signify* surplus for others to value, take pleasure in, or extract violence from; it is embedded in her body, for her, and for other Black women. The Candomblé goddess of the sea also has all her usual markers of beauty and vanity: the long, wavy blue hair, bright lipstick, eyeliner, eye shadow, a beauty mole, nail polish, and an array of maritime-based jewelry such as seashell earrings and water drops (which also signify perfume). She is adorned with a constellation of beauty, rendering her and other ordinary Black women beautiful and desirable.

Around the globe, societies use a Eurocentric aesthetic sensibility to portray Black women as ugly, relying on a pervasive fatphobia that signifies Black women's bodies as diseased, filthy, and contaminated (Strings, 2019). This sensibility idealizes a slender and toned body. Even Black diasporic beauty standards heavily privilege Black women who are what T. Denean Sharpley-Whiting calls "ascriptive mulattas" (2008), African-descended women whose racially "in-between" beauty is transcendent, conveying ideal beauty, hypersexuality, and sexual accessibility (p. 27). This occurs in Brazil: society values women with European features combined with other African physical attributes. For example, the *mulata* has a slender body frame, including arms, stomach, and ankles, like the Eurocentric ideal; some accentuated erogenous physical features, like the buttocks, hips, and breasts, that signify Blackness; and other physical features that, while not European, are much less African, like curly hair instead of kinky hair, a narrower nose, and lighter skin tone. Brazilian society maps desirable attributes of Black femininity onto an otherwise European body frame, accenting some features and diminishing others. This is similar to Kobena Mercer's notion of racial "cropping" (1999), when a photographer emphasizes certain Black bodily attributes, like the phallus or muscles, in their photography. Racial cropping marks only certain parts of Black people as beautiful and discards the rest, a practice of dehumanizing fetishization. In the Brazilian example, the desire is to take the racially cropped-off parts of Black people's bodies and paste them onto European bodies. When people participate in racial cropping of Black people's bodies, they are denying a full and holistic embrace of Black people's Black embodied beauty.[6]

Sista Katia's representation of "gordiva" signifies that Black women can be whole, beautiful, and divine without racial cropping. In my 2014 interview with her, Sista Katia discussed how she uses Iemanjá to intervene in Black women's dehumanization. She wanted to represent alternative possibilities of Black womanhood, including sexuality and motherhood. She told me:

> This graffiti, I make these characters large because in graffiti, the girls that have been painting in Brazil always create the same thematic: feminine figures with white characteristics. They're little white female characters, all cute and cuddly, with blue eyes, with red hair, blonde hair. They don't really have the aesthetic of real women [that you see] day-to-day. The aesthetics of "the doll" has always gravitated more towards Barbie than toward the crazy Black woman [*nega maluca*], you know?

I want to situate the *nega maluca* within a broader social context and then consider its importance within the field of visual representation. The *nega maluca* is a derogatory stereotype of Black women. In Portuguese, *maluca* is the feminine adjective for crazy as well as lunatic, weird, wild, and mad. The word *nega* is, like the word *nego* for *negro*, a shortened colloquial expression for *negra*, or Black woman. The *nega maluca*, or crazy Black woman, is a sambo-like figure that Brazilian society uses to pathologize Black women and stigmatize their bodies as ugly and undesirable. Many white actors use blackface to perform as the *nega maluca* and fortify existing deprecating stereotypes of Black women.[7] In her visual politics, Sista Katia takes the *nega maluca* figure, disrupts its dominant meanings, and links her to a radical Black beauty. She upsets existing racial and gender hierarchies that compound one another by working through instead of avoiding controlling images.

Sista Katia told me that her goal is to shift ideal beauty away from the Barbie and to the *nega maluca*, disrupting the way people visually read Black women. This insight reveals much about Brazil's racialized and gendered notions of beauty, human hierarchies, and their social consequences. Her use of the "Barbie" is a shorthand for ideals of white femininity. White women can more easily claim their humanity, as people who count, on racial grounds even if they do not entirely conform to Man on gendered grounds. In Brazil, people view white women as more than ideal beauty subjects; they are also ideal wives and mothers. They may view Black women as hypersexual, sexually desirable, and sexually available, but they do not see them as beautiful or as potential partners or mothers. In relation to one another, white women have asserted their womanhood and claim to humanism by negating Black women's womanhood and humanity on racial and gender grounds. There is also a class element: white women are more acceptable in middle- and upper-class communities, while people assume that Black women are poor and "the help." White women also participate in representing Black women as *nega malucas*, which fortifies white women's position as the apex of feminine ideals of beauty, partnership, and motherhood.

Sista Katia's graffiti murals represent Black women with cultural meanings that assert their womanhood and their humanity without conforming to white ideals of femininity and humanism. Rather than use the iconography of a more palpable Eurocentric body closer to Man, Sista Katia anchors Iemanjá in the images of the "real women" that Black people see every day on the margins, in the lower class. They are dark in skin tone. They are mothers. And they are fat. These are not the women Brazilian society represents as beautiful in media, popular culture, and other visual representations. They are not even the *mulata* who circulates in Brazilian public spaces. Instead of "idealized" women in the middle and upper classes, these are "real women" that ordinary Black Brazilians see in their poor and working-class communities. They are shop workers, teachers, food vendors, and neighbors. Juxtaposing Iemanjá and ordinary Black women attaches the former's qualities of femininity, motherhood, and beauty to the latter instead of to white women, which all too often happens in Brazil.

There is another reason that Sista Katia's representation of Iemanjá as the *nega maluca* merits attention. More than refusing racist and sexist tropes of Black womanhood, Sista Katia challenges the way society sees Black women as "crazy," signifying an inherent condition of being unable to possess reason, and instead reclaims them from their supposed irrationality to unsettle two interrelated signifying processes that overrepresent Man as the human. Sylvia Wynter outlines two variations of Man, what she calls Man1, a religious figure, and Man2, a political figure. During earlier periods of colonialism, slavery, and genocide, European Christian colonizers deemed non-Europeans subhuman beasts if they rejected Christianity, because only Christians are able to transcend their state of nature and be humans (Wynter, 1989, 1994, 2003; Wynter and McKittrick, 2015). This distinction was the basis of the earliest "racial contract" (Mills, 1997), a sociopolitical and moral agreement among white people, who designate themselves as fully human and categorize nonwhite people as morally inferior with second-class citizenship. In the era of Man1, European colonizers portrayed non-Christian Black people as irrational, linking reason to race as some sort of biological fact. This logic can be mapped onto Eurocentric beauty standards where people valorize the Barbie over the *nega maluca*. To recognize Black women as beautiful is to recognize their humanity, an aesthetic, moral, and political impossibility that travels across the boundaries of reason and into the territory of craziness. To recognize Black women as beautiful and thus human is also to call the viewer crazy, just like the *nega maluca*. Sista Katia's mural disrupts Man1 as a moral and ruling figure with his own structures of reason that everyone else should aspire to.

Eurocentric beauty standards are prevalent in global, Brazilian, and Black diasporic communities, including the Bahian hip-hop movement and the larger Brazilian hip-hop community. Sista Katia's representation of Iemanjá as a "real woman" challenges the Bahian hip-hop movement's own particular misogynoir that stigmatizes and pathologizes Black women. She specifically points out that it is graffiti artists who are reproducing Eurocentric beauty standards, depicting white women as the apex of femininity just like Bahian society overrepresents Iemanjá as a white woman. Many Black women and even white women in the Bahian hip-hop movement express frustration that Black men preach but do not practice racial solidarity as well as criticize but do not reject the Brazilian racial democracy ideology, especially the objectification of Black women and their displacement from Black communities.[8] That is, many Black men date only or mostly white women. Others will date Black women only if they are very fair-skinned. They marginalize Black women in the romantic economy. One result is that Salvador has the highest rate of unpartnered Black women in the country (Pacheco, 2013).[9] Many Black women say they are not against interracial dating but add that they see how many of these Black men in the hip-hop movement valorize white women and otherwise commit to misogynoir against Black women, as Visi00nárias pointed out in the previous chapter.[10]

Sista Katia does not simply replace the *mulata* by swapping out one image of Black women for another. No. Twinning Iemanjá with ordinary Black women or "real women" means creating a racial icon that rewrites the genre of the human from the vantage point of those pushed furthest away. Similar to a diva, an icon is "a term of divination ... rooted in a desire to represent, and thus produce, God" (Fleetwood,

2015, p. 5). In this context, ordinary Black women do not need to be spectacular like the *mulata* for Brazilians to consider them beautiful. More importantly, Black women do not need to be non-Black for others to perceive them as divine, iconic, and venerated. Putting this mural in a space such as the Kilombo Bar means that socially excluded Black people will see Iemanjá represented as not only a darker and fatter Black woman but also a woman figure who is ubiquitous in their own lives as well.

Radical Modes of Black Motherhood

Here I focus on how Taís Ribeiro (better known by her graffiti name, Tata) depicted Iemanjá at Nossa–Casa Colaborativa, a now defunct artist workspace in Rio Vermelho, a once bohemian artist neighborhood that is rapidly gentrifying. In many ways, her Iemanjá is very similar to Sista Katia's: darker in tone and more voluptuous in body shape than dominant images. Like Sista Katia, Tata challenges how other artists represent Iemanjá as a slender white woman, a choice that establishes whiteness as a race-gender fulcrum of the libidinal economy and human value.

Visually, Tata's Iemanjá also differs from Sista Katia's, though it does not critique her work. Whereas Sista Kati's Iemanjá is a "gordiva" and chubby all over, Tata's is somewhere between a "gordiva" and thin. Her Iemanjá has a slight frame, evidenced by her shoulders, slender arms, upper torso, and small waist; her lower torso is beautifully adorned with panniculus, or belly fat, that gently lies on top of each hip and also rolls over her stomach. Iemanjá's fleshiness is also shown in her lower hips and her thighs, which are glittering from mermaid scales like aqua-green sequins, as if she is ready for a night of dancing under the moonlight. Her forearms cover her bare breasts, denying the viewer her nipples, and her hands slide underneath her left ear to gently cradle her head, finding peace. With her eyes closed, she opens a smile so wide, so white, so beautiful that her beauty is undeniable and irresistible. The mural visually offers the Black body as a site of refuge, its own *quilombo* that protects Black women from optical regimes of power and objectification.

In this last graffiti mural I analyze, I want to read Tata's representation of Iemanjá as a Black woman as a point of divine orientation that articulates a different genre of the human, which emergent *quilombos*

Figure 7.4. Tata's mural of Iemanjá; photo used with permission of the artist (2016)

can radically organize themselves around. Here, Iemanjá is a mother who establishes Black people's humanity in a dialogical fashion, a process where Black people can recognize their self as human with other Black people as also human by working through instead of negating their differences with one another. This counters a familiar dynamic in which Black women experience a double negation of their humanity: as Black and as women. Rather than beginning with a human subject, namely Man, whose existence depends on the negation of his raced and gendered other, Tata's representation of Iemanjá as a Black mother is the point from which Black people imagine and practice another humanity with and through one another.

Rather than tying Iemanjá to existing tropes of Black womanhood, Tata orients Black womanhood to Iemanjá's existing discourses, which creates a circularity between Iemanjá and Black mothers, as opposed to Black women as mothers/lovers and Black men as sons/lovers. This charts a different way of seeing Black mothers through Iemanjá, representing her as embodying what Judith Hoch-Smith calls a "radical

Yoruba female sexuality" that uses witchcraft for "mystic retribution and protection against all evil," that is, a militant opposition against male dominance, class differences, unequal resource distribution, and Western technocratic structures (Thompson, 1984, pp. 74–75). Rather than deriding Black mothers as bad, as sites of punishment and responsible for producing the enemies of the Brazilian state, we can reorient to a different society where Black women are on the front lines against Brazil's inherent anti-Black racism, sexism, and classism. It means that an emergent *quilombo* must start with Black mothers, not a Black patriarchal leader like Zumbí, as the point of scaffolding alternative social, cultural, and political systems that revolve around a different conception of who is the human.

In Brazil, people associate the Black mother with failure: failure to keep a man because she is too strong, too angry, and too difficult; failure to adhere to heteronormativity, such as having children with more than one partner; failure to economically support her children; and failure to supervise her children and raise them morally. In particular, the state and media visually represent pregnant Black women, those soon-to-be mothers, especially from the periphery, as moral failures: the pregnancy is evidence that she is sexually loose and irresponsible about birth control (as if it is only the woman's responsibility) (M. A. Soares, 2012). Pregnant Black women pose a social problem for the Brazilian nation-state. People view them as producing more Black people, which means more criminals, responsible for the chaos and violence in Brazilian society (M. A. Soares, 2012, p. 86). Society blames Black mothers for their children's violent behavior and/or for their violent deaths at the hands of the state. Many Brazilians vocally support punishing Black women via involuntary sterilization, incarceration, and incessant public shaming. The stigma, the threats, the actual practices of unequal health care, and the premature deaths of their sons are pushing Black mothers to their own premature death (C. Smith, 2016b).

I want to read Tata's Iemanjá as a visual representation of refusing Eurocentric beauty standards and *marronage* in her own body, taking refuge from visual regimes of power that portray larger Black bodies as diseased, unhealthy, and undesirable. This refusal can be located in her closed eyes, a flight from how racialization depends on a visual regime that centers on embodiment (Hall, 2017). She resists looking back at her viewer. In the mural, Iemanjá is also covering her breasts, a signifier that she is refusing how subjects look at Black women and sexualize them, such as the hypersexual *mulata*. In this moment, she also looks at peace, as she rests her head, and filled with joy, with a wide-open smile. Within a *quilombo* framework, the viewer can see her as participating in an embodied *petit marronage* (Price, 1996). While *petit marronage* usually means an act of truancy, such as visiting a relative or a lover, it applies here as well: Iemanjá is removing herself from the visual regimes of gendered racialization that dehumanize her. Often, *petit marronage* is temporary, usually as a means of rest, recovery, and renewal (J. Reis, 1995). We see this relief in how Iemanjá rests her head on her hands, smiling and relaxed with her eyes closed. Her body is her site of *aquilombamento* (Raquel Gerber, 2008; C. Smith, 2016c). In the same way that the enslaved ran away and stole back their bodies, Iemanjá, representing Black women more broadly, is taking back her body and in that act finding refuge.

While people expect Iemanjá to care for and bring peace to Black men, as in Calongos's mural, Tatá shows us Iemanjá bringing peace and relief to Black women from dehumanizing Eurocentric body standards. Tata's Iemanjá does not conform to this beauty regime of racial cropping for Black women's bodies, instead showing and embracing how ordinary Black women's bodies change over time. I read the bodily and fleshy rolls on Tata's Iemanjá in a way that emerges from Black women's realities and lived experiences, who are then idealized as Iemanjá. Rather than life imitating art, we see the inverse: art is imitating real life. Why might Iemanjá, like many Black women, have these rolls? She has simply gotten older. Her metabolism has slowed down. She is not restricting her diet to stay thin and remain desirable. Perhaps she likes to drink beer and has a nice beer belly. As Black women earn the least in Salvador, her diet may not be the highest quality, because fried street food is cheaper. Remembering that Iemanjá is both lover and mother, pregnancy has left her skin not as "tight" as it was in her younger days. She might not only have to work for wages during the day but also then come home in the evening and work the "second shift," doing the extra unpaid domestic labor that women perform in the home, including but not limited to cooking, cleaning, and child care. If Black mothers are working two shifts but compensated for only one, then when do they have time to work out? Right. They rarely do.

In Tata's Iemanjá mural, there is a refusal and escape, a flight to an embodied *petit marronage* where Black women are combating visual regimes that reduce them to objects and deny them personhood. I want to develop a deeper meaning in her mural that disrupts a subject-object dialectic that negates Black women's humanity and turns instead to a dialogical method that affirms Black women's humanity and thus opens up a more expansive notion of the human.

Tata's representation of Iemanjá refuses to engage in subject-object relationships where the affirmation of one person's humanity requires the denial of another's. Black diasporic feminists have long critiqued how dominant conceptions of the human result in denying Black women their humanity on raced, gendered, and classed terms. Michelle Wright (2004) illustrates the racial and gender dynamics of liberal subjectivities in both Western/white and Afrocentric/Black processes. First, she critiques the Hegelian dialectical method, in which a liberal subject actively looks at an external entity, a looked-upon object, and proceeds to categorize, describe, and order the object. When the subject names the object, they assert their Self as a human subject, assume a dominant position, and subordinate the object as the Other, a position of difference and a displacement from human selfhood. To do this, the object participates by looking at the subject who is looking at them, a symbol of recognizing the subject as the self. In the modern world, Western white Man reduces Black people to objects that they name, assign meaning to, and locate at the bottom of a racial hierarchy. "Man" then labors to overrepresent his perspective as universal, negating situated vantage points that would challenge his authority and ordering of the world. Wright illustrates that the white masculine liberal subject (thesis) rests upon the "sublation," which means to both abolish and preserve, of the racial Other (antithesis) to achieve synthesis.[11] However, Wright points out that there is little difference between the thesis and synthesis: they both reify whiteness and masculinity as the subject and negate Black people as the Other.

Black communities, especially Black men, have retooled the subject-object relational process, internalizing this Western dialectical process with their own people. Black men (thesis) sublate Black women as the Other (antithesis) to achieve synthesis as a liberal subject (Wright, 2004). Black men assert their humanity as an active social subject by reducing Black women to an object they name, describe, and situate. As such, they turn Black women into the "Other of the Other" (Wallace, 1990), a double displacement from the self and ultimately from Western human subjectivity.

Tata's mural of Iemanjá as a "real woman" points to a different zone of being that does not reify whiteness and masculinity but instead affirms Black femininity as the orienting space of humanity outside abject Blackness and Man's zone of being. Instead of becoming a subject and an agent of history through dialectical processes, Black women are too often objects whose histories, lives, and cultures are narrated for them. As bell hooks (1989) argues, there are unbalanced relations of power in terms of who can define not only themselves but also others, and on what terms: "As subjects, people have the right to define their own reality, establish their own identities, name their history. As objects, one's reality is defined by others, one's identity created by others, one's history named only in ways that define one's relationship to those who are subjects" (pp. 42–43). Who are subjects and who are objects *matters* because the distinction is often mapped out along racial lines of who is a citizen and who is a noncitizen; who belongs in the zone of being and who is in the zone of nonbeing; and who is human and who is nonhuman. Men, from different races, write Black women's realities, identities, and histories for them: white men through a notion of the Brazilian nation; white women through a notion of (white) feminism; or Black men through the Black community. In all cases, they use Black women as a sublated Other, or Other of the Other, to assert their subjectivity as active subjects of history.

How do Black women assert themselves as subjects then? I want to keep pushing this Black diasporic feminist reading of Tata's Iemanjá to an egalitarian and collective model of humanism. Black women assert their subjectivity through omnivocality via the pillars of circularity, collectivity, and difference. Drawing on Mae Gwendolyn Henderson, Wright (2004) argues that "'omnivocality' possesses the far greater power of being able to connect with others and *recognize* their subjectivities" (pp. 141–142). Intersubjectivity is important because this process does not require the sublation of an Other. As Black women are often the sublated Other, they have shifted toward other modalities of human recognition and inclusion. As Wright argues, this omnivocality rests upon a *dialogical* method that brings multiple subjects together and works through difference, variation, and multiple positionalities. A dialogical omnivocal subjectivity does not desire a liberalism or the sublation of the Other; it turns to the collectivity that bridges the past, present, and future.

Continuing to think with Wright, dialectical processes of subjectivity rest upon masculinity, fatherhood, and nationalism. As she notes, men beget other men who become the active agents of history in the nation. Women are but passive vessels who produce men's offspring and the next generation of the nation's subjects. Wright argues for turning toward Black mothers as the "point of orientation" (p. 178) for dialogical processes of omnivocal subjectivity that affirm rather than negate Black women. In her analysis of poems by Carolyn Rodgers and Audre Lorde, Wright illustrates that the Black mother engenders a different set of meanings for Black subjectivity: "Neither Rodgers nor Lorde ever position[s] [the Black mother] as an absolute origin—rather, she is the point of orientation for *all Black subjects*, the medium through which, willingly or not, they negotiate their intersubjectivity (p. 178; emphasis added). In other words, we should refuse the myth of "Mama Africa" (P. Pinho, 2010) that associates racial origins with particular essences, appearances, and tendencies as well as a nurturing and timeless matriarchy that negates Black women's humanity as subjects. As a "point of orientation," affirming Black mothers establishes all Black people's humanity without establishing a patrilineage back to Africa or measuring one's self against Man. Wright's theorization of Black motherhood points to refusals of and flight from a folkloric Blackness that rests upon a particular heteromasculine nationalist project.

Tata's mural Iemanjá and Black motherhood in general point to an orientation in the Bahian hip-hop movement that refuses the various masculinist nationalisms that reduce Black women to nonhuman objects. What would it mean to shift the orientation from hypermasculinity to Black motherhood in the Bahian hip-hop movement? Bahian feminist hip-hop scholars point out how the movement is not hospitable to mothers (Sobral Freire, 2018). What happens is that women are included only insofar as they are put into a subordinate relation to Black men. Black men rap about their sexual conquests with women and/or relationships to their mothers or girlfriends in their lyrics. In practice, Black men will not make space for women; they will be outright hostile to them, or will not advocate for women in concert and festival lineups, or will pay women less than they would men.

Syncretizing Iemanjá with Black mothers as the point of orientation for the Bahian hip-hop movement's *aquilombamento* is useful when considering the circularity between the juxtaposition of the two. If seeing Black mothers as Iemanjá means that they are militant witches opposing technocratic structures of oppression, then what does that mean for seeing Iemanjá in Black mothers? That is, how do we re-see Black mothers? It means seeing them, not Black men/fathers, as the focal point of Black communities, politico-cultural resistance, and a truly limitless humanism. Black motherhood is the site of cultural inheritance, not as the slave but rather as a different type of humanism.

Following Hortense Spillers (1987), it is "the power of 'yes' to the 'female' within" (p. 80). Hip-hop feminists have already established a link between Black motherhood and radicalism. Tricia Rose argues we need to have "radical feminist modes of pregnancy and motherhood" (quoted in Dery, 1994, p. 218). As Rose goes on, she drops this knowledge bomb: "The key is for feminist women to have as much power and as many babies as they want to, creating universes of feminist children" (p. 221). Rather than seeing Black women with many children as a socially deviant and irresponsible action, having "as many babies as they want to" is a feminist practice and a means for Black women to assert their power. And there is no more supreme and powerful mother than Iemanjá with the innumerable children she has birthed. Real Black women who are the mothers in our lives are thus the site of a radical Blackness central to contemporary *aquilombamento* practices.

Refusing Man, Taking Flight to Other Modalities of the Human

Through a Black diasporic feminist lens that establishes Black motherhood, femininity, and diaspora as the vortex for Black people's humanity, we can see that these three visual representations of Iemanjá reconnect her, a Candomblé deity central to Salvador's iconography, with Black Bahian mothers who (among other things) give birth to and raise Salvador's predominantly Black population. Even though the hegemonic power-bloc juxtaposes Iemanjá, the supreme deity of beauty and motherhood, with the Virgin Mary and by extension whiteness and Christianity, these murals portray her through hip-hop and abject Blackness, depicting Black women as divine, loving, and lovable, as political actors and radical mothers. In relation to dominant representations of whiteness as ideal femininity, we can map out a politics of refusal, flight, and *aquilombar-se*. This juxtaposition links Iemanjá with a different mode of Black life and human orientation.

Black visual hip-hop artists are redefining who belongs in Black sovereign spaces by redescribing who the "human" is and thus who is a member of the polis. Rather than negating Black women and reducing them to biological vessels who beget sons for fathers, these murals point to a reading of Black women embodying and practicing philosophies of dialogism and omnivocality that stress the collective totality as a means of survival against social stigma, dehumanizing conditions, and premature death.

All three murals gesture toward an alternative model of the human, one that has existed for centuries. The Jamaican critical theorist Sylvia Wynter (2003) argues that the hegemonic construction of the human is defined as "Man": Western, white, bourgeois, masculine, and male. She notes that our conception "overrepresents itself as if it were the human itself" (p. 260). The imperative of securing the well-being of Man as the overrepresentation of the human constitutes the coloniality of Being/Power/Truth/Freedom (p. 260). This coloniality depends on Man signifying the human at the level of both language and mythology. As Wynter goes on to beautifully illuminate, those who are not Man cannot just begin decolonization by trying to occupy Man's position. Or as Fanon frames it, Black people cannot become human by attempting to emulate Man in his geography, language, cultural affinities, social mobility, occupational excellence, desire, gender expression, and quotidian performances. It is not Man's template that needs to expand. Rather, it is our notion of the human: as Wynter points out, "one cannot 'unsettle' the 'coloniality of power' without a redescription of the human outside the terms of our present descriptive statement of the human, Man, and its overrepresentation" (2003, p. 268). Calongos, Sista Katia, and Tata all visually communicate a "redescription" of the human by turning not to Man but toward Black women as a more liberatory notion of the human.

Rather than the normative, we can follow Iemanjá as a point of human orientation toward the deviant, the denigrated, and the depraved. By doing so, we refuse the individual as the state of being that naturalizes the nation and masculinity (Fanon, 1963). In each example I discuss, Iemanjá is used in a modality of circularity between the street vendor, the large Black woman, and the Black mother. My reading of these depictions is not only that Iemanjá is a Black woman but also that Black women are the starting point of any decolonizing effort that dismantles Man as our ethno-class of the human and forges a *dialogical* process that emphasizes the collective, the omnivocality, and our differences. I emphasize foregrounding Black people's humanity not by pursuing Man but rather through or with other Black people, and by centering Black women. This is the Black radical tradition where we find the "historical struggle for liberation ... motivated by the shared sense of obligation to preserve the collective being, the ontological totality" (Robinson, 2000, p. 171). Black visual artists in the Bahian hip-hop movement establish Black motherhood as the humanist compass in their emergent *quilombo* social, cultural, and political practices in Salvador.

Coda
A Diasporic Love Letter

Ultimately, this book is a love letter. It blooms out of a deep and profound love for all Black people across the globe. The preceding pages are dedicated to every one of us, a challenge to the way the world hates us and wants us to hate ourselves. Each word is meant to love on and cherish Black people whom various societies view as disposable, undesirable, and unlovable. We are valuable (and not in the capitalistic way). We are desirable. We are lovable in ways beyond what we can even imagine. And we are already loving each other in ways that are so, so, so radical. These practices must be amplified and expanded because they are literally blueprints for our eventual liberation.

This book has been difficult for me to write. Like many of us, I wrote my dissertation in a fury of righteous rage. I was so angry. And I still am. But I was also bitter, in a way that was not necessarily productive. First, I was angry at the extreme level of violent hostility toward Black people and how its treachery circulates globally, penetrating the very fabric of our social, cultural, and political worlds. Moreover, I was angry at how global gendered anti-Blackness ruthlessly limits and hinders our imaginations of what is possible, so that many of us can imagine liberation only through the nation-state. I was also angry at the inadequacies of my doctoral discipline (communication) to grapple with this anti-Blackness. Moreover, I was quite frustrated at the multiple gaps in Black studies, Latin American studies, cultural studies, anthropology, and diaspora studies that make certain forms of Black culture and people visible while also making Black suffering invisible or seen as less worthy of serious study. I despised the way we internalize hierarchies within our own local, regional, national, diasporic, and global communities that make some of us worthy and others not. We are *all* worthy.

I want all of this to burn down. And by "this," I mean this symbolic and material violence. I will never not be furious about this. And I will not apologize for this. The question I faced after my dissertation was, What do we build after we tear down inhumane, utterly atrocious, and destructive systems? I want to return to James Baldwin one more time, who wrote, "I imagine one of the reasons people cling to their hates so stubbornly is because they sense, once hate is gone, they will be forced to deal with pain." We are dealing with that pain now. And once we heal, we must reckon with what we want to build in its place. We can be angry all we want, but there comes a time when we have to face the aftermath. The rubble is smoldering. The ashes are blowing. And we are there looking at one another, like "What next?" We must trade the tool of destruction for the tool of building, a tool that can construct radical communities. To be honest, I'm terrified that we might rebuild a world based on the same blueprint of the world we exist in now. We cannot afford to do that if we are to ever be free.

When we build, I want it to be out of love. Deep, never-ending, and abundant love. To slightly riff off Audre Lorde, we can heal, but only collectively by loving those who are never meant to be loved. This is a Black diasporic feminist praxis, a love not just of the "good ones" or the "respectable ones" or the "nice ones." For me, this means loving those who are most marginalized, most vulnerable, most precarious in our communities. I'll be honest: this book goes only so far, but I would like to think it is steering us in the right direction. The work is not done with this book. But I dedicate this love letter to the poor and working-class Black people and their social, cultural, and political worlds around the globe. One reason why I love poor and working-class Black people is their radical love of the popular and their innovative uses of the profane, the grotesque, the kitsch, the copy, and the artificial. Dismiss it at your own peril. It beautifully scrapes against beloved notions of the pure, the bourgeois, the original, the avant-garde, the respectable, the highbrow, and the normative. And by doing this, we often radically love the people who are not meant to be loved, valorized, and adored. It's a whole different way of building social systems and ultimately what it means to be human.

After years of working through this shift from anger to love, I have come to engage with and embrace *quilombos* as a deep political and philosophical praxis that teaches us to build out of love and not just destroy out of bitter anger. I am constantly inspired by *quilombos*, past and present. In the sociopolitical context of colonial slave society, the risk that Black people took when they said enough is enough is a radical politics of Black sociality, which is to say, of Black love. They said, "We must go." And this decision was literally a matter of life and death. They refused slavery, fled the plantation, escaped into the hills, and then built something that colonialism and slavery would never permit. This something is based on African social and institutional models that protect one another, models that are not bellicose, but rather are founded on an incessant commitment to love and peace. *Quilombos* are models of creating and practicing social, cultural, and political systems of liberation that demand we lovingly depend upon one another. More importantly, they begin by imagining and creating their notion of the human through a Black collective framing.

Simply stated, *quilombos* coalesce around the remarkable yet ordinary social, cultural, and political systems, alternative relations, and modes of assembly that socially excluded Black people create, perform, and practice in anticipation of a collective liberation that far exceeds what emancipation can ever produce and provide. As Abdias Nascimento (1980) writes, a *quilombo* is always in a "constant process of revitalization and remodernization, attending to the needs of the various historical times and geographical environments" (p. 153). That is, it is contextual, adapting to the contemporary conjuncture (Hall, 2016). Not constrained by Eurocentric and white supremacist notions of history or even geography, *quilombos* continue to form whenever, wherever, and however Black people on the margins practice these principles that fracture the colonial logic which still undergirds Western modernity and our notions of the human built upon white supremacy, anti-Blackness, heteropatriarchy, and global hypercapitalist exploitation. They take those who are discarded and create worlds anew with them.

As Black people continue to reinvigorate *quilombo* systems, beliefs, and practices according to the various and complex conditions they must confront, I have sought to demonstrate how the Bahian hip-hop movement is a contemporary *quilombo* that manifests in their material conditions, ideologies, socialities, space-making, aesthetics, concepts of sovereignty, and human orientations. More importantly, I want to reemphasize that it is an emergent *quilombo*. An emergent *quilombo* emphasizes taking flight from not only the systems of white supremacy, anti-Blackness, heteropatriarchy, and racial capitalism but also the limited and tenuous forms of Black inclusion that the nation-state uses to insidiously weave its own linear narratives of racial progress dependent on adherence to colonial logics, practices, and systems. When Black people refuse and escape, they must also refuse and escape from the politics of bourgeois respectability that would redeem us under a Judeo-Christian matrix never meant to bestow citizenship or even basic human rights on us. The diaspora must be seen as a project that does not sit neatly within the nation-state; it is a powerful tool used to understand, critique, and tear down the nation-state, its borders, and its sovereign power to bestow and deny political citizenship based on racist ideologies, philosophies, and codifications of belonging. It is into the unknown of the diaspora that Black liberation, which will mean collective liberation, beckons us as a site of radical imagination and choreography, and a blueprint for the more just and caring worlds we will eventually build.

I must note that not everything is a *quilombo*. I am weary of the proliferation and uncritical application of *marronage* in Black studies. Not everything is refusal and escape. Not everyone is a maroon. Not everything is part of the Black radical tradition. *Aquilombamento* is not just any grouping of Black people or a Black space. As I elucidate in this book, there are many Black spaces, organizations, and assemblies that rely upon bourgeois respectability politics, class differentiation, patriarchy, misogyny, and state paternalism. That is, they still depend on certain structures of permissibility to carve out space and legitimation in Brazilian society. In doing so, they reproduce "afro-nationalism" (C. Smith, 2016a), multiculturalism (A. E. da Costa, 2014), or the racial democracy mythos. We must remain committed to ensuring our units of analysis and, more importantly, our politics align with our theories.

Quilombos are ultimately about love, a love for and by Black people that the entire semantic world is afraid of because it would undermine and destroy Western modes of being, thinking, and relations to one another. They are a radical love built upon interbeing, interdependency, and the growth of ourselves and one another that creates intense modes of intimacy between us (hooks, 2001, 2004, 2018). They are committed to tearing down this world and building new ones. They foster spaces for those least loved and most marginalized to be brought into the fold, have their humanity recognized as is and even centered, and become part of a collective that is responsible for and by one another. *Quilombos* are a political philosophy that Black people put into practice to imagine the impossible and provide a blueprint, or better yet a choreography, of not only how we get free but also what systems and forms of relations we want to normalize when we do get free. It is a liberation for the not yet but soon to come. As countless Black hip-hop artists have taught me, "só um caminho," it's just a journey, and one day we're going to get there and create the worlds that the earliest *quilombos* such as Palmares have imagined and forged. We must keep fleeing and *aquilombar-se* into the diaspora, that beautiful dark abyss of radical possibility for worlds otherwise beyond the limited one we occupy now.

Notes

Introduction

1. By social death, I refer to Orlando Patterson's framework, which is based on gratuitous violence, general dishonor, and natal alienation.
2. For concrete examples, consider Brazil's agreement with England to stop participating in and eventually end the slave trade. Brazil was dependent upon the slave trade, especially because Portugal was central to it, and preferred to bring more enslaved Africans rather than creating a system that would produce Brazilian-born Black people. To be clear: Brazil preferred working Black people to death over feeding, housing, and caring for their progeny. Brazil did not move to stop participating in the transatlantic slave trade until after the 1835 Malê Revolt in Salvador da Bahia, the ninth one since 1807. Many Bahian white elites were afraid Bahia would become the next Haiti. In fact, the English sought to end the slave trade after the 1791 Haitian Revolution, which produced the first nation to abolish slavery and the second free republic in the Americas. European metropoles and the United States were all afraid of rebellious Africans in the Western Hemisphere and the cocktail for Black revolution, especially in colonies with a majority Black population. See J. Reis (1995).
3. The United States was and still is much more tolerant toward white ethnic difference than Black ethnic difference. This is most obvious with the histories of Italian, Jewish, and Irish immigration and assimilation into white communities. See Roediger (2018) and Ignatiev (1995).
4. Even though he did not coin the term, Gilberto Freyre created the racial democracy mythological template in his book *The Masters and the Slaves: A Study in the Development of Brazilian Civilization* (1986). The argument is based on the following. The Portuguese were more benign and cosmopolitan colonizers than their British, French, and Spanish counterparts. This tolerance for ethnic difference is attributed to Portugal's exposure to the

Moors during their occupation of the Iberian Peninsula. In Brazil, the Portuguese "freely" mingled with African and Indigenous peoples, picking up many of their social and cultural practices. Portuguese men often lost their virginity to enslaved African/Black women. Rather than obscure this common (and violent) practice, Freyre, and subsequently Brazilian thought, has praised it because it produced a large *mestiço* (mixed race) population that constitutes the national body politic. Today, this means that in Brazil everyone has some African biological or ethnic heritage on their body or in their soul (p. 278). If every Brazilian is racially or ethnically mixed, then there are no racial divisions in the nation, only color gradations. Therefore, Brazilians cannot be racist because that would mean they would be racist against themselves. In this framework, racism is a matter of individual prejudice rather than something structural and systemic.

5. I want to thank Nadine Naber for stressing the importance of doing this even as ethnographer self-reflexivity has seemed to pass as a fad. In the Women of Color Feminism course I took with her at the University of Michigan, we read Kamala Visweswaran's *Fictions of Feminist Ethnography* (1994) and discussed the transnational feminist politics of ethnographic "homework" as well as the need to disrupt the omnipresent Euromasculinity of the ethnographic gaze. Who we are and how we come to do research are super-fucking important in how we interact with communities we perform research with.

Chapter 1: Racial Conditions

1. Here, I am referencing Amado's assertion that Brazil's most famous export is the *mulata* woman. See Eliana Ramos Bennett's interrogation of the sexual economy of trafficking the *mulata* image and performance around the world in "Gabriela Cravo e Canela: Jorge Amado and the Myth of the Sexual Mulata in Brazilian Culture" (2001).
2. The *baiana* dress consists of a white petticoat, a long white skirt with material tied around the waist, a white headwarp, a white lacy bodice, and lots of colorful jewelry, especially around the neck.
3. This information is culled from a community document titled "Quilombo Urbano—Ladeira da Preguiça." It has circulated on the internet for a while. It is also printed out and posted at the local community center.
4. I want to thank Rachel Afi Quinn for emphasizing the importance of continued critical self-reflection not only during ethnographic fieldwork but also in one's manuscript. Too often, ethnographers reduce this important facet to one paragraph in the introduction, framing it as a listing of identities without illustrating how it works in the field. See her book talk with the Association for the Study of the Worldwide African Diaspora.

5. As Cedric Robinson argues in *Black Marxism: The Making of the Black Radical Tradition* (2021), racialism was already a feature of Western societies before the transatlantic slave trade. He traces racialism back to the Greeks and Romans, and follows it through European feudal society and into the modern world. He argues that racialism, the racialization of groups intertwined in power differentials that produce racism, is fundamental to capitalism. For him, capitalism is not a break from the feudal order, but rather a continuation of it. His theoretical insights point out how racialism was transformed when it moved away from European internal differences and toward global differences between Europe and the rest of the world. For further insights on racial capitalism, see Robin Kelley's "What Did Cedric Robinson Mean by Racial Capitalism?" (2017). Carole Boyce Davies (2008, 2009) extends the racial capitalism framework to incorporate gender. Minkah Makalani elaborates on the often-murky understandings of racialism in "Cedric Robinson and the Origins of Race" (2021).
6. It is common among critical race scholars in sociology to analyze socioeconomic data along a white-nonwhite axis in Brazil. This groups *parda/os* and *preta/os* together. See Telles (2004) and Mitchell-Walthour (2017).

Chapter 2: Hip-Hop *Aquilombamento*

1. Of course, this framing derives from Stuart Hall's groundbreaking essay "Encoding/Decoding" (1980a), which argues that media texts are encoded by their producers with particular meanings but that the decoding by audiences is done in three ways: dominant, oppositional, and negotiated. What I am calling attention to here is how hip-hop artists are decoding Brazilian popular music in oppositional ways to incorporate them in the encoding processes of their hip-hop texts as part of a Black *conscientização*.
2. For more on the Black Movement, see Michael Hanchard's *Orpheus and Power: The Movimento Negro of Rio de Janeiro and Sao Paulo, Brazil, 1945–1988* (1994).
3. For more on the React or Be Killed! movement, see Christen Smith's *Afro-Paradise: Blackness, Violence, and Performance* (2016a).
4. For more on this, see the report commissioned by the Latin American Studies Association: *Report of the LASA Fact-Finding Delegation on the Impeachment of Brazilian President Dilma Rouseff* (Chalhoub et al., 2017).
5. Comissões Parlamentares de Inquérito recommended that Bolsonaro be charged with crimes against humanity for the way he handled the nation's COVID-19 response. See https://www.cnn.com/2021/10/20/americas/brazil-bolsonaro-covid-19-intl-hnk/index.html.

Chapter 3: Black Spaces of Culture

1. The music video did receive some backlash because the two women do not (openly) identify as lesbian, bisexual, or queer in their lives.
2. The Haitian Revolution resulted in many significant world-historical events. Haiti was the first nation to abolish slavery. It was the first and only nation that emerged from a slave revolt. Also, it was the second free nation in the Americas. Without the Haitian Revolution, Napoleon may or may not have sold the Louisiana Territory, of which he had just regained control in 1800, to the United States, more than doubling the size of the latter.

Chapter 4: Intimacy

1. For more on Palmares, see Edison Carneiro's *O Quilombo dos Palmares: 1630–1695* (1947), Flavío dos Santos Gomes's *De Olho em Zumbi dos Palmares: Histórias, símbolos e memória social* (2011), Robert Nelson Anderson's "The Quilombo of Palmares: A New Overview of a Maroon State in Seventeenth-Century Brazil" (1996), and R. K. Kent's "Palmares: An African State in Brazil" (1965).
2. While many scholars, activists, and *quilombos* would like to think so, Palmares was not a democracy. As it was ruled by a monarch, it was not and could not be a democratic state. It seems that many conflate freedom with democracy. However, Palmares was not a totally free state either. Many of the newly arrived *quilombolas* were considered prisoners until they were able to replace themselves with a newly arrived *quilombola*. While the term "prisoner" is far from our modern conception of the term, the political position of newly arrived *quilombola* could not be considered entirely free, as they could be not full members of the *quilombo* right away.
3. There are references to Palmares even as far back as 1597 (F. dos S. Gomes [2011]).
4. In the Brazilian colony, the Portuguese monarch would assign captaincy, a land grant fifty leagues wide, to a captain major or captain donatary, who exercised administrative and governing control over that area. Many of these captaincies crumbled quickly. The Pernambuco captaincy is one of two successful captaincies, along with São Vicente. See E. Bradford Burns, *A History of Brazil* (1993).
5. The Dutch colonized parts of Northern Brazil, then called "New Holland," from 1630 to 1654.
6. São Thome is now called São Tomé, an African island that the Portuguese colonized beginning in the late fifteenth century to produce sugarcane with enslaved African labor they would bring from elsewhere. As in continental Africa and in the Americas, Black people also revolted against slavery,

plantation economies, and colonial violence. The 1595 revolt is especially notable in São Tomé's history. See Caldeira (2011), Seibert (2013), and Vogt (1973).
7. The "-UH" ending is nuanced, as it might suggest a feminine-gendered "EMOCIONADA" where the "-UH" replaces the "-A." However, Vandal throws an "H" onto the end of everything, like *TIPOLAZVEGAZH*, and does not change the sound of the word. Therefore, the "U" correlates to how the "O" is pronounced in Brazilian Portuguese, making it a masculine articulation of "EMOTIONAL." The song is a refusal of US hip-hop masculinities and how the US movement counters the Bahian hip-hop movement, but not necessarily of hip-hop culture. In particular, Vandal responds to the emphasis on Black men's physical capabilities that neglects his emotional needs and wants. Having everything he wants according to the US hip-hop iconography of money, women, respect, and power leaves him unsatisfied.
8. His eight-minute short film "Bluesman" won him the 2019 Cannes Grand Prix award. A mélange of various songs accompanies the short film. It was the co-winner with "This Is America" by Childish Gambino. Ironically, it beat out Beyoncé and Jay-Z's "Apeshit."
9. For an illuminating book on the blues in the US South, see Clyde Woods's *Development Arrested: The Blues and Plantation Power in the Mississippi Delta* (2000).

Chapter 5: Artifice

1. I want to reiterate to researchers who go to do ethnographic research, especially abroad, that it is okay if you miss something. Ethnography can be exhausting, tiring, and stressful, and can push your body to the brink. Your health is important, and it is okay to skip out on something. This is advice I never received in graduate school training and that I have rarely, if ever, read in ethnographic research, methodologies, and methods. The work is important, but so is your health.
2. For a phenomenal exploration of this critique, see the conclusion in Michael Hanchard's *Orpheus and Power: The Movimento Negro of Rio de Janeiro and São Paulo, Brazil, 1945–1988* (1994).
3. This is all the more interesting considering the racist episode with his current football team, Paris Saint-Germain, in 2020. During a match that year, an official made a racist remark toward an opposing coach. After hearing it, Neymar and his teammate Mbappé accused the official of racism and walked off in protest.
4. I would like to thank Luciana Mesquita and her presentation on Bianca Santana and Afro-Brazilian women's literature at the 2019 Association for the

230 | Notes to Chapters 5 and 6

Study of the Worldwide African Diaspora biennial conference. Her insights are helpful in this discussion.

5. For readers unfamiliar with hair type and systems, see a diagram and explanations at https://www.naturalhairrules.com/hair-type/.
6. In Candomblé, *orí* literally means "head" and symbolizes one's spiritual intuition and destiny. In this case, DJ Nai Kiese is taking *orí* as an aesthetic concept as well, symbolizing her hair transformation and new beginnings.
7. Issa Rae explores this brilliantly in "The Stop Sign" episode in season 1 of *Awkward Black Girl* on her YouTube series.
8. Even though these are the police officer's words, I still can't reproduce the slur in this book. You can probably figure out what it is. The "worker" question is quasi-ironic because being called a worker is not an insult by itself. Here, I read it as suggesting that he's not even a worker, one who labors for his income. Instead, the officer is suggesting that Diego is a "thief" and "vagabond," in opposition to a worker, who makes his money through illegal means.
9. "Elephant print" refers to the design on the classic Jordan 3 black/cement and white/cement colorways.
10. The term "baseball hat" refers to a style of hat, not a hat bearing the name of a baseball team.
11. While R&B is not usually included in hip-hop cultures, a shift in the 1990s paired rappers and R&B singers.
12. My use of "permissible Blackness" is informed by Christen A. Smith (2016a), who adopts it from Charles Hale's notion of the permissible indio (2004).

Chapter 6: Mediating *Quilombo* Politics

1. I base this assessment on the numerous other times I have seen young Black men endure these searches. In addition, I too have been subjected to this process.
2. The duo broke up recently and no longer perform together. They are each pursuing their own careers.
3. As numerous Black Brazilian feminists illustrate, the inverse happens within mainstream feminist movements. As in the United States, Brazilian feminism centers on white femininity and pushes questions of race and racism aside. As a result, many feminist movements ostracize Black women, especially because white women make their gains at the expense of Black women whom society "superexploits" (to borrow a word from Claudia Jones) and who perform the domestic labor that white women leave behind when they join the workforce.
4. Like many other words that marginalized groups reappropriate, the word in one context can be endearing and empowering but in others can be

derogatory and provoking. Women call each other a *piriguete,* and sometimes even men are called a *piriguete.* This is usually among friends. If a stranger calls a woman a *piriguete,* there is probably going to be a confrontation. There can also be problems if *piriguete* is used among friends but in a way that demeans someone.
5. DJ KL Jay is the famous DJ from the São Paulo–based group Racionais MCs. Racionais MCs are considered by many the greatest Brazilian rap group and are deeply revered throughout Brazil.
6. My good brother, Dr. Kyle T. Mays, always brings up a good point: If Black women were free, would *everyone* be free? His line of questioning comes from an Indigenous studies perspective. We can eradicate racism, sexism, homophobia, and classism, but what about issues of land? Indigenous peoples' issues revolve around dispossession and sovereignty. This is by no means to undermine the Combahee River Collective. Where would we be without their foundational insights? Instead, I take his line of questions as an opportunity to imagine how to expand on their incredible contributions, tackle different groups' pressing needs, and think about our collective liberation in more complicated ways.
7. Interestingly enough, the antagonist is Santos's partner in real life.

Chapter 7: Real Women

1. While many scholars used to refer to this as "syncretism," it is more common to use "juxtaposition."
2. Some Candomblé communities assert that they have never juxtaposed their deities with Catholic saints.
3. In particular, I am thinking of the works of both Beatriz Nascimento and Cedric Robinson. In her *quilombo* theory, Nascimento (1985) illustrates the way that Black people in Brazil have reterritorialized African cosmologies in the Americas. Reasserting African-derived ways of life in the Americas is part of a journey of Black liberation that does not depend upon the modern nation-state. Similarly, Robinson, in his Black radical tradition, illustrates how African-derived cultures factor into an "emergent African people" (2000, p. 170) which resists and undermines slavery, racial capitalism, and the coloniality of the world. Anthropologist Christen Smith has put Nascimento's work in conversation with Gilroy's Black Atlantic, but it would be quite the endeavor to put Nascimento in conversation with Robinson, especially because their works on Black radicalism were published at nearly the same time.
4. In Salvador, a *piriguete* can mean both a tiny beer and a sexually free woman. However, the latter definition is the only one that is nearly universal in Brazil. The former is typically confined to Bahia. I make this point to reference

how the Bahian sexual economy is embedded in the language of commercial transaction and consumption.
5. This of course builds on the Frankfurt School's notion of the cultural industry. See Theodor Adorno and Max Horkheimer, whose work explicates how television, media, radio, and popular culture create an imagined notion of belonging in which people are the same, part of a mass, and void of the individualization that is created in part through socioeconomic and political positionings (T. Adorno and Horkheimer, 1993; T. W. Adorno, 2001).
6. I want to expand on Mercer's notion of cropping. In his analysis of Robert Mapplethorpe's photos, Mercer illustrates how the famed white gay photographer crops Black men's bodies and focuses on particular body parts, such as the penis or the face, which signify the exotic Other. Here, I want to extend this cropping to illustrate how Black people are often deemed desirable if certain body parts of erogenous excess are cropped onto a Eurocentric body template. In particular, I am alluding to how the standard hypersexual *mulata* is desirable because of her buttocks but at the same time has less African phenotypes and still has a flat stomach, slim waist, and slender arms. The buttocks have been cropped off a Black body and pasted onto a white one.
7. I would like to thank Kim D. Butler's comments about the role of the *nega maluca* in the context of Afro-Bahian culture and dominant representations of Blackness.
8. There is also a dangerous and pervasive line of thinking that Black women are using their sexual appeal to collude with white men, emasculate Black men, whiten their babies, gain access to power, and destroy the Black community. Black men purport to embrace racial solidarity but still express racist and sexist attitudes toward Black women.
9. In *Mulher negra: Afetividade e solidão* (2013), Ana Cláudia Lemos Pacheco explores the racial and gender affect of Black women in the romantic economy. Black women in Salvador have the highest rates of being single anywhere in Brazil. As I argue here, Pacheco shows how militant Black men preach racial pride, self-esteem, and unity but then only date white women. Many Black Bahian women I know, and not just in the hip-hop movement, have expressed to me how they often feel the least valued and desired in Salvador da Bahia. Even though Salvador is predominantly Black, many Black people have internalized Eurocentric constructions of beauty in how they self-style as well as in how they select their partners. Due to the combination of anti-Black racism and sexism, Black women are too often viewed as less than desirable or even as unfit romantic partners. Sure, people want to have sexual relations with Black women, but they do not want to date them.
10. As so often happens, we lose origins and genealogies of important and critical concepts that address, critique, and enable us to imagine beyond oppression. In that regard, I want to point my readers again to Moya Bailey's term

"misogynoir" connotating the anti-Black sexism spewed at Black women (Bailey, 2021).
11. In German, the word is *aufheben* or *Aufhebung*, two terms that share contradictory meanings: to suspend, abolish, cancel, lift up, or preserve (as a verb) or the acts of doing so (as a noun). Since the nineteenth century, people have translated this as "sublation," at least in roughly philosophical contexts. Even though it is uncommon, I use "sublation" rather than, say, "negation," because it represents a dual action that denies something and yet keeps that absence in one's presence. Sublation requires the presence of that which is denied instead of wholly exterminating a subjugated entity.

Reference List

A Tarde Online, A. T. O. (2019, November 11). *Acusado de matar Moa do Katendê é condenado a mais de 22 anos de prisão*. Portal A TARDE. http://www.atarde.com.br/bahia/salvador/noticias/2109794-acusado-de-matar-moa-do-katende-e-condenado-a-mais-de-22-anos-de-prisao.

Adorno, T., Benjamin, W., Bloch, E., Brecht, B., & Lukacs, G. (2007). *Aesthetics and politics*. Verso.

Adorno, T., & Horkheimer, M. (1993). The culture industry: Enlightenment as mass deception. In S. During (Ed.), *The cultural studies reader* (pp. 29–43). Routledge.

Adorno, T. W. (2001). *The culture industry: Selected essays on mass culture* (J. M. Bernstein, Ed.; 2nd ed.). Routledge.

Agamben, G. (1998). *Homo sacer: Sovereign power and bare life* (D. Heller-Roazen, Trans.). Stanford University Press.

Aidoo, L. (2018). *Slavery unseen: Sex, power, and violence in Brazilian history*. Duke University Press.

Albuquerque, W. R. de. (1999). *Algazarra nas ruas: Comemorações da independência na Bahia (1889–1923)*. Editora da UNICAMP.

Alim, H. S., Ibrahim, A., & Pennycook, A. (Eds.). (2009). *Global linguistic flows: Hip hop cultures, youth identities, and the politics of language*. Routledge.

Almeida, S. (2019). *Racismo estrutural*. Pólen Livros.

Althusser, L. (1998). Ideology and ideological state apparatuses. In J. Storey (Ed.), *Cultural theory and popular culture: A reader* (2nd ed., pp. 153–164). University of Georgia Press.

Amado, J. (1984). *Sea of death* (G. Rabassa, Trans.). Avon Books.

Amnesty International. (2005). *Brazil: "They come in shooting": Policing socially excluded communities*. Amnesty International. https://www.amnesty.org/en/documents/AMR19/025/2005/en/.

Amnesty International. (2015). *You killed my son: Homicides by military police in the city of Rio de Janeiro*. Amnesty International.

Anderson, B. (2006). *Imagined communities: Reflections on the origin and spread of nationalism* (2nd ed.). Verso.

Anderson, R. N. (1996). The quilombo of Palmares: A new overview of a maroon state in seventeenth-century Brazil. *Journal of Latin American Studies, 28*(3), 545–566. https://doi.org/10.1017/S0022216X00023889.

Andrade, E. N. (Ed.). (1999). *Rap e educação: Rap é educação.* Selo Negro Edições.

Ansell, A. (2014). *Zero hunger: Political culture and antipoverty policy in Northeast Brazil.* University of North Carolina Press.

Apter, A. (1991). Herskovit's heritage: Rethinking syncretism in the African diaspora. *Diaspora: A Journal of Transnational Studies, 1*(3), 235–260.

Armstrong, P. (1999). The aesthetic escape hatch: Carnaval, blocos afro and the mutations of baianidade under the signs of globalisation and re-Africanisation. *Journal of Iberian and Latin American Research, 5*(2), 65–98. https://doi.org/10.1080/13260219.1999.10431798.

Armstrong, P. (2001). Moralizing Dionysus and lubricating Apollo: A semantic topography of subject construction in Afro-Bahian Carnival. *Luso-Brazilian Review, 38*(2), 29–60.

Azevedo, T. (1955). *As elites de cor: Um estudo de ascenção social.* Companhia Editora Nacional.

Bacelar, J. (1997). Blacks in Salvador: Racial paths. *Macalester International, 5*(1), 96–109.

Báez, J. M. (2018). *In search of belonging: Latinas, media, and citizenship.* University of Illinois Press.

Bailey, M. (2021). *Misogynoir transformed: Black women's digital resistance.* NYU Press.

Baldwin, J. (2021). *The Price of the ticket: Collected nonfiction: 1948–1985.* Beacon Press.

Barreto, R. de A. (2005). *Enegrecendo o feminismo ou feminizando a raça: Narrativas de libertação em Angela Davis e Lélia Gonzalez.* Unpublished master's dissertation, Pontifíca Universidade Católica do Rio de Janeiro.

Bastide, R. (1978). *The African religions of Brazil: Toward a sociology of the interpenetration of civilizations* (H. Sebba, Trans.). Johns Hopkins University Press.

Bauman, Z. (1997). *Postmodernity and its discontents.* Polity.

Beatriz dos Santos, A., Nascimento-Mandingo, F., & Chazkel, A. (2020). React or be killed: The history of policing and the struggle against anti-Black violence in Salvador, Brazil. *Radical History Review, 137,* 157–176. https://doi.org/10.1215/01636545-8092834.

Benjamin, W. (2003). On the concept of history. In H. Eiland & M. W. Jennings (Eds.), *Walter Benjamin: Selected Writings* (E. Jephcott et al., Trans.), Volume 4: *1938–1940.* Harvard University Press.

Berry, M. J., Argüelles, C. C., Cordis, S., Ihmoud, S., & Estrada, E. V. (2017). Toward a fugitive anthropology: Gender, race, and violence in the field. *Cultural Anthropology, 32*(4), 537–565. https://doi.org/10.14506/ca32.4.05.

Bey, M. (2019). Black fugitivity un/gendered. *The Black Scholar*, 49(1), 55–62. https://doi.org/10.1080/00064246.2019.1548059.

Bispo dos Santos, A. (2015). *Colonização, quilombos, modos e significados*. Patria Educadora.

Bispo dos Santos, A. (2020, August 7). We belong to the land. Agitate! Unsettling Knowledges. https://agitatejournal.org/we-belong-to-the-land/.

Bobo, J. (1998). The color purple: Black women as cultural readers. In J. Storey (Ed.), *Cultural theory and popular culture: A reader* (2nd ed., pp. 310–318). University of Georgia Press.

Bourdieu, P. (1984). *Distinction: A social critique of the judgement of taste*. Harvard University Press.

Bowen, M. (2016). Who owns paradise? Afro-Brazilians and ethnic tourism in Brazil's quilombos. *African and Black Diaspora: An International Journal*. https://doi.org/10.1080/17528631.2016.1189689.

Bowen, M. (2021). *For land and liberty: Black struggles in rural Brazil*. Cambridge University Press.

Boxer, C. R. (1962). *The golden age of Brazil 1695–1750: Growing pains of a colonial society*. University of California Press.

Braga, J. (1992). Candomblé: Força e resistência. *Afro-Ásia*, 15, 13–17.

Burdick, J. (1998). *Blessed Anastacia: Women, race and popular Christianity in Brazil*. Routledge.

Burns, E. B. (1993). *A history of Brazil* (3rd ed.). Columbia University Press.

Butler, K. (2001). Defining diaspora, refining a discourse. *Diaspora: A Journal of Transnational Studies*, 10(2), 189–219.

Butler, K. D. (1998). *Freedoms given, freedoms won: Afro-Brazilians in post-abolition São Paulo and Salvador*. Rutgers University Press.

Butler, K. D. (2017). Masquerading Africa in the Carnival of Salvador, Bahia, Brazil 1895–1905. *African and Black Diaspora: An International Journal*, 10(2), 203–227. https://doi.org/10.1080/17528631.2016.1189690.

Caldeira, A. M. (2011). Learning the ropes in the tropics: Slavery and the plantation system on the island of São Tomé. *African Economic History*, 39, 35–71.

Caldwell, K. L. (2004). "Look at her hair": The body politics of Black womanhood in Brazil. *Transforming Anthropology*, 11(2), 18–29.

Caldwell, K. L. (2006). *Negras in Brazil: Re-envisioning Black women, citizenship, and the politics of identity*. Rutgers University Press.

Caldwell, K. L. (2017). *Health equity in Brazil: Intersections of gender, race, and policy*. University of Illinois Press.

Calógeras, J. P. (1933). *A History of Brazil* (P. Martin, Trans.). University of North Carolina Press.

Camargos, R. (2015). *Rap e politica: Percepcoes da vida social brasileira no rap*. Boitempo.

Campos, A. (2005). *Do quilombo à favela: A produção do "espaço criminalizado" no Rio de Janeiro*. Bertrand Brasil.

Cardoso, F. H., & Enzo, F. (1979). *Dependency and development in Latin America*. University of California Press.
Carlim. (2015, March 7). Opanijé—Opanijé. *Oganpazan*. https://oganpazan.com.br/opanije-opanije/.
Carneiro, E. (1947). *O quilombo dos Palmares: 1630–1695*. Editora Brasiliense Ltda.
Carneiro, E. (1958). *O quilombo dos Palmares* (2nd ed.). Companhia Editora Nacional.
Carneiro, E. (1974). *Folguedos tradicionais*. Conquista.
Carneiro, E. (1980). *A cidade do Salvador 1549: Uma reconstituição histórica* (2nd ed.). Civilizacao Brasileira.
Carneiro, S. (1995). Gênero, raça e ascenção social. *Estudos Feministas*, 3(2), 544–552.
Carneiro, S. (2011). *Racismo, sexismo e desigualidade no Brasil*. Selo Negro Edições.
Carneiro, S. (2019a). *Escritos de uma vida*. Pólen Livros.
Carneiro, S. (2019b). Gênero e raça na sociedade brasileira. In *Escritos de uma vida* (pp. 150–184). Pólen Livros.
Carneiro, S. (2019c). Mulher Negra. In *Escritos de uma vida* (pp. 13–59). Pólen Livros.
Carril, L. de F. B. (2005). Quilombo, território e geografia. *Agrária*, 3, Article 3. https://doi.org/10.11606/issn.1808-1150.v0i3p156-171.
Carvalho, I., & Barreto, V. (2007). Segregação residencial, condição social e raça em Salvador. *Cadernos Metrópole*, 18, 251–273.
Carvalho, I., & Pereira, G. (2015). Segregação socioespacial e desigualidades em Salvador. *Cadernos do CEAS*, 235, 5–22.
Carvalho, J. J. (1996). Images of the Black man in Brazilian popular culture. *Série Antropologia*, issue 20.
Celeste, M. (2018). "What now?" The wailing Black woman, grief, and difference. *Black Camera*, 9(2), 110–131.
Chalhoub, S., Collins, C., Llanos, M., Pachón, M., & Perry, K.-K. (2017). *Report of the LASA fact-finding delegation on the impeachment of Brazilian president Dilma Rouseff*. Latin American Studies Association.
Chang, J. (2005). *Can't stop, won't stop: A history of the hip-hop generation*. Picador.
Chang, J. (2007). It's a hip-hop world. *Foreign Policy*, 163, 58–65.
Ciconello, A. (2015). Police killings in Brazil: "My taxes paid for the bullet that killed my grandson." Amnesty International. https://www.amnesty.org/en/latest/news/2015/03/police-killings-in-brazil-my-taxes-paid-for-the-bullet-that-killed-my-grandson/.
Clark Hine, D. (2014). A Black studies manifesto. *Black Scholar*, 44(2), 11–15. https://doi.org/10.1080/00064246.2014.11413683.
Clarke, K. M. (2006). Mapping transnationality: Roots tourism and the institutionalization of ethnic heritage. In K. M. Clarke & D. A. Thomas (Eds.),

Globalization and race: Transformations in the cultural production of Blackness (pp. 133–153). Duke University Press.

Cohen, C. (1997). Punks, bulldaggers, and welfare queens: The radical potential of queer politics? *GLQ, 3,* 437–465.

Collins, J. F. (2015). *Revolt of the saints: Memory and redemption in the twilight of Brazilian racial democracy.* Duke University Press.

Collins, P. (2000). *Black feminist thought: Knowledge, consciousness, and the politics of empowerment* (2nd ed.). Routledge.

Combahee River Collective. (2015). A Black feminist statement. In C. Moraga & G. Anzaldua (Eds.), *This bridge called my back: Writings by radical women of color* (4th ed., pp. 210–219). SUNY Press.

Conquergood, D. (2013). *Cultural struggles: Performance, ethnography, praxis* (E. P. Johnson, Ed.). University of Michigan Press.

Costa, E. (2000). *The Brazilian empire: Myths and histories* (2nd ed.). University of North Carolina Press.

Costa Lima, A. C. (2006). *Saltando e quebrando: O Rap ... pensar identidades no trânsito entre Bahia e o Maranhão.* Unpublished master's dissertation, Universidade Federal da Bahia.

Couto, E. S. (2010). *Tempo de festas—homenagens a Santa Barbara, Nossa Senhora da Conceição.* EDUFBA.

Cox, O. C. (1964). *Capitalism as a system.* Monthly Review Press.

Da Costa, A. E. (2014). *Reimagining Black difference and politics in Brazil: From racial democracy to multiculturalism.* Palgrave Macmillan.

Da Silva, C. (2019). *#Parem de nos matar!* Pólen Livros.

Da Silva, S. (2019). *O protagonismo das mulheres quilombolas na luta por direitos em comunidades do Estado de São Paulo (1988–2018).* Pontifíca Universidade Católica de São Paulo.

Davies, C. (2008). *Left of Karl Marx: The political life of Black communist Claudia Jones.* Duke University Press.

Davies, C. (2009). Sisters outside: Tracing the Caribbean/Black radical intellectual tradition. *Small Axe, 13*(1), 217–229. https://doi.org/10.1215/07990537-2008-017.

Davis, A. Y. (1998). Reflections on the role of the Black woman in the community of slaves. In J. James (Ed.), *The Angela Y. Davis Reader* (pp. 111–128). Blackwell.

De Almeida, P. (2019). Reports on the wars against Palmares by Pernambuco. In J. N. Green, V. Langland, & L. M. Schwarcz (Eds.), *The Brazil reader: History, culture, politics* (2nd ed., pp. 80–82). Duke University Press.

Dery, M. (1994). Black to the future: Interviews with Samuel R. Delany, Greg Tate, and Tricia Rose. In M. Dery (Ed.), *Flame wars: The discourse of cyberculture* (pp. 179–222). Duke University Press.

Diawara, M. (1992). Afro-Kitsch. In G. Dent (Ed.), *Black popular culture* (pp. 285–291). Bay Press.

Dimitriadis, G. (1996). Hip hop: From live performance to mediated narrative. *Popular Music, 15*(2), 179–194. https://doi.org/10.1017/S0261143000008102.

Dimitriadis, G. (2009). *Performing identity/performing culture: Hip hop as text, pedagogy, and lived practice* (2nd ed.). Peter Lang.

Durham, A. (2014). *Home with hip hop feminism: Performances in communication and culture.* Peter Lang.

Edu, U. F. (2019). Aesthetics politics: Negotiations of Black reproduction in Brazil. *Medical Anthropology, 38*(8), 680–694. https://doi.org/10.1080/01459740.2019.1665671.

Fagan, B. (1993). Timelines: Brazil's Little Angola. *Archaeology, 46*(4), 14–19.

Fanon, F. (1963). *The wretched of the earth* (C. Farrington, Trans.). Grove Press.

Fanon, F. (2004). *The wretched of the earth* (R. Philcox, Trans.). Grove Press.

Fanon, F. (2008). *Black skin, white masks* (R. Philcox, Trans.). Grove Press.

Farfán-Santos, E. (2016). *Black bodies, Black rights: The Politics of quilombolismo in contemporary Brazil.* University of Texas Press.

Ferguson, R. A. (2014). Race. In B. Burgett & G. Hendler (Eds.), *Keywords for American cultural studies* (2nd ed., pp. 207–211). NYU Press.

Fernandes, F. (1969). *The Negro in Brazilian society.* Columbia University Press.

Ferreira Bastos, R. C. (2009). *Hip hop e educação popular.* Unpublished bachelor's thesis in communication and licensure in journalism, Universidade Federal da Bahia.

Ferreira da Silva, D. (2001). Towards a critique of the socio-logos of justice: The analytics of raciality and the production of universality. *Social Identities, 7*(3), 421–454. https://doi.org/10.1080/13504630120087253.

Fiske, J. (2010). *Understanding popular culture* (2nd ed.). Routledge.

Fleetwood, N. R. (2015). *On racial icons: Blackness and the public imagination.* Rutgers University Press.

Franco, M. (2014). *Upp—a redução da favela a três letras: Uma análise da política de segurança pública do estado do Rio de Janeiro.* Unpublished master's dissertation, Universidade Federal Fluminense.

Frazier, E. F. (1939). *The Negro family in the United States.* University of Chicago Press.

Freelon, K. (2020, May 28). *Your hairstyle can cost you your life in Brazil.* Medium. https://level.medium.com/your-hairstyle-can-cost-you-your-life-in-brazil-2705f963b8ea.

Freire, P. (2000). *Pedagogy of the oppressed.* Continuum.

Freitas, H. (2016). *O arco e a arkhé: Enasios sobre literatura e cultura.* Editora Ogum's Toques Negros Ltda.

Freyre, G. (1986). *The masters and the slaves: A study in the development of Brazilian civilization* (S. Putnam, Trans.; 2nd ed.). University of California Press.

Funari, P. P. A., & de Carvalho, A. V. (2016). Palmares: A rebel polity through archaeological lenses. In F. D. S. Gomes & J. J. Reis (Eds.), *Freedom by a thread: The history of quilombos in Brazil* (pp. 19–42). Diasporic Africa Press.

Gibson, T. A. (2000). Beyond cultural populism: Notes toward the critical ethnography of media audiences. *Journal of Communication Inquiry, 24*(3), 253–273.

Gillam, R. (2022). *Visualizing Black lives: Ownership and control in Afro-Brazilian media*. University of Illinois Press.

Gilmore, R. W. (2007). *Golden gulag: Prisons, surplus, crisis, and opposition in globalizing California*. University of California Press.

Gilroy, P. (2004). It's a family affair. In M. Forman & M. A. Neal (Eds.), *That's the joint! The hip-hop studies reader* (pp. 87–94). Routledge.

Globo. (2020, February 3). Moradores filmam agressão policial a adolescente em Salvador: "Você para mim é ladrão, olha esse cabelo", diz PM; VÍDEO. Globo.com. https://g1.globo.com/ba/bahia/noticia/2020/02/03/moradores-registram-agressao-policial-a-jovem-no-suburbio-de-salvador-voce-para-mim-e-ladrao-olha-esse-cabelo-disse-pm-video.ghtml.

Gomes, F. dos S. (2011). *De Olho em Zumbi dos Palmares: Histórias, símbolos e memória social*. Claro Enigma.

Gomes, F. dos S., & Reis, J. J. (Eds.). (2016). *Freedom by a thread: The history of quilombos in Brazil*. Diasporic Africa Press.

Gomes da Silva, D. F. (2019). *Hip-hop salvação: Afro-narratives of the hip-hop generation in São Paulo, Brazil or how hip-hop showed us the way out!* Unpublished doctoral dissertation, University of Texas.

Gomes da Silva, J. C. (1999). Arte e educação: A experiência do movimento hip hop paulistano. In E. N. Andrade (Ed.), *Rap e educação: Rap é educação* (pp. 23–38). Selo Negro Edições.

Gomes da Silva, J. C. (2015). *Rap na cidade de São Paulo: Juventude negra, música e segregação urbana (1984–1998)*. EDUFU.

Gomes do Nascimento, C. (2009). *Entrelaçando corpos e letras: Representações de gênero nos pagodes baianos*. Unpublished doctoral thesis, Universidade Federal da Bahia.

Gomes do Nascimento, C. (2010). "Piriguetes em cena: Uma leitura do corpo feminino a partir dos pagdoes baianos." Paper presented at Diásporas, Diversidades, Deslocamentos Conference. http://www.fg2010.wwc2017.eventos.dype.com.br/resources/anais/1278379755_ARQUIVO_Pirigue tesemcena.pdf.

Gonzalez, L. (1984). Racismo e sexismo na cultura brasileira. *Revista Ciências Sociais Hoje*, 223–244.

Gonzalez, L. (1988a). A categoria político-cultural de amefricanidade. *Tempo Brasileiro, 92/93*, 69–82.

Gonzalez, L. (1988b). Por um feminismo afrolatinoamericano. *Revista Isis Internacional, 9*, 133–141.

Gonzalez, L. (2018a). A categoria político-cultural da amefricanidade. In *Lélia Gonzalez: Primavera para as rosas negras* (pp. 321–334). Editora Filhos da África.

Gonzalez, L. (2018b). A mulher negra na sociedade brasileira: Uma abordagem polítco-econômica. In *Lélia Gonzalez: Primavera para as rosas negras* (pp. 34–53). Editora Filhos da África.

Gonzalez, L. (2018c). Odara Dudu: Beleza negra. In *Lélia Gonzalez: Primavera para as rosas negras* (pp. 295–297). Editora Filhos da África.

Gonzalez, L. (2021). Racism and sexism in Brazilian culture (B. Barros, Feva, J. Oliveira, & L. Reis, Trans.). *WSQ: Women's Studies Quarterly, 49*(Fall/Winter), 371–394. https://doi.org/10.1353/wsq.2021.0027.

Gopinath, G. (2005). *Impossible desires: Queer diasporas and South Asian public cultures.* Duke University Press.

Gordon, L. R. (1995). *Bad faith and antiblack racism.* Humanity Books.

Green, J. N., Langland, V., & Schwarcz, L. M. (Eds.). (2019). *The Brazil reader: History, culture, politics* (2nd ed.). Duke University Press.

Guimarães, A. S. A. (1999). *Racismo e anti-racismo no Brasil.* FUSP.

Gumbs, A. P. (2016a). M/other ourselves: A Black queer feminist genealogy for radical mothering. In A. P. Gumbs, C. Martens, & M. Williams (Eds.), *Revolutionary mothering: Love on the front lines* (pp. 19–31). PM Press.

Gumbs, A. P. (2016b). *Spill: Scenes of Black feminist fugitivity.* Duke University Press.

Hafiz, J. (2016, February 25). The Cabula 12: Brazil's police war against the Black community. Aljazeera America. http://america.aljazeera.com/watch/shows/america-tonight/articles/2016/2/25/the-cabula-12-brazil-police-war-blacks.html.

Hale, C. (2004). Rethinking indigenous politics in the era of the "Indio permitido." *NACLA Report on the Americas, 38*(2), 16–20.

Hale, C. (Ed.). (2008). *Engaging contradictions: Theory, politics, and methods of activist scholarship.* University of California Press.

Hall, S. (1980a). Encoding/decoding. In *Culture, media, language* (pp. 128–138). Routledge.

Hall, S. (1980b). Race, articulation and societies structured in dominance. In *Sociological theories: race and colonialism* (pp. 305–345). UNESCO.

Hall, S. (1981). Notes on deconstructing "the popular." In R. Samuel (Ed.), *People's history and socialist theory* (pp. 227–240). Routledge.

Hall, S. (1990). Cultural identity and diaspora. In J. Rutherford (Ed.), *Identity: Community, culture, difference* (pp. 222–237). Lawrence and Wishart.

Hall, S. (1992). What is this "Black" in Black popular culture? In G. Dent (Ed.), *Black popular culture* (pp. 21–33). Bay Press.

Hall, S. (1996). Introduction: Who needs "identity"? In S. Hall & P. du Gay (Eds.), *Questions of cultural identity* (pp. 1–17). Sage.

Hall, S. (Ed.). (1997). *Representation: Cultural representations and signifying practices.* Open University.

Hall, S. (2016). *Cultural studies 1983: A theoretical history* (J. D. Slack & L. Grossberg, Eds.). Duke University Press.

Hall, S. (2017). *The fateful triangle: Race, ethnicity, nation* (K. Mercer, Ed.). Harvard University Press.

Hall, S., Critcher, C., Jefferson, T., Clarke, J., & Roberts, B. (Eds.). (2013). *Policing the crisis: Mugging, the state, and law and order* (2nd ed.). Palgrave Macmillan.

Hanchard, M. (1994). *Orpheus and power: The Movimento Negro of Rio de Janeiro and Sao Paulo, Brazil, 1945–1988*. Princeton University Press.

Hanchard, M. (2008). Black memory versus state memory: Notes toward a method. *Small Axe, 12*(2), 45–62. https://doi.org/10.1215/-12-2-45.

Harding, R. E. (2000). *A refuge in thunder: Candomblé and alternative spaces of Blackness*. Indiana University Press.

Harney, S., & Moten, F. (2013). *The undercommons: Fugitive planning & Black study*. Minor Compositions.

Harrison, F. V. (Ed.). (1997). *Decolonizing anthropology: Moving further toward an anthropology for liberation* (2nd ed.). American Anthropological Association.

Harrison, F. V. (2008). *Outsider within: Reworking anthropology in the global age*. University of Illinois Press.

Hartman, S. (2008). *Lose your mother: A journey along the Atlantic slave route*. Farrar, Straus and Giroux.

Hautzinger, S. J. (2007). *Violence in the city of women: Police and batterers in Bahia, Brazil*. University of California Press.

Henrique, K. (2011, October 20). Dandara: A face feminina de Palmares. *Geledés*. https://www.geledes.org.br/dandara-a-face-feminina-de-palmares/.

Henson, B. (2016a). Bahian hip-hop and diaspora: A contextual analysis of Coscarque's "Scarface." *Words, Beats & Life: The Global Journal of Hip-Hop Culture, 6*(2), 49–61.

Henson, B. (2016b). Real recognize real: Local hip-hop cultures and global imbalances in the African diaspora. In M. A. Peters (Ed.), *Encyclopedia of educational philosophy and theory*. Springer. https://doi.org/10.1007/978-981-287-532-7_504-2.

Henson, B. (2019). Low frequencies in the diaspora: The Black subaltern intellectual and hip-hop cultures. In J. Retis & R. Tsagarousianou (Eds.), *Handbook of diasporas, media, and culture* (pp. 461–473). Wiley-Blackwell.

Henson, B. (2020). Black invisibility: Reframing diasporic visual cultures and racial codes in Bahia. *African and Black Diaspora: An International Journal, 13*(3), 241–255. https://doi.org/10.1080/17528631.2019.1666498.

Herschmann, M. (2005). *O funk e o hip-hop invadem a cena* (2nd ed.). Editora UFRJ.

Hill, M. L. (2009). *Beats, rhymes, and classroom life: Hip-hop pedagogy and the politics of identity*. Teachers College Press.

hooks, bell. (1989). *Talking back: Thinking feminist, thinking Black*. South End Press.

hooks, bell. (2001). *Salvation: Black people and love.* William Morrow Paperbacks.
hooks, bell. (2003). *We real cool: Black men and masculinity.* Routledge.
hooks, bell. (2004). *The will to change: Men, masculinity, and love.* Washington Square Press.
hooks, bell. (2014). *Ain't I a woman: Black women and feminism* (2nd ed.). Routledge.
hooks, bell. (2018). *All about love: New visions.* William Morrow Paperbacks.
Hudson, P. J. (2018, February 20). *Racial capitalism and the dark proletariat.* Boston Review. http://bostonreview.net/forum/remake-world-slavery-racial-capitalism-and-justice/peter-james-hudson-racial-capitalism-and.
IBGE. (2010). *Instituto Brasileiro de Geografia e Estatística censo 2010.* http://www.censo2010.ibge.gov.br/painel/?nivel=mn.
Ignatiev, N. (1995). *How the Irish became white.* Routledge.
Ilê Aiyê. (n.d.). *Ilê Aiyê oficial—Noite da Beleza Negra.* Retrieved March 18, 2020, from http://www.ileaiyeoficial.com/noite-da-beleza-negra/.
Iton, R. (2008). *In search of the Black fantastic: Politics and popular culture in the post-civil rights era.* Oxford University Press.
Jackson, J. L. (2008). Toward an ethnographic lingua franca: Communication and anthropology. *Journal of Communication, 58*(4), 664–678. https://doi.org/10.1111/j.1460-2466.2008.00407.x.
Jackson, R. L., II. (2006). *Scripting the Black masculine body: Identity, discourse, and racial politics in popular media.* SUNY Press.
Jones, C. (2009). An end to the neglect of the problems of the Negro woman! In M. Marable & L. Mullings (Eds.), *Let nobody turn us around: An African American anthology* (2nd ed., pp. 316–326). Rowman and Littlefield.
Junior, J. (2019, April 29). *É tempo de se aquilombar.* Revista Fórum. https://revistaforum.com.br/noticias/e-tempo-de-se-aquilombar/.
Kaba, M. (2021). *We do this 'til we free us: Abolitionist organizing and transforming justice.* Haymarket Books.
Kelley, R. (2000). Foreword. In C. Robinson, *Black Marxism: The making of the Black radical tradition* (2nd ed., pp. xi–xxvi). University of North Carolina Press.
Kelley, R. D. G. (1998). *Yo' mama's disFUNKtional! Fighting the culture wars in urban America.* Beacon Press.
Kelley, R. D. G. (2017, January 12). "What did Cedric Robinson mean by racial capitalism?" Boston Review. http://bostonreview.net/race/robin-d-g-kelley-what-did-cedric-robinson-mean-racial-capitalism.
Kent, R. K. (1965). Palmares: An African state in Brazil. *Journal of African History, 6*(2), 161–175. https://doi.org/10.1017/S0021853700005582.
Krasner, S. D. (2001). *Problematic sovereignty: Contested rules and political possibilities.* Columbia University Press.
Kurtz, E. V. (2020). Guerreira tactics: Women warriors' sonic practices of refusal in capoeira Angola. *Women and Music: A Journal of Gender and Culture, 24*(1), 71–95. https://doi.org/10.1353/wam.2020.0014.

Lacerda, T. de C. (2019). Tereza de Benguela: Identidade e representatividade negra. *Revista de Estudos Acadêmicos de Letras, 12*(2), Article 2.

Leite, M. L. dos S. (2020). Lutando com Dandara de Palmares: Feminismos e representatividade na literatura contemporânea. *RELACult: Revista Latino-Americana de Estudos em Cultura e Sociedade, 6*(1), Article 1. https://doi.org/10.23899/relacult.v6i1.1864 zoot.

Lewis, J. L. (1992). *Ring of liberation: Deceptive discourse in Brazilian capoeira*. University of Chicago Press.

Lima, A. (2001). A legitimação do intelectual negro no meio acadêmico brasileiro: Negação de inferioridade, confronto ou assimilação intelectual? *Afro-Ásia, 25–26*, 281–312.

Lima, A. (2016). *Uma crítica cultural sobre o pagode Baiano: Música que se ouve, se dança e se observa*. Pinaúna Editora.

Lipsitz, G. (2011). *How racism takes place*. Temple University Press.

Lugones, M. (2007). Heterosexualism and the colonial/modern gender system. *Hypatia, 22*(1), 186–209.

Maca, N. (2013, December 28). Feliz Ano Velho, Sankofa. *Correio*. http://www.correio24horas.com.br/detalhe/noticia/nelson-maca-feliz-ano-velho-sankofa/?cHash=aaedce64179f2d12711482f7b06f7174.

Maca, N. (2015). Díaspora. In *Gramática da ira* (pp. 71–75). Blackitude.

Machado Larangeira, L. Q. (2016). *Mulheres perigosas: Uma análise da construção da categoria piriguete*. Unpublished master's dissertation, Universidade Federal do Rio de Janeiro.

Madison, D. S. (2003). Performance, personal narratives, and the politics of possibility. In Y. S. Lincoln & N. K. Denzin (Eds.), *Turning points in qualitative research: Tying knots in a handkerchief* (pp. 469–486). Rowman and Littlefield.

Madison, D. S. (2005). *Critical ethnography: Method, ethics, and performance*. Sage.

Maia, S. (2019). Espaços de branquitude: Segregação racial entre as classes médias em Salvador, Bahia. *Século XXI: Revista de Ciências Sociais, 9*(1), Article 1. https://doi.org/10.5902/2236672536942.

Maia, S., & Reiter, B. (2021). Racial capital and white middle class territorialization in Salvador, Brazil. *Latin American and Caribbean Ethnic Studies, 17*(2), 243–260. https://doi.org/10.1080/17442222.2021.1915445.

Makalani, M. (2014). *In the cause of freedom: Radical Black internationalism from Harlem to London, 1917–1939*. University of North Carolina Press.

Makalani, M. (2021, February 2). Cedric Robinson and the origins of race. *Boston Review*. https://bostonreview.net/articles/minkah-makalani-cedric-robinson-and-origins-race/.

Maldonado-Torres, N. (2007). On the coloniality of being. *Cultural Studies, 21*(2–3), 240–270. https://doi.org/10.1080/09502380601162548.

Maldonado-Torres, N. (2008). *Against war: Views from the underside of modernity*. Duke University Press.

Malveaux, J. (1992). Popular culture and the economics of alienation. In G. Dent (Ed.), *Black popular culture* (pp. 200–208). Bay Press.

Marcuse, H. (1979). *The aesthetic dimension: Toward a critique of Marxist aesthetics* (E. Sherover, Trans.). Beacon Press.

Massey, D. (1994). *Space, place, and gender.* University of Minnesota Press.

Matory, J. L. (2005). *Black Atlantic religion: Tradition, transnationalism, and matriarchy in the Afro-Brazilian Candomblé.* Princeton University Press.

Matsunaga, P. (2006). *Mulher no hip hop: Identidades e representações.* Unpublished master's dissertation, Universidade Estadual de Campinas.

Matsunaga, P. (2008). As representações sociais da mulher no movimento hip hop. *Psicologia & Sociedade, 20*(1), 108–116.

Mbembe, A. (2003). Necropolitics. *Public Culture, 15*(1), 11–40.

Mbembe, A. (2019). *Necropolitics.* Duke University Press.

McCarthy, C. (1998). *The uses of culture: Education and the limits of ethnic affiliation.* Routledge.

McClintock, A. (1995). *Imperial leather: Race, gender, and sexuality in the colonial contest.* Routledge.

McKittrick, K. (2006). *Demonic grounds: Black women and the cartographies of struggle.* University of Minnesota Press.

Menezes, J. (2017, May 14). Emicida estará no Conexões Sonoras na Concha dia 21. *Portal Soteropreta.* http://portalsoteropreta.com.br/emicida-estara-no-conexoes-sonoras-na-concha-dia-21/.

Mercer, K. (1994). *Welcome to the jungle: New positions in Black cultural studies.* Routledge.

Mercer, K. (1999). Reading racial fetishism: Photographs of Robert Mapplethorpe. In J. Evans & S. Hall (Eds.), *Visual culture: The reader* (pp. 435–447). Sage.

Mesquita, L. (2019). "Afro-Brazilian literature in perspective: 'When I found myself Black,' by Bianca Santana." Paper presented at the Association for the Study of the Worldwide African Diaspora, Williamsburg, VA.

Messias, I. dos S. (2015). *Hip hop, educação e poder: O rap como instrumento de educação.* EDUFBA.

Miles, S. (2021, May 10). Afro Brazilians love "Everybody Hates Chris." *Hub News.* https://thehub.news/afro-brazilians-love-everybody-hates-chris/.

Mills, C. W. (1997). *The racial contract.* Cornell University Press.

Mintz, S. W., & Price, R. (1992). *The birth of African-American culture: An anthropological perspective.* Beacon Press.

Miranda, J. H. de A. (2006). Relação de mercado e trabalho social no hip-hop. *Cadernos Do CEAS, 223.*

Miranda, J. H. de A. (2014). *Bahia com H de Hip-Hop.* Segundo Selo.

Mitchell-Walthour, G. (2017). Racial discrimination and Afro-Brazilian perceptions of economic well-being during better times. *Journal of Black Studies, 48*(7), pp. 675–697.

Moten, F. (2018). *Stolen life*. Duke University Press.
Moura, C. (1981). *Os quilombos e a rebelião negra*. Editora Brasiliense Ltda.
Munanga, K. (2009). *Negritude—usos e sentidos* (3rd. ed.). Autêntica Editora.
Nascimento, A. (1980). Quilombismo: An Afro-Brazilian political alternative. *Journal of Black Studies, 11*(2), 141–178.
Nascimento, A. (2014). My painting and Candomblé. In A. Winter, E. L. Nascimento, & J. Collins (Eds.), *Abdias Nascimento: Artist, activist, author* (pp. 20–25). Godwin-Ternbach Museum, Queens College CUNY/IPEAFRO.
Nascimento, B. (1985). O conceito de quilombo e a resistência cultural negra. *Afrodiaspora, 3*(6–7), 41–50.
Nascimento, B. (2005). Kilombo e memória comunitária: Um estudo de caso. In A. Ratts (Ed.), *Eu sou Atlântica: Sobre a trajetória de vida de Beatriz Nascimento* (pp. 109–116). Imprensa Oficial.
Nascimento, B. (2018a). A mulher negra no mercado de trabalho. In *Beatriz Nascimento, quilombola e intelectual: Possibilidade nos dias da destruição* (pp. 80–85). Editora Filhos da África.
Nascimento, B. (2018b). Historiografia do quilombo. In *Beatriz Nascimento, quilombola e intelectual: Possibilidade nos dias da destruição* (pp. 125–165). Editora Filhos da África.
Nascimento, B. (2018c). Negro e racismo. In *Beatriz Nascimento, quilombola e intelectual: Possibilidade nos dias da destruição* (pp. 50–56). Editora Filhos da África.
Nascimento, B. (2018d). O Conceito de quilombo e a resistência cultural negra. In *Beatriz Nascimento, quilombola e intelectual: Possibilidade nos dias da destruição* (pp. 273–294). Editora Filhos da África.
Nascimento, B. (2018e). Por uma história do homem negro. In *Beatriz Nascimento, quilombola e intelectual: Possibilidade nos dias da destruição* (pp. 42–49). Editora Filhos da África.
Nascimento, B. (2018f). Quilombo: Em Palmares, na favela, no Carnaval. In *Beatriz Nascimento, quilombola e intelectual: Possibilidade nos dias da destruição* (pp. 189–194). Editora Filhos da África.
Nascimento, B. (2018g). "Quilombos": Mudança Social e conservantismo? In *Beatriz Nascimento, quilombola e intelectual: Possibilidade nos dias da destruição* (pp. 66–79). Editora Filhos da África.
Nascimento, B. (2018h). Zumbi de N'Gola ou de Angola Pequena ou do Quilombo de Palmares. In *Beatriz Nascimento, quilombola e intelectual: Possibilidade nos dias da destruição* (pp. 104–111). Editora Filhos da África.
Nascimento, B. (2021). The concept of quilombo and Black cultural resistance (C. Smith, A. Davies, & B. Gomes, Trans.). *Antipode, 53*(1), 298–304.
Nascimento, J. (2011). Cultural and racial consciousness: The "calling" of Racionais MC's. In A. D. Tillis (Ed.), *(Re)considering Blackness in contemporary Afro-Brazilian (con)texts* (pp. 165–185). Peter Lang.

Neal, M. A. (2001). *Soul babies: Black popular culture and the post-soul aesthetic.* Routledge.

Neal, M. A. (2013). *Looking for Leroy: Illegible Black masculinities.* NYU Press.

Nito, M. K. da S., & Scifoni, S. (2018). Ativismo urbano e patrimônio cultural. *arq.urb, 23,* Article 23.

Ogunnaike, A. (2020). What's really behind the mask: A Reexamination of syncretism in Brazilian Candomblé. *Journal of Africana Religions, 8*(1), 146–171. https://doi.org/10.5325/jafrireli.8.1.0146.

Omi, M., & Winant, H. (2014). *Racial formation in the United States* (3rd ed.). Routledge.

Opanijé. (2020). "E hoje é #SextaFeira, e na sexta #EuvistoBranco 'A pele preta, a roupa branca reluzindo o dia Minha vitória é iminente não é utopia.'" Instagram. https://www.instagram.com/p/CCM_wdJFO9y/.

Otovo, O. T. (2016). *Progressive mothers, better babies: Race, public health, and the state in Brazil, 1850–1945.* University of Texas Press.

Oyěwùmí, O. (1997). *The invention of women: Making an African sense of Western gender discourses.* University of Minnesota Press.

Pacheco, A. C. L. (2013). *Mulher negra: Afetividade e solidão.* EDUFBA.

Pardue, D. (2008). *Ideologies of marginality in Brazilian hip-hop.* Palgrave Macmillan.

Paschel, T. S. (2009). Re-Africanization and the cultural politics of bahianidade. *Souls, 11*(4), 423–440. https://doi.org/10.1080/10999940903417334.

Patterson, O. (1982). *Slavery and social death: A comparative study.* Harvard University Press.

Patterson, T. R., & Kelley, R. D. G. (2000). Unfinished migrations: Reflections on the African diaspora and the making of the modern world. *African Studies Review, 43*(1), 11–45. https://doi.org/10.2307/524719.

Pereira, J. A. (2015). Quilombos urbanos. In C. da Silva (Ed.), *Africanidades e relações raciais: Insumos para políticas na área do livro, leitura, literatura e bibliotecas no Brasil* (pp. 48–50). Fundação Cultural Palmares.

Perry, I. (2004). *Prophets of the hood: Politics and poetics in hip hop.* Duke University Press.

Perry, K.-K. (2012). State violence and the ethnographic encounter: Feminist research and racial embodiment. *African and Black Diaspora: An International Journal, 5*(1), 135–154. https://doi.org/10.1080/17528631.2011.629440.

Perry, K.-K. (2013). *Black women against the land grab: The fight for racial justice in Brazil.* University of Minnesota Press.

Perry, M. (2008). Global Black self-fashionings: Hip hop as diasporic space. *Identities: Global Studies in Culture and Power, 15*(6), 635–664.

Pierson, D. (1944). *Negroes in Brazil: A study of race contact at Bahia.* University of Chicago Press.

Pinho, O. (1999). "Só se vê na Bahia": A imagem típica e a imagem crítica do pelourinho afro-baiano. In J. Bacelar & C. Caroso (Eds.), *Brasil: Um país de negros?* (pp. 87–110). PALLAS/CEAO.

Pinho, O. (2005). Etnografias do brau: Corpo, masculinidade e raça na reafricanização em Salvador. *Estudos Feministas, 13*(1), 127–145.

Pinho, O. (2008). Relações raciais e sexualidades. In O. Pinho & L. Sansone (Eds.), *Raça: Novas perspectivas antropológicas* (2nd ed., rev., pp. 257–283). EDUFBA.

Pinho, O. (2018). Black bodies, wrong places: Rolezinho, moral panic, and racialized male subjects in Brazil. In M. Seigel (Ed.), *Panic, transnational cultural studies, and the affective contours of power* (pp. 158–178). Routledge.

Pinho, O. (2021). *Cativeiro—antinegritude e ancestralidade*. Segundo Selo.

Pinho, O., & Rocha, E. (2011). Racionais MC's: Cultural afro-brasileira contemporânea com política cultural. *Afro-Hispanic Review, 30*(2), 101–114.

Pinho, P. (2010). *Mama Africa: Reinventing Blackness in Bahia* (E. Langdon, Trans.). Duke University Press.

Pinho, P. (2015). The dirty body that cleans: Representations of domestic workers in Brazilian common sense. *Meridians, 13*(1), 103–128. https://doi.org/10.2979/meridians.13.1.103.

Pinho, P. (2018). *Mapping diaspora: African American roots tourism in Brazil*. University of North Carolina Press.

Prefeitura vai demolir três "cascas" de imóveis na Ladeira da Preguiça. (2015, May 18). [Bahia Notícias]. R7.com. https://noticias.r7.com/bahia/prefeitura-vai-demolir-tres-cascas-de-imoveis-na-ladeira-da-preguica-28082015.

Preta-rara. (2019). *Eu, empregada doméstica—a senzala moderna é o quartinho da empregada*. Letramento.

Price, R. (1996). Introduction: Maroons and their communities. In R. Price (Ed.), *Maroon societies: Rebel slave communities in the Americas* (3rd ed., pp. 1–30). Johns Hopkins University Press.

Quilombo Vivo. (2020). *Quilombo Vivo*. SoundCloud. https://soundcloud.com/quilombo-vivo.

Ramos, A. (1951). *The Negro in Brazil*. Associated Publishers.

Ramos Bennett, E. G. (2001). Gabriela cravo e canela: Jorge Amado and the myth of the sexual mulata in Brazilian culture. In I. Okpewho, C. B. Davies, & A. A. Mazrui (Eds.), *The African diaspora: African origins and New World identities* (pp. 227–233). Indiana University Press.

Rana, J. (2011). *Terrifying Muslims: Race and labor in the South Asian diaspora*. Duke University Press.

Rana, J. (2020). Anthropology and the riddle of white supremacy. *American Anthropologist, 122*(1), 99–111. https://doi.org/10.1111/aman.13355.

Ransby, B., & Matthews, T. (1993). Black popular culture and the transcendence of patriarchal illusions. *Race & Class, 35*(1), 57–68.

Raquel Gerber (Director). (2008). *Orí*. Distr. Angra Filmes. https://www.youtube.com/watch?v=DBxLx8D99b4.

Rede de Observatórios da Segurança. (2021). *Pele-Alvo: A cor da violência policial*. CESeC. https://static.poder360.com.br/2021/12/relatorio-Rede-Observatorios-Seguranca-violencia-policial-14-dez-2021.pdf.

Reis, I. A. (2020). *O grafite como discurso de (re)existência na ladeira da preguiça*. Unpublished doctoral thesis, Universidade do Estado da Bahia.

Reis, J. (1995). *Slave rebellion in Brazil: The Muslim uprising of 1835 in Bahia* (A. Brakel, Trans.). Johns Hopkins University Press.

Reis, J. J. (2016). Slaves and the Coiteiros in the quilombo of Oitizeiro, Bahia, 1806. In F. D. S. Gomes & J. J. Reis (Eds.), *Freedom by a thread: The history of quilombos in Brazil* (pp. 288–325). Diasporic Africa Press.

Reis, J. J., & Gomes, F. (2016). Introduction: A history of freedom. In J. J. Reis & F. Gomes (Eds.), *Freedom by a thread: The history of quilombos in Brazil* (pp. 3–18). Diasporic Africa Press.

Ribeiro, T. R. (2016). *Narrar a rua: Hibridação cultural potencializada pelos dispositivos móveis*. Universidade do Estado da Bahia.

Roberts, D. (2012). *Fatal invention: How science, politics, and big business re-create race in the twenty-first century*. New Press.

Robinson, C. (2000). *Black Marxism: The making of the black radical tradition* (2nd ed.). University of North Carolina Press.

Robinson, C. (2021). *Black Marxism: The making of the black radical tradition* (3rd. ed.). University of North Carolina Press.

Roca, R. S. (2005). Catholic saints, African gods, Black masks and white heads: Tracing the history of some religious festivals in Bahia. *Portuguese Studies*, 21, 182–200.

Rodney, W. (2018). *How Europe underdeveloped Africa*. Verso.

Roediger, D. R. (2018). *Working toward whiteness: How America's immigrants became white: The strange journey from Ellis Island to the suburbs* (2nd ed.). Basic Books.

Romo, A. A. (2010). *Brazil's living museum: Race, reform, and tradition in Bahia*. University of North Carolina Press.

Rose, D. G. (2012). *Visual methodologies: An introduction to researching with visual materials* (3rd. ed.). Sage.

Rose, T. (1994). *Black noise: Rap music and Black culture in contemporary America*. Wesleyan University Press.

Roth-Gordon, J. (2009). Conversational sampling, race trafficking, and the invocation of the gueto in Brazilian hip hop. In *Global linguistic flows: Hip hop cultures, youth identities, and the politics of language* (pp. 63–78). Routledge.

Said, E. W. (1978). *Orientalism*. Vintage.

Santana, B. (2015). *Quando me descobri negra*. SESI-SP.

Santana, G. S. L., & Sobrinho, B. (2020). *Aquilombamento digital*. Clube de Autores.

Santos, D. (2002). *O racismo na determinação da suspeição policial*. Unpublished doctoral thesis, Universidade Federal da Bahia.

Santos, G. (2015). Ladeira da preguiça: Ativistas são detidos e guarda municipal agredido. *Jornal CORREIO*. https://www.correio24horas.com.br/noticia/nid/ladeira-da-preguica-ativistas-sao-detidos-e-guarda-municipal-agredido/.

Santos, J. L. (2016). Hip-hop and the reconfiguration of Blackness in Sao Paulo: The influence of African American political and musical movements in the twentieth century. *Social Identities, 22*(2), 160–177. https://doi.org/10.1080/13504630.2015.1121573.

Santos, M. (2021). *The nature of space* (B. Baletti, Trans.). Duke University Press.

Schmitt, C. (2006). *Political theology: Four chapters on the concept of sovereignty* (G. Schwab, Trans.). University of Chicago Press.

Schmitt, C. (2007). *The concept of the political* (G. Schwab, Trans.; expanded ed.). University of Chicago Press.

Schreiber, M. (2020, February 1). Iemanjá tem cor? Por que a divindade de origem africana se transformou em "mulher branca" no Brasil. *BBC News Brasil*. https://www.bbc.com/portuguese/brasil-51341828.

Schwartz, S. (1995). *Slaves, peasants, and rebels: Reconsidering Brazilian slavery.* University of Illinois Press.

Seibert, G. (2013). São Tomé & Príncipe: The first plantation economy in the tropics. In R. Law, S. Schwarz, & S. Strickrodt (Eds.), *Commercial agriculture, the slave trade and slavery in Atlantic Africa* (pp. 54–78). Boydell and Brewer.

Seigel, M. (2020). Places without police: Brazilian visions. *Radical History Review, 2020*(137), 177–192. https://doi.org/10.1215/01636545-8092846.

Sexton, J. (2008). *Amalgamation schemes: Antiblackness and the critique of multiracialism.* University of Minnesota Press.

Sexton, J. (2010). People-of-color-blindness: Notes on the afterlife of slavery. *Social Text, 28*(2), 31–56.

Sharpe, C. (2016). *In the wake: On Blackness and being.* Duke University Press.

Sharpley-Whiting, T. D. (2002). *Negritude women.* University of Minnesota Press.

Sharpley-Whiting, T. D. (2008). *Pimps up, ho's down: Hip hop's hold on young Black women.* NYU Press.

Silva de Oliveira, A. V., Santos Amancio, I. M., Luiz de Oliveira, R., Meneghelli Cassilhas, F. H., Araujo, K., Banke Palhano, L. Y., & Pitanga Gonçalves, T. B. (Eds.). (2021). *Transvivências negras entre afetos e aquilombamentos: Contando histórias afro-diaspóricas.* Devires.

Skidmore, T. E. (1993). *Black into white: Race and nationality in Brazilian thought* (2nd ed.). Duke University Press.

Skidmore, T. E. (2009). *Brazil: Five centuries of change* (2nd ed.). Oxford University Press.

Smith, C. (2016a). *Afro-paradise: Blackness, violence, and performance in Brazil.* University of Illinois Press.

Smith, C. (2016b). Facing the dragon: Black mothering, sequelae, and gendered necropolitics in the Americas. *Transforming Anthropology, 24*(1), 31–48. https://doi.org/10.1111/traa.12055.

Smith, C. (2016c). Towards a Black feminist model of Black Atlantic Liberation: Remembering Beatriz Nascimento. *Meridians: Feminism, Race, Transnationalism, 14*(2), 71–87. https://doi.org/10.2979/meridians.14.2.06.

Smith, C., Davies, A., & Gomes, B. (2021). "In front of the world": Translating Beatriz Nascimento. *Antipode, 53*(1), 279–297.

Smith, C. (2021). Counting frequency: Un/gendering anti-Black police terror. *Social Text, 39*(2), 25–49. https://doi.org/10.1215/01642472-8903591.

Smitherman, G. (1977). *Talkin and testifyin: The language of Black America.* Wayne State University Press.

Soares, K. dos R. A., & Ferreira, A. P. (2021). A transexualidade e a tradição do candomblé: Gênero e cultura em debate. *Interfaces Científicas—Humanas e Sociais, 9*(2), Article 2. https://doi.org/10.17564/2316-3801.2021v9n2p134-153.

Soares, M. A. (2012). Look, Blackness in Brazil! Disrupting the grotesquerie of racial representation in Brazilian visual culture. *Cultural Dynamics, 24*(1), 75–101.

Sobral Freire, R. (2018). *Hip-hop feminista? Convenções de gênero e feminismos no movimento Hip-hop soteropolitano.* EDUFBA/NEIM.

Sojoyner, D. M. (2017). Another life is possible: Black fugitivity and enclosed places. *Cultural Anthropology, 32*(4), 514–536. https://doi.org/10.14506/ca32.4.04.

Somerville, S. (2014). Queer. In B. Burgett & G. Hendler (Eds.), *Keywords for American cultural studies* (2nd ed., pp. 203–207). NYU Press.

Souza, A. L. S. (2011). *Letramentos de reexistência: Poesia, grafite, música, dança: Hip hop.* Parábola.

Souza, B. O. (2008). *Aquilombar-se: Panorama histórico, identitário e político do movimento quilmbola brasileiro.* Unpublished master's dissertation, Universidade de Brasília. https://repositorio.unb.br/handle/10482/2130.

Spillers, H. (1987). Mama's baby, papa's maybe: An American grammar book. *Diacritics, 17*(2), 64–81.

Sterling, C. (2012). *African roots, Brazilian rites: Cultural and national identity in Brazil.* Palgrave Macmillan.

Storey, J. (2015). *Cultural theory and popular culture: An introduction* (7th ed.). Routledge.

Strings, S. (2019). *Fearing the Black body: The racial origins of fat phobia.* NYU Press.

Tate, S. A. (2009). *Black beauty: Aesthetics, stylization, politics.* Routledge.

Telles, E. (2004). *Race in another America: The significance of skin color in Brazil.* Princeton University Press.

Teperman, R. (2015). *Se liga no som: As transformações do rap no Brasil.* Claro Enigma.

Terra, L. M. (2010). *Negro suspeito, negro bandido: Um estudo sobre o discurso policial.* Unpublished master's dissertation, Universidade Estadual Paulista.

Thompson, R. F. (1984). *Flash of the spirit: African & Afro-American art & philosophy.* Vintage.

Tinsley, O. N. (2008). Black Atlantic, queer Atlantic. *GLQ, 14*(2–3), 191–215.

Trabazo, C., & Lahiri, V. (2013, November 11). DJ Sankofa conta trajetória de Gana até Salvador. *Jornal Correio*. https://www.correio24horas.com.br/noticia/nid/dj-sankofa-conta-trajetoria-de-gana-ate-salvador/.

UNESCO. (2020). *Historic Centre of Salvador de Bahia*. UNESCO World Heritage Centre. https://whc.unesco.org/en/list/309/.

Visweswaran, K. (1994). *Fictions of feminist ethnography*. University of Minnesota Press.

Vogt, J. L. (1973). The early Sao Tome-Principe slave trade with Mina, 1500–1540. *International Journal of African Historical Studies*, 6(3), 453–467. https://doi.org/10.2307/216611.

Waiselfisz, J. (2014). *Mapa da violência 2014: Os jovens do Brasil*. Secretaria-Geral da Presidência da República. http://www.mapadaviolencia.org.br/pdf2014/Mapa2014_JovensBrasil.pdf.

Waiselfisz, J. (2015). *Mapa da violência 2015: Homicídio de mulheres no Brasil*. Secretaria-Geral da Presidência da República. http://www.onumulheres.org.br/wp-content/uploads/2016/04/MapaViolencia_2015_mulheres.pdf.

Walcott, R. (2015). The problem of the human: Black ontologies and "the coloniality of being." In S. Broeck & C. Junker (Eds.), *Postcoloniality—decoloniality—Black critique: Joints and fissures* (pp. 93–105). Campus Verlag.

Walcott, R. (2021). *The long emancipation: Moving toward Black freedom*. Duke University Press.

Wallace, M. (1990). *Invisibility blues: From pop to theory*. Verso.

Wallerstein, I. (2004). *World-systems analysis: An introduction*. Duke University Press.

Weheliye, A. (2008). Pornotropes. *Journal of Visual Culture*, 7(1), 65–81.

Weheliye, A. (2014). Introduction: Black studies and Black life. *Black Scholar*, 44(2), 5–10. https://doi.org/10.1080/00064246.2014.11413682.

Wilderson, F. B. (2003). Gramsci's Black Marx: Whither the slave in civil society. *Social Identities*, 9(2), 225–240.

Wilderson, F. B. (2010). *Red, white & black: Cinema and the structure of U.S. antagonisms*. Duke University Press.

Williams, E. (2013). *Sex tourism in Bahia: Ambiguous entanglements*. University of Illinois Press.

Williams, R. (1978). *Marxism and literature*. Oxford University Press.

Williams, R. (1985). Aesthetic. In *Keywords: A vocabulary of culture and society* (rev. ed., pp. 31–33). Oxford University Press.

Winant, H. (1994). *Racial conditions: Politics, theory, comparisons*. University of Minnesota Press.

Woods, C. (2000). *Development arrested: The blues and plantation power in the Mississippi Delta*. Verso.

Wright, M. (2004). *Becoming Black: Creating identity in the African Diaspora*. Duke University Press.

Wynter, S. (1989). Beyond the word of man: Glissant and the new discourse of the Antilles. *World Literature Today*, 63(4), 637–648.

Wynter, S. (1994). No humans involved: An open letter to my colleagues. *N.H.I. Knowledge for the 21st Century, 1*(1), 42–73.

Wynter, S. (2003). Unsettling the coloniality of being/power/truth/freedom: Towards the human, after man, its overrepresentation—an argument. *CR: The New Centennial Review, 3*(3), 257–337.

Wynter, S., & McKittrick, K. (2015). Unparalleled catastrophe for our species? Or to give humanness a different future: Conversations. In K. McKittrick (Ed.), *Sylvia Wynter: On being human as praxis* (pp. 9–89). Duke University Press.

Zulu Inform@. (2013, August 18). *Notícias da Bahia: Reação Sankofa—Entre nessa luta*... Zulu Nation. http://zulunationbrazil.blogspot.com/2013/08/noticias-da-bahia-reacao-sankofa-entre.html.

Index

Page numbers in *italics* indicate an illustration. The letter *t* following a page number indicates a table.

"1/3 da tropa" (Visi00nárias), 178–183

abject Blackness: aesthetic aspects of, 136–137, 153–156; diasporic Blackness in relation to, 13; displacement and, 32, 35; gendered aspects of, 19–20; hair and, 145; Iemanjá and, 194; nature and significance of, 9–10, 11; Pelourinho and, 91; transformation of, 165
aesthetics, natural, 133–136
aesthetics of the artifice. *See* Black aesthetics
afoxés, 91, 162
Afreeka, 149–150
African Americans and folkloric Blackness, 80
africanidade, 60
Afro-blocs, 11, 77, 78, 85, 91, 131
Afro-Catholicism, 191–192
"Afrohiphop resistance," 58
Afro-kitsch, 52
Almeida, Pedro de, 109–110

alternative political and social systems: in "1/3 da tropa," 178–183; Iemanjá and, 201–203; masculinity in relation to, 25, 123–129, 201; motherhood and, 212; in music videos, 160–161, 168–171; Nascimento on, 165; sovereignty and, 172–177
Amado, Jorge, 96–97, 194, 196–197, 201
Amnesty International, 46
ancestralidade (ancestrality): in Bahian hip-hop, 56; Carlos and, 69–70; concept of, 67; Mestre Môa and, 162; negritude and, 71–72; Opanijé and, 68; significance of, 24; of Visi00nárias, 179–180
androgyny, 142, 143
anger and love, 219–222
Angola, 183
Anitta, 78
Aparelha Luzia, 18
AquaHertz Beats, 161

aquilombamento: aesthetic aspects of, 136; Black feminist, 181; bodily, 213; *conscientização* and, 57–58; fashioning, 145–153; intimacy and, 123; nature of, 55–56; *quilombo* in relation to, 7; space and, 95; technology and, 16; ungendering in relation to, 20–21
aquilombar-se: aesthetic aspects of, 136; Black feminism in relation to, 17–18; and *conscientização*, 56–57; criminalization of, 155; defined, 7; religious aspects of, 192, 195, 217; spatial aspects of, 78–79
artifice, the, 25, 136–137, 141, 153. See also Black aesthetics
ascriptive mulattas, 206
Aspri RBF, 161
"Áurea Abolicionista" (Abolitionist Áurea) (Semiseria), 55
authenticity, 121
axé, 118
Azevedo, Thales, 40

Baco Exu do Blues, 115, 118–122, 229n8
Badu, Erykah, 96, 97, 103
Bahia. See Salvador da Bahia
Bahia com H de Hip-Hop (Hilton), 74
Bahian (*baiana/o*), the term, 24
Bahian hip-hop: Black feminist approach to, 17–21; elements of, 55–56; as emergent quilombo, 4–5; historical aspects of, 5–6; nature and significance of, 14–15; origins of, 58–60; as *quilombo*, 15–16; role and significance of, 3; as a social movement, 72–76. See also emergent *quilombos*; graffiti and graffiti artists; music videos
"Baiana" (Emicida), 77, 228n1
baiana dress, 29, 226n2
bailes black (Black dances), 58

Bailey, Moya, 178, 232n10
bairro (district), the term, 23
'BALLAH IH FOGOH' (Vandal), 115
barbershops, 143–144
Barbie, 207
beauty standards, 205–209, 212, 232n9
benevolent patriarchs, 112
Benguela, Tereza de, 18
Bey, Marquis, 20
big chop, the, 142
Black, the term, 23
Black aesthetics: as artifice, 136–137, 154; Blackening, 139–140; fashion, 146; freedom linked to, 155–156; hair and, 138–145; historical aspects of, 60; nature and significance of, 135
Black *conscientizacão* (critical consciousness): ancestrality linked to, 67, 68; Carla and, 71; gendered aspects of, 64–65; hair and, 138; João on, 61–62, 66; nature and significance of, 56–60; negritude and, 60–63; Night of the Black Beauty and, 132; significance of, 24; social change and, 72, 76; space and, 81
Blackening, 137, 139
Black feminism: Blackening and, 139; *conscientizacão* and, 65; hair and, 137–138; hip-hop feminists, 97–98; humanism and, 214; justice through, 177–183; love and, 220; mainstream feminism in relation to, 230n3; in music videos, 166; nature and significance of, 17–21. See also Black women; gender; sexuality
Black fugitives, 18, 52, 148, 172, 186
Black humanity, 88, 194–196, 207–208, 211, 214–215

Blackitude, 83
Black Marxism (Robinson), 227n5
Black masculinity: alternative forms of, 25, 123–129, 201; Baco and, 119–122; bodily aesthetics and, 144–145; constructions of, 19–20; feminists on, 97–98, 216; patriarchal, 111–114; queering, 151–152; in US hip-hop, 99–100, 229n7; Vandal and, 115–118; Zumbí as, 107, 111
Black men: intimacy and, 114; physical prowess of, 113, 117, 120, 124, 229n7; relations with Black women, 209, 232n7. *See also* intimacy
Black motherhood, 193, 203–204, 210–217
Blackness: Candomblé and, 195; modern, 14; negritude as, 60; non-synchrony of, 164–165; permissible, 230n12; queering, 12–13, 151–152, 202–203; race in relation to, 8; racial democracy in relation to, 11–12; as resistance, 51; rethinking, 20; types of, 9–10
Black radical tradition, 4, 169, 218
Black sovereignty, 172–177, 180, 183–187
Black spaces: diasporic connections and, 92–95; educational, 95–100; hip-hop feminism and, 100–104; nature and significance of, 79; the quilombo as, 25, 105; reafricanization and, 91; repression of, 85–88; Sankofa Bar, 81–84; whitening of, 89–92
Black studies, 222
Black women: Carla and Camila on, 64–65; hair and, 142–143; in hip hop, 65–66; hypersexualization of, 10, 64, 170–171, 197, 203, 206; Iemanjá as, 192–193, 195, 196; income distribution and, 45; as leaders, 18; leadership of, 170–171; mothers, 50; orixás, 26; performing masculinity, 128; rappers, 96–97, 103; as real women, 193; relations with Black men, 209, 232n7; representations of, 96–99; significance of, 218; violence against, 181–182; in the workforce, 19. *See also* Black motherhood; Iemanjá
Bluesman (Baco), 118, 119, 229n8
bodily sovereignty, 172–173, 180, 183
Bolsonaro, Jair, 74, 138
boné, 147–148
Boogie Naipe (Brown), 2
braids, 139–140
branca/os, salary of, 43t
Brazil: African cultural symbols of, 10; Brazilian Academy of Letters, 197; Brazilian Public Security Annual Report (ABSP), 48; Dutch colonization of, 228n5; economic history of, 166–167; homicide rates in, 164; justice system of, 177; racial segregation in, 38. *See also* colonial Brazil
Brazil: They Come in Shooting (Amnesty International), 46
Brooklyn, New York, 93–94
Brown, Mano, 1–3
Bruta Flor (Brutal flower) (Savoli), 98
Butler, Kim D, 232n6

Cabral, Sérgio, 50
Cabula, 106
Cabula massacre, 157–159
Calongos, 197–204
Camila (MC), 46–47, 72, 128–129
"Campaign against the criminalization of Black spaces of culture," 86

Candomblé: African traditions in, 190–191; ancestrality and, 67; Baco and, 118; Blackness and, 195; Catholicism juxtaposed to, 191; Iemanjá in, 189–190; justice through, 179–183; A. Nascimento on, 195; Opanijé and, 68; *orí* in, 230n6; orixás, 26; *terreiros*, 85, 195; whitening of, 194
Capoeira, 162
captaincies, 109, 228n4
Cardi B, 78
Cardozo, Wall, 161, 163–164
care and protection, practice of, 123–129, 201
Carla (MC): ancestrality and, 72; on *conscientizacâo*, 64; on Criolo, 63–64; on liberation, 72; on negritude, 71; performing masculinity, 128–129; on racism, 46–47; on women rappers, 103
Carlim (writer), 68
Carlos (producer): aesthetics of, 141–142; *ancestrality and*, 69; on Candomblé, 67–68; intimacy and, 125–127; on public transportation, 42; on Salvador, 35–36, 37
Carnival, 85, 91
Casa Fundação de Jorge Amado, 29, 77
Catholicism, 191–192, 194, 196, 231n2
Central Pacção, 63
"Chapa" (Emicida), 203
Chiba D, 68
Childish Gambino, 229n8
Chinaski, Diomedes, 118
Christianity, 182, 191–192, 193, 194, 208–209, 231n2
class: geographic aspects of, 37–39; humanism and, 208; in music videos, 165; *piriguetes* and, 170–171; rethinking, 17–18; in Salvador, 43–45; Salvador as class-based, 37–38
clothes and fashion, 145–153
colonial Brazil: Black women and, 18, 203; captaincies in, 228n4; freedom in, 155; gender and, 20, 100; *kilombo* and, 5, 111–112; Palmares *quilombo* in, 107–110, 228n2; *quilombo* formation in, 51–52; space-making in, 79; violence in, 90
colorism, 140
Combahee River Collective, 231n6
conquering self, 166
conscientizacâo (critical consciousness). See Black *conscientizacâo* (critical consciousness)
cornrows, 141
Correio, 81, 87, 88
Coscarque, 173–177
Costa, Rui, 159
cost of living, 40–41
criminalization of Black people, 49–50, 52, 86, 155
Criolo, 63, 71
critical visual methodology, 196
cultural industry, 232n5

dad hats, 148
Dandara, 18, 105, 123
Dark MC, 72
Darlene (graffiti artist), 137–138
deindustrialization, 166
"Desculpa Me Jay-Z" (Baco), 118, 119–122
Detroit, Michigan, 148–149
dialogism, 215–216, 217
diasporic Blackness: Black spaces and, 92–95; cultural encounters, 80–81; fashion and, 146–150; in music videos, 165; nature and significance of, 12–13; political aspects of, 91; in religion, 195
Didá, 78

divas, 205, 209
DJ Bandido, 53
DJ KL Jay, 231n5
DJ Kool Herc, 15
DJ Larissa, 93, 94, 95
DJ Nai Kiese, 68, 142–143, 230n6
DJ Sankofa, 81, 85–86
domestic violence, 113
domestic workers, 18, 19
dreadlocks, 131, 142

educational tools and spaces, 16, 60–61, 95–100
Elem, Brena. See "1/3 da tropa" (Visi00nárias); "Visionárias" (Visi00nárias)
emergent *quilombos*: diasporic Blackness and, 12; formation of, 20, 52, 137, 155; justice in, 179, 181; nature and significance of, 4–8, 187, 221–222. See also alternative political and social systems; Bahian hip-hop; Black feminism; Black spaces
Emicida, 71, 77–78, 192, 203, 228n1
"EMOCIONADUH" (Vandal), 116
"Encoding/Decoding" (Hall), 227n1
enegrecendo (Blackening), 137, 139
Eré, Lázaro, 68, 164
Esú (Baco), 118
ethnic difference, 10, 225n3
Expressão Ativa, 71
Exú, 152
eyebrow shaping, 143–144

Fall Classico, 69
Fanon, Frantz: abject Blackness and, 9; *Black Skin, White Masks*, 57; on colonialism, 50; on humanity, 218; masculinity and, 121; and the non-synchrony of Blackness, 164; on primitivism, 89
fashion, diasporic aspects of, 146–150

fashion, gendered aspects of, 151–152
favela, the term, 23
femininity: constructions of, 19–20; humanism and, 208, 214–215; queering, 151; representations of, 97–99; white, 207
feminism, Black. See Black feminism; hip-hop feminists
festa de Iemanjá (Festival of Iemanjá), 189, 191, 199, 200
Filhas de Gandhi, 77
folkloric Blackness: aesthetic aspects of, 135, 153–154; diasporic Blackness in relation to, 13; displacement and, 32; geographic aspects of, 14; hypervisibility of, 30; Iemanjá and, 194; motherhood and, 216; nature and significance of, 9, 11–12; Pelourinho as, 32; space and, 80
freedom, 155, 165, 186–187
Freire, Pablo, 57
Freire, Rebeca Sobral, 73
Freyre, Gilberto, 225n4
fugitives, Black. See Black fugitives
fugitive un/gendering, 20

Ganga-Zumba, 109, 110
gangsta rap, 65
gangsta trope, 113
gender: anti-Black solidarity and, 9; capitalism and, 227n5; *conscientizacão* and, 64–65; and the diaspora, 12; fashion and, 151–152; hair and, 142, 145; humanistic aspects of, 207–208; income distribution and, 44t, 45; masculinity and, 19–20; rethinking, 17–18; slavery and, 100, 111–112; socioeconomic aspects of, 41; ungendering, 20–21; violence and, 181–182. See also Black feminism; Black masculinity; femininity

gentrification, 35, 167
German Complex, 84
Ghetto Union and Hip-Hop Culture Family. *See* Ugangue Familia
Gil, Gilberto, 107
Gilroy, Paul, 231n3
Giroux, Henry A., 171
globalization, 150
gordivas, 204–210
Gordon, Lewis, 49
graffiti and graffiti artists: as activism, 34; Calongos, 197–204; Darlene, 137–138; as an educational tools, 100–103; Iemanjá and, 193; Marisa, 40–41, 96–97, 98, 103; New Boys Crew, 123; Ronaldo, 124, 125; significance of, 26, 196, 217–218; Sista Katia, 193, 204–210
Gramática da Ira (Maca), 90
gueto (ghetto), the term, 23

Haddad, Fernando, 74
hair, politics of, 137–145
Haitian Revolution, 225n2, 228n2
Hall, Stuart, 24, 155, 227n1
Harding, Rachel E., 195
hats, 147–151
Henderson, Mae Gwendolyn, 215
high culture, 16–17
Hill, Lauryn, 96, 97, 103
Hilton, Jorge, 74–75, 103
hip-hop. *See* Bahian hip-hop
Hip-Hop e Educação Popular (Hip-Hop and popular education), 60–61
Hip-hop feminista? (Freire), 73
hip-hop feminists: educational aspects of, 100; on masculinity, 113–114; masculinity, 216; on motherhood, 217; role and significance of, 97–98; space making practices, 100–104

hip-hop masculinities. *See* Black masculinity
"Historiografia do Quilombo" (The quilombo historiography) (Nascimento), 75
Hoch-Smith, Judith, 211–221
homicide rates, 48–49, 164
hooks, bell, 215
A Hora da Guerra (The hour of war) (Amado), 197
humanity, Black, 88, 194–196, 207–208, 211, 214–215
hygienification, 35

Iansã, 181, 182, 191
Iemanjá: Black women as, 192–193; Calongos mural of, 197–204; festival of, 189, 191, 199, 200; house of, 189–190; racialization of, 194; as real Black women, 195, 196; significance of, 26, 218; Sista Katia mural of, 204–210; Tata mural of, 210–214, 216
Ilê Aiyê, 91, 131–133, 135, 153
illegible masculinity, 114
imaginative geographies, 89
imagined community, 12, 13
Imbangala group, 5
income distribution, 43–45
income inequality, 40
Indigenous people's, 231n6
internal enemies, 46, 52
intimacy: in *aquilombamento*, 123; Baco and, 119–120, 122; Black men and, 114; practice of, 125–127; social aspects of, 111; Vandal and, 116

Jackson, Michael, 77, 78
Jay-Z, 119–122
J Dilla, 148–149
João (MC): aesthetics of, 141, 148; on *conscientizacão*, 66;

influences of, 68–69; intimacy and, 125–126; on justice, 48; on negritude, 61–62; on Salvador, 39; on violence, 46
Jones, Claudia, 230n3
Jorge (graffiti artist), 93, 94, 95, 104
Julio (rapper), 144
Junior, Joselicio, 7
justice, Black feminist, 177–183
justice defined, 46

Kilombo Bar, 146
kilombos, 5–6, 183–187
knowledge in Bahian hip-hop, 59

Ladeira da Preguiça (Lazy Slope), 32, 33–34, *102*
Lee, Spike, 77
Lima, Maria, 158
loneliness and isolation, 115, 124
Lorde, Audre, 216
love and anger, 219–222
Lôzaro Erê, 164
Lula, 73
Luz, Larissa, 192
Luzia, Aparelha, 18

Maca, Nelson, 83, 86–88, 90, 161, 163
Macaido, Justine Lloyd Ankai, 81
Maceo (rapper), 148
Mães de Maio (Mothers of May), 203
Magno, Marcia, 107
Makalani, Minkah, 227n5
Malê Revolt, 225n2
Malunguinho, Erica, 18
Mama Africa, 216
Man in Christianity, 182, 193, 195, 208–209, 214
Marisa (graffiti artist), 40–41, 96–97, 98, 103
masculinity. *See* Black masculinity

Masters and the Slaves (Freyre), 225n4
Matory, J. Lorland, 194
matriarchy, Black, 202–203
Mays, Kyle T., 231n6
McLaren, Peter, 171
"Me Gusta" (Anitta), 78
Mercer, Kobena, 232n6
Mesquita, Luciana, 229n4
mestiçagem (racial mixing), 10, 226n5
Mestre Môa da Katende, 161–163, 164
methodology, 21–23, 229n1
militancy, Black radical, 170
Miranda, Jorge Hilton de Assis. *See* Hilton, Jorge
misogynoir, 178–179, 180, 209, 233n10
mixed Blackness: aesthetic aspects of, 153–154; in the Bahian imaginary, 30; concept of, 9, 10–11, 12; diasporic Blackness in relation to, 13; Pelourinho as, 32; spatial aspects of, 91. *See also* the *mulata* figure
Môa da Katende, 161–163
"Moço Lindo Do Badauê" (Beautiful Boy from Badauê) (AquaHertz Beats), 161, 163–164, *165*
modernity, Black, 13, 14
monthly minimum salary (MMS), 43–44
Moten, Fred, 6
motherhood, Black, 193, 203–204, 210–217
mother-lover trope, 202
movimento negro (the Black movement), 73
mulata figure, the, 96–97, 153, 205, 206, 226n1, 232n6
murals. *See* graffiti and graffiti artists; Iemanjá

music videos: "1/3 da tropa," 178–183; "Baiana," 77, 228n1; Black feminism in, 166; "Chapa," 203; "Me Gusta," 78; "Moço Lindo Do Badauê," 161, 163–164, 165; motherhood in, 203; necropolitics in, 159–160; Pelourinho in, 77–79; political aspects of, 161, 163–164, 173–177, 178–183; "Scarface," 173–177; significance of, 165, 184–185
MV Bill, 63

Naber, Nadine, 226n5
Nada como um dias após o outro dia (Nothing like a day after the other day) (Racionais), 2
Nascimento, Abdias, 195–196, 221
Nascimento, Beatriz: on Black humanity, 88; on Candomblé, 195; on freedom, 165; hip-hop linked to, 75–76; "Historiografia do Quilombo," 75; on peace, 112; on the periphery, 105; on *quilombos*, 31, 128–129, 183–184; on resistance, 51; Robinson in relation to, 231n3; significance of, 6, 186
National Historic and Artistic Heritage Institute (IPHAN), 34
native bourgeoisie, 117
natives' zone, 89
natural aesthetics, refusing, 133–136, 139
necropolitics: alternatives to, 168–171, 173–177, 181–183; in music videos, 161; nature and significance of, 159–160
nega maluca, 207, 208, 232n7
Nego Juno, 53, 54
negra/os, 43t
negritude/*négritude*, 56, 60–67, 71, 162
Negrizu, 163

"Negro Drama" (Brown), 2
"Negro Fugido" (Quilombo Vivo), 53
Negro Original 100+ ou– (Black original 100 + or–) (Quilombo Vivo), 53
negrx/a/o, the term, 23
Neto, Antônio Carlos Magalhães, 41
New Boys Crew, 34, 123
New Era baseball hats, 147–151
New Holland, 228n5
Neymar, 138, 229n3
Night da Beleza Negra (Night of the black beauty), 131–133
non-synchrony of Blackness, 164–165
Nossa-Casa Colaborativa, 210
Nova Era, 63

Olodum, 77, 78, 91, 132
Olukemi, Zeze, 68, 192
omnivocality, 215, 217
O Pais do Carnaval (The country of the Carnival) (Amado), 196–197
Opanijé, 68, 161, 164, 192
orí, 230n6
orixás, 195–196

Pacheco, Ana Cláudia Lemos, 232n9
pagodé, 95
Palmares *quilombo*, 107–110, 228n2
Panorama Percussivo Mundial (Global Percussion Panorama), 1–3
parda/os, salary of, 43t
pardx/a/o, the term, 23
patriarchical masculinity, escaping, 114–118
patriarchical masculinity, historical aspects of, 111–114
patriarchy: Baco and, 119; combating, 178–183; feminists on, 97; impact of, 117; masculinity in relation to, 113; *padrão* in relation to, 99–100; plantation patriarchy, 20, 112
Patterson, Orlando, 225n1

Pedagogy of the Oppressed (Freire), 57–58
Pelourinho: Brooklyn compared to, 93–94; displacement in, 32, 36–37; folkloric Blackness and, 80; in music videos, 77–78; Panorama Percussivo Mundial in, 1–3; representation of, 77–79; "SALVADOR" block letters in, 28; Sankofa Bar in, 81–82; as settlers' zone, 89; as a space of Black culture, 91–92; as a white space, 89–90; Zumbí statue in, 107–108
Pereira, Germino, 161, 162
performance of possibilities, 171
periphery: freedom linked to, 165; hip-hop origins in, 58–59; political aspects of, 168–171; public services in, 176–177; race and racism in, 36–39; in Rio de Janeiro, 84; as sovereign space, 160–161; the term, 23–24; transportation in, 42; as urban *quilombo*, 104–106
Pernambuco captaincy, 228n4
petit marronage, 195, 213
phenomenal beauty, 134
Pierson, Donald, 40
piriguete, 170–171, 230n4, 231n4
plantation patriarchy, 20, 112
Police Pacification Unit, 84
police violence: Amnesty International on, 47; Cabula massacre, 157–159; Diego and, 144–145, 230n8; João on, 46; racial conditions in relation to, 46–48
polis, the term, 45
political and social systems, alternative. *See* alternative political and social systems
pornotroping, 182
Portela, Adriana Pereira, 78
Possee Orí, 67
preta/os, salary of, 43t

preta surburbana, 167, 170, 171
Preto Jacó, 53
pretx/a/o, the term, 23

Quando Me Descobri Negra (When I discovered I am a Black woman) (Santana), 138
Quariterê *quilombo*, 18
queering Blackness: aesthetic aspects of, 136, 151–152; alternative socialities and, 25; diasporic aspects of, 12–13; Iemanjá and, 201–202; motherhood and, 202–203
Queiros, Viviam Caroline de Jesus, 78
quilombos (maroon communities): Black feminist approach to, 17–21; defined, 31, 52; formations, 51–52; geographic aspects of, 125; hip-hop compared to, 15–16; hip-hop linked to, 54–56; historical aspects of, 52, 105–110, 228n2; *kilombos* juxtaposed to, 183–187; nature and purpose of, 128–130; nature and significance of, 3–4, 221–223; the periphery as, 104–106; *quilombismo*, 16; *quilombola*, 6; urban, 104–106; values of, 75–76. *See also* alternative political and social systems; Bahian hip-hop; emergent *quilombos*
"Quilombo Urbano–Ladeira da Preguiça," 34, 226n3
Quilombo Vivo, 5, 53, 54–55, 57–58
Quinn, Rachel Afi, 226n4

racial capitalism, 100, 197–198, 227n5
racial conditions: concept of, 30; displacement and, 31–32, 35; hip-hop in relation to, 14–15; Quilombo Vivo on, 53; socioeconomic aspects of, 39–45; structural aspects of, 39; violence and, 45–51

racial cropping, 206–207, 213, 232n6
racial democracy myth: Amado and, 197; Black men and, 209; Blackness in relation to, 11–12; challenging, 60; concept of, 10; Iemanjá linked to, 195; in *Masters and the Slaves*, 225n4; *mestiçagem* and, 226n5; racial exclusion and the, 29–30
racial profiling, 157
racial segregation, 38
Racionais MC, 1–3, 63, 71, 231n5
racism, structural, 30–31, 160, 178
radical Yoruba sexuality, 211–212
Rae, Issa, 230n7
Rael, Ludmilla, 71
Raiz Afro Mae (Afro Mother roots), 163
Rapaziada da Baixa Fria (RBF), 71, 72, 164
Rap Etnia, 63
reafricanization movement, 77, 133–134, 135, 153–154
reaja ou seja morto! (React or be Killed!), 73, 158
Reconcâvo region, 24, 55
Rede Aiyê Hip-hop, 60
rehumanization, 112
Ribeiro, Taís. *See* Tata
Rio de Janeiro: Cabral and, 50; deaths in, 48; German Complex, 84; hip-hop in, 14; homicide rates in, 47, 49; the periphery in, 77; *zona sul*, 165
"Risca Mina, Rima Mina" mural, 102–103
Robinson, Cedric, 197–198, 227n5, 231n3
Rodgers, Carolyn, 216
Rodrigues, Pero, 110
Rodrigues, Raimundo Nina, 35
Ronaldo (graffiti artist), 124, 125
Ron DumDum, 68
roots tourism, 80, 92

Rose, Tricia, 217
Rousseff, Dilma, 73

Sabotage, 63
safety and security, 124, 125
Salvador da Bahia: Amado and, 197; Bahian imaginary of, 30; block letters, 28; the center in relation to, 37–39; class in, 37–38, 43–45; contextualized, 24; deindustrialization in, 166; homicide rates in, 48–49; income distribution in, 43t; income inequality in, 40. *See also* Pelourinho; periphery
Samba, Neguinho do, 77, 78
Sankofa Bar, 81–84, 85–88
Santana, Bianca, 138, 229n4
Santana, Paulo Sérgio Ferreira de, 161–165
Santos, Udi. *See* "1/3 da tropa" (Visi00nárias); "Visionárias" (Visi00nárias)
São Paulo: Aparelha Luzia in, 18; Bahia compared to, 99; Emicida of, 71, 77–78, 192, 203, 228n1; Haddad and, 74; homicide rates of, 49; industrialization in, 167; police violence in, 48
São Tomé, 228n6
Sarau Bem Black, 83
Savoli, Cintia, 98
"Scarface" (Coscarque), 173–177
Schmitt, Carl, 186
Sea of Death (Amado), 201
Security Observatory Network, 48
segregation, racial, 38
Seixas, Raul, 71
self, conquering, 166
Semiseria, Áurea, 55
Senzala do Barro Preto Associação Cultural Ilê Aiyê, 131
Sergio (graffiti artist), 58

settlers' zone, 89
sexual harassment, 64
sexuality: beauty standards and, 152; Black women's use of, 232n7; Calongo mural on, 199, 203; fashion and, 144–145; hypersexuality, 10, 64, 170–171, 197, 203, 206; Marisa on, 98; queer in relation to, 12; race and class in relation to, 128; radical Yoruba, 211–212; rethinking, 17–18; Sista Katia on, 207–208
Sharpley-Whiting, T. Denean, 206
signifyin,' 173
Silva, Cidinha da, 160
Silva, Luiz Inácio Lula da, 73
Simples Rap'ortagem, 72, 74–75
Sista Katia, 193, 204–210
slavery, 111–112, 203, 225n2, 228n2, 228n6. *See also* colonial Brazil
Smith, Christen A., 230n12, 231n3
Soares, Elza, 71
Sobrevivendo no Inferno (Surviving in Hell) (Racionais), 2
soteropagotrap, 95
soterpolitanx/a/o (Soterpolitan), 24
Souza, Deborah de, 78
sovereignties, 172–177, 180, 183–187
space-making practices. *See* Black spaces
spaces, periphery. *See* periphery
spaces of Black culture, 79, 92
spatial displacement, 32–39
Spillers, Hortense, 182, 217
"Stop killing us!" mantra, 164
street vendors, 198–204
subject-object relations, 214–215
sublation, 233n11
subúrbio (suburb), the term, 23
"Sulicído" (Baco), 118

superexploits, 230n3
Superintendence for Municipal Control and Land use Planning (SUCOM), 85
syncretism, 231n1

Tata, 210–214, 216
technology and *quilombismo*, 16
terminology, 23–24
terreiros (worship compounds), 85, 118, 195
territorial sovereignty, 172–173, 180, 183
Tharles (rapper), 93, 94, 95
Theodore, Helena, 194
"They Don't Care About Us" (Jackson), 77
"This is America" (Childish Gambino), 229n8
Tícia, 69
'TIPOLAZVEGAZH' (Vandal), 115, 116
tourism, 80, 89, 92, 157, 167
Towers, Myke, 78
transforming reality, 72–76
transportation, public, 41–42, 84
trap music, 95
twists hair style, 139–140

Ugangue Familia, 173–175
unemployment, 39–40
UNESCO World Heritage site, 92
ungendering, 20–21, 111–114
Urban Municipal Secretary (SUCOM), 34
urban *quilombos*, 104–106, 187
US hip-hop, 95–97, 99–100, 117, 119–122, 229n7

vagabonds, 89–90
Vandal de Verdade, 115–118, 122, 229n7
Vila Canaria *subúrbio*, 104

violence: against Black people, 219–220; Cabula massacre, 157–159; colonial, 90; domestic, 113; economies of, 45–51; gendered, 179; by police, 46–48, 144–145, 157–159, 230n8; against *quilombos*, 185–186; the racial condition of, 32; against women, 181–182
Virgin Mary, 191–192, 195
Visi00nárias. *See* "1/3 da tropa" (Visi00nárias); "Visionárias" (Visi00nárias)
"Visionárias" (Visi00nárias), 166, 167–171

white Brazilians, 82, 84–85
whitening, 194–195
white redemption, 182
white spatial imaginary, 80, 89

white womanhood, 193, 207–208
Williams, Raymond, 134
Winant, Howard, 30
women, Black. *See* Black feminism; Black motherhood; Black women
Worker's Party, 73–74, 159
Wright, Michelle, 193, 214, 215–216
Wynter, Sylvia, 208

Xarope MC, 161, 164

"Yemanjá é preta" (Iemanjá is Black) (Luz), 192
You Killed My Son (Amnesty International), 46

Zero Hunger, 41
Zumbí, 105, 107–111, 113, 174
"Zumbí (The Warrior of Happiness)" (Gil), 109